THE POLITICS OF PIRACY

CORNELL UNIVERSITY PRESS
Ithaca and London

THE POLITICS OF

Piracy

INTELLECTUAL

PROPERTY IN

CONTEMPORARY

China

Andrew Mertha

Cornell University Press gratefully acknowledges receipt of a grant from Washington University in St. Louis, which aided in the production of this book.

First published © 2005 by Cornell University Press

Printed in the United States of America

Library of Congress Cataloging-in-Publication Data

Mertha, Andrew C., 1965–
   The politics of piracy : intellectual property in contemporary China / Andrew C. Mertha.
      v. cm.
   Includes bibliographical references and index.
   Contents: Foreign pressure and China's IPR—The structure and process of exogenous pressure—Patents and faux consolidation of China's administrative patent regime—The copyright problem—Trademarks and anticounterfeiting—Evaluating the argument and analysis—Casting a wider net.
   ISBN-13: 978-0-8014-4364-0 (cloth : alk. paper)
   ISBN-10: 0-8014-4364-4 (cloth : alk. paper)
   1. Intellectual property—China. 2. Piracy (Copyright)—China. 3. Product counterfeiting—China. 4. United States—Foreign economic relations—China. 5. China—Foreign economic relations—United States. I. Title.
   KNQ1155.M47 2005
   346.5104'8—dc22   200512284

Cornell University Press strives to use environmentally responsible suppliers and materials to the fullest extent possible in the publishing of its books. Such materials include vegetable-based, low-VOC inks and acid-free papers that are recycled, totally chlorine-free, or partly composed of nonwood fibers. For futher information, visit our website at www.cornellpress.cornell.edu.

Cloth printing   10 9 8 7 6 5 4 3 2 1
Paperback printing   10 9 8 7 6 5 4 3 2 1

to Isabelle

Contents

Tables and Figures

Preface

In 1997, I secured the position of program officer for the National Bureau of Asian Research (NBR), a research and policy institute based in Seattle, Washington. The year before, as part of an ongoing project, *Advancing Intellectual Property Rights in China,* co-directed by Michel Oksenberg and Pitman Potter, the Bureau had published "Advancing Intellectual Property Rights: Information Technologies and the Course of Economic Development in China," which to this day remains one of the very few analyses on intellectual property rights (IPR) in China that uses a nonlegal, political focus.[1] The program officer was to lay the groundwork for the second module of the project, an IPR conference in southwestern China. From February through September 1998, I was based in the city of Chongqing, the site of the conference, from where I made repeated trips to Beijing, Shanghai, Chengdu, Guiyang, and Kunming municipalities.

One of my responsibilities was to recruit government officials, scholars, lawyers, and businesspeople in China and invite them to attend or formally participate in the conference. It was a tremendous opportunity to make contacts with Chinese government officials and others in China's IPR policy community. I was able to get my foot in the door, gaining access to these officials and establishing professional and eventually, in many cases, personal relationships with them. In addition, I worked with my two sponsoring agencies, the Chongqing Municipal Foreign Affairs Office and the Science and Technology Commission, which provided a type of access not often available to the foreign researcher in China. By the end of 1998, after more than eight months of intensive interaction with these

---

1. Michel C. Oksenberg, Pitman B. Potter, and William B. Abnett, "Advancing Intellectual Property Rights: Information Technologies and the Course of Economic Development in China," *NBR Analysis* 7, no. 4 (November 1996).

officials—as well as with their friends and associates in other parts of the country, whom I also got to know—I had mapped out China's intellectual property apparatus.

In addition, beginning in 1998 and 1999, I interviewed more than a dozen current and former officials from the Office of the United States Trade Representative (including a former United States trade representative, a deputy U.S. trade representative, an assistant U.S. trade representative, and a deputy chief negotiator for China and Hong Kong), the Department of State, and the Department of Commerce, as well as several representatives from the International Intellectual Property Alliance, the Motion Picture Association of America, the Business Software Alliance, the International Federation of Phonograph Industries, the Pharmaceutical Research and Manufacturers Association of America, the International Anti-Counterfeiting Coalition, the China Anti-Counterfeiting Coalition,[2] and the International Trademark Association.[3] I was also granted unfettered access to documents in the Office of the United States Trade Representative Reading Room.

In February 1999, I returned to China for six additional months of intensive fieldwork as a visiting scholar at the Research Center on Contemporary China (RCCC) at Beijing University, an excursion made possible by a Fulbright-Hays Fellowship from the U.S. Department of Education. The RCCC allowed me to conduct my research with an extraordinary degree of independence, while also helping me over a number of bureaucratic hurdles. As in 1998, I was able to interview, in some cases multiple times, officials across different parts of the country (Chongqing, Guizhou, Jiangsu, Shanghai, Sichuan, and Yunnan) as well as at the national level in Beijing. This, combined with hundreds of cold calls to lawyers, businesspeople, and, especially, private investigation agencies, helped me flesh out the story and to present a more nuanced, accurate, and complex picture of the IPR situation in China.

One particularly fortunate accident was the discovery that several national-level officials I was interviewing in late summer 1999 about their own domestic bureaucracies turned out to have participated as agency representatives during the Sino-U.S. IPR negotiations. As a result, I was able to interview U.S. and Chinese officials from both sides of the negotiating table.

Since then I have conducted fieldwork in many of the same areas, often re-interviewing people in China and the United States while also making new contacts. These trips in June 2001, June through August 2002, March

2. It has since been renamed the Quality Brands Protection Committee (QBPC), as discussed in chapter 5.

3. These individuals also availed themselves to me for follow-up questions. In addition, during my fieldwork in 1998 and 1999, many other U.S. officials directly and indirectly involved in the negotiations were extraordinarily helpful in providing me with data and very charitable with their time.

and July 2003, and August 2004 allowed me to track recent changes and developments in China's intellectual property regime.

I have learned a great deal since my arrival in Chongqing in early 1998. It is often counterproductive to go digging for dirt or to search for the smoking gun when researching the Chinese political process—almost always, a story that seems too good to be true is precisely that. One can gain important insights simply finding out how things work. This tactic requires considerable patience in the quest to amass information from as many credible sources as possible.

The researcher often does not control which research sites will be visited and which individuals interviewed. Nor is it often possible to establish optimal conditions for interviewing. For instance, I began my fieldwork in the Southwest and moved outward from there. Given the access that I enjoyed, I tried to identify how the Southwest differed from other parts of China—levels of economic development, contact with the outside, degree of legal infrastructure in existence, etc. Having identified these dimensions, I focused further research on field sites with different characteristics.

Although most of my interviews began with a fairly standard questionnaire, my interviewees often took the conversation in other directions. Conversely, in those (mercifully) rare instances when an official read from a prepared text, I knew that I could punctuate the "lesson" with only two or three substantive questions that were not on the official agenda. I endeavored to interview officials in the various bureaucracies under review in each location, specifically officials with the same ranks and titles in each setting. Some officials were more forthcoming than others, some painted an impossibly rosy picture, some became openly hostile to my questions, and some were extraordinarily matter-of-fact and forthcoming.[4] By replicating interviews in different locales, by following up in subsequent months and years, and by "triangulating," I slowly built the necessary degree of confidence in my data.

To cite just one example, in 1999 a national-level official told me that the "strike down fakes" (*dajia*) leadership small group was being dismantled (described in chapter 5). In the summer of 2003, however, several county-level officials told me that this group was still in existence in their county. This not only contradicted what my 1999 source had told me about the leadership small group but potentially discredited all the information that this particular source had provided. A few days later, I was talking with provincial-level officials in a different province and asked them about this

4. I should note that I encountered these problems at least as much, and often even more, from the non-Chinese governmental and commercial actors interviewed for this project. In addition, it was also necessary to evaluate the degree to which these sources actually knew the subject being discussed. Almost every foreigner in China prides him- or herself on being some form of "China expert," to a degree often inversely proportional to the length of time that person has actually spent in China. In this setting, details such as the conditionality of the person's responses contributed to his or her credibility as a source of information.

inconsistency. They told me that this leadership small group was still in existence at the local level and that it was being transformed into another quasi-formal body: "standardize the market economy" leadership small groups (*guifan shichang jingji lingdao xiaozu*). This was consistent with what my 1999 source had told me—but the pace of change was largely left to the localities. Some still had the old group; others had already changed to a new, less controversial body. All this was subsequently confirmed by other sources.

During my fieldwork from 1998 to 2003, I was asking questions about events that had taken place up to ten years earlier. One of the biggest challenges was that the configuration of Chinese bureaucracy changes over time: officials retire, get promoted, fall from grace. And, being human, they forget or embellish or otherwise color their recollections, consciously or unconsciously. This problem extended to something as seemingly "objective" as organizational charts. It took months to come up with an accurate map of the National Copyright Administration (NCA). Several NCA officials provided different versions of the NCA's internal divisions, accounts that were contradicted by subsequent interviewees. By narrowing down the inconsistencies, by re-interviewing some officials, and, finally, by arriving early for an interview so that I could walk through the NCA offices and jot down the various physical subdivisions in my notebook, I built what I believe is an accurate description of the NCA.

In this book I shed some light on an often misunderstood and highly sensitive policy issue in China. It is embedded in a complicated institutional context, one in which change is often swift and dramatic—and uneven—and its future trajectory remains largely uncertain. My hope is that I have provided more than a snapshot or an instance of "comparative statics," and offer instead a chronologically grounded analysis that explains political and organizational developments in China up through the present, and one that anticipates some of the changes and continuities to be confronted by the Chinese state in the years that lie ahead.

Acknowledgments

At the University of Michigan I was trained as a political scientist and as a student of China. My first debt of gratitude goes to Kenneth Lieberthal, Harold Jacobson, Michel Oksenberg, Robert Pahre, and Ernest Young. Ken did more than any other individual to initiate and deepen my fascination with, and love for, China. I owe him a debt that cannot be repaid. Even as he worked as special assistant to the president and senior director for Asian affairs at the National Security Council, Ken made time to read my drafts and to offer alternatively trenchant and supportive but always useful comments. However, I will never forget his confession to me over the phone during the crisis in East Timor in 1999: "I meant to get to your chapter this week, but . . . East Timor!" "Jake" combined his unfailing good nature with an emphasis on scholarly rigor and showed me the many different ways one can see the world analytically. Mike took on the role of mentor and colleague when we were in China together. Our month of collaborative fieldwork during the spring of 1998 was one of the great experiences of my professional career. Even though he is no longer with us, Mike continues to inspire. Bob is a valued colleague and friend whose thinking outside the "International Political Economy (IPE) box" fueled his genuine interest in a topic that was in many ways quite different from the traditional IPE canon. Ernie was a wonderful mentor and supportive committee member; his great humanity is matched only by his peerless knowledge and sage advice.

At Michigan, I was the beneficiary of training and advice from Chris Achen, John Campbell, Pradeep Chhibber, Paul Huth, Don Kinder, C. K. Lee, Doug Lemke, Liang Hsin-hsin, Albert Park, and Jennifer Widner, as well as from two wonderful visiting professors, Ellis Joffe and T. J. Cheng. I also gained a great deal from numerous colleagues. A few stand out: Dan Lynch (now at USC), Pierre Landry (now at Yale), Jeremy Schiffman (now at Syracuse), and Ben Goldsmith (now at the National University of Singapore). I thank them for their collegiality and am grateful for their continued friendship.

During my three years at Washington University, all of my colleagues in the department of political science have lent their support at various times. I am obliged to all of them. I thank former department chairs Jack Knight and Lee Epstein for using a perfect combination of the carrot and the stick to keep me motivated and focused on this project. In addition, Lisa Baldez, Frances Foster, John Haley, Nate Jensen, Bill Jones, Gary Miller, Sunita Parikh, and Andy Sobel all read parts of the manuscript and were extremely generous with their time and consistently on the mark with their advice. I also thank Bob Hegel and Rebecca Copeland for their encouragement. Steve Smith and the Weidenbaum Center on the Economy, Government, and Public Policy provided considerable moral and financial support to help see this project through.

Other scholars and experts who have read parts of what would become this book include William Abnett, William Alford, Jerome Cohen, Neil Diamant, Ken Foster, Mark Frazier, Mary Gallagher, Bill Hurst, Scott Kennedy, Stanley Lubman, Keith Maskus, Kevin O'Brien, John Odell, Pitman Potter, Stanley Rosen, Susan Sell, Susan Shirk, Joe Simone, Andy Sun, Scot Tanner, Karen Zeng, and four anonymous reviewers. I thank them all for their contributions. Chapter 5 is adapted from an essay in *Engaging the Law in China: State, Society and Possibilities for Justice*, edited by Neil J. Diamant, Kevin O'Brien, and Stanley Lubman (Stanford: Stanford University Press, 2005); it is reprinted here with permission of the publisher. Part of the discussion in chapter 6 is drawn from an article, "'Policy Enforcement Markets': How Bureaucratic Redundancy Contributes to Effective IPR Policy Implementation in China," which is forthcoming in *Comparative Politics*.

I am also grateful to former and current individuals at the Office of the United States Trade Representative, the Department of Commerce, the Department of State, the Business Software Alliance, the International Anti-Counterfeiting Coalition, the International Federation of Phonograph Industries, the International Intellectual Property Alliance, the International Trademark Association, the Motion Picture Association of America, the Pharmaceutical Research and Manufacturers Association of America, and the Quality Brands Protection Committee. In addition, countless individuals from the private sector in China, the United States, and Hong Kong were extraordinarily generous in making time for me despite their busy schedules—and incurring considerable opportunity costs in terms of billable hours.

I am indebted to the scores of anonymous government and Party officials, judges, lawyers, businesspeople, private investigators, and others throughout China who were willing to meet with me and who provided information I had no conceivable means of acquiring were it not for their generosity. I regret that I am unable to acknowledge these individuals by name. Within the Chinese government, these include officials in the National Patent Bureau/State Intellectual Property Office, the National Copyright Administration, the Administration for Industry and Commerce, the Quality Technical Supervision Bureau, the Ministry of Culture, the State Science and Technology Commission (now Ministry), the General Administration of Customs, and their local counterparts. At the subnational level, I am also beholden to individuals from the Finance Bureaus, the Committees for the Composition of Government Offices, the Intellectual Property Rights Working Groups, and the Foreign Affairs Offices in Chongqing, Guangdong, Guizhou, Jiangsu, Shanghai, Sichuan, and Yunnan provinces. I also thank the Chinese trade negotiators, judges, lawyers, and businesspeople who agreed to be interviewed for this project. This book would have been unthinkable without their help.

Others in China considerably mitigated the stress of fieldwork and provided logistical assistance (couches to sleep on or similar acts of kindness). These include Thierry Borel, Tara Boyce, Kevin Crowe, Shep Driver, Jim Nicholson, Shen Mingming, Wade and Grace Shepard, Graeme Smith, Junko Takada, Wu Shufang and Chen Lizhen, and especially Mindy Liu, Kevin O'Connell and Zhou Min. My colleagues at Beijing University and Fudan University also deserve thanks, as do individuals at the Sichuan, Yunnan, and Guizhou academies of social science.

Field research from 1999 through 2003 was made possible by a Fulbright-Hays Fellowship from the U.S. Department of Education, a Foreign Language and Area Studies (FLAS) Fellowship from the Center for Chinese Studies at the University of Michigan, a Washington University Grimm Fellowship, and several Weidenbaum Center small grants. I thank the selection committees at each of these institutions for their support.

Roger Haydon, my editor at Cornell University Press, saw the potential of this book several drafts ago and has been unsparing and unsurpassed in his professionalism, constructive criticism, and support. I also thank Chuck Myers and Muriel Bell for their consideration. Karen Laun has been the epitome of professionalism throughout this process. Dan O'Neill provided yeoman service in proofreading the final manuscript. Ultimately, I am responsible for any errors contained herein.

I am thankful to my parents, Eva Foreman and Gustav Mertha, and their spouses, Jerry Foreman and Valerie Mertha, as well as Jay Foreman for their interest throughout this process. My daughter, Sophie, also helped by establishing a pattern of sleep in relatively unbroken twelve-hour intervals.

However, the individual who has made the greatest sacrifices and contributed the most to this book is my wife and muse, Isabelle. It is to her that this book, and all the work that went into it, is gratefully dedicated.

THE POLITICS OF PIRACY

CHAPTER 1

Foreign Pressure and China's IPR Regime

On July 3, 1998, after a successful summit between U.S. President Bill Clinton and Chinese General Secretary Jiang Zemin, the U.S. delegation returned home to Washington. The only glitch came when United States Trade Representative Charlene Barshefsky was stopped by the U.S. Customs Service; her bags were found to contain forty-odd counterfeit "Beanie Babies" (a highly popular stuffed toy at the time) she had purchased in Beijing. This caused considerable embarrassment, given Barshefsky's pivotal role in pressuring Beijing to strengthen China's intellectual property rights (IPR) regime. The ensuing "Beaniegate" scandal was short-lived, as U.S. trade officials sought to play down the story. The Beanie Babies themselves—which became known collectively as "the Beijing 40"—were confiscated and, although originally intended to be donated to needy children, were eventually incinerated in Alexandria, Virginia, along with a shipment of Cuban cigars.[1] Chagrined officials at the U.S. Embassy in Beijing were given the thankless task of drawing up a memorandum to prevent such snafus in the future.[2]

1. Barshefsky was faulted not for purchasing *counterfeit* Beanie Babies but rather for failing to comply with the U.S. Customs Service rule (which was a response to a request by the manufacturer, Ty, Inc., since rescinded) that stated that individuals could only bring back one Beanie Baby purchased abroad. "Official Chagrined by Beanie Babies," *New York Times,* July 11, 1998. Although a Barshefsky representative asserted that these were not counterfeit but rather production overruns (factory seconds, not intended for sale), recent communications with Ty, Inc.'s legal representative confirms that they were, indeed, counterfeit. "Squeeze on Bogus Beanie Babies: Customs Agents Seize 256,000 Counterfeit Toys Worth $1.8 Million," *Knight-Ridder Tribune News,* December 23, 1998; "Daily Briefing," *Seattle Times,* September 2, 1998.
2. "U.S. Government employees in China have a special obligation to uphold U.S. law, including U.S. agreements with China, and not to undercut U.S. policy. The United States Embassy strongly recommends that all employees, family members, and official visitors exercise caution in their shopping in China in order to avoid purchasing goods which may be counterfeit." Administrative Notice, American Embassy, Beijing, number 007, January 19, 1999.

Quite apart from placing Barshefsky in an unflattering light, this anecdote illustrates the central problem facing U.S. efforts to obtain compliance from China in enforcing its own intellectual property laws. That even a high-profile U.S. trade official could purchase counterfeit products in the Chinese capital—only a short drive from where the actual meetings with the Chinese head of state had taken place, and while under the glare of the media spotlight—underscores the gaping holes that exist in China's IPR enforcement regime. It goes without saying that countless ordinary Chinese and foreigners in China can—and do—engage in this behavior every day in the absence of such scrutiny and without being caught. Moreover, having embraced the entrepreneurial spirit that is a mainstay of today's China, many IPR violators have developed increasingly sophisticated methods of manufacturing and selling pirated and counterfeit goods, ranging from cigarettes to computer software to auto parts, and in some cases even copying the factories that produce them.[3]

Frustrated by growing financial losses due to intellectual property theft in China, many in the U.S. IPR community argue that the best way to get China to act is by exerting pressure, to compel Beijing through the use (or threat) of sanctions and blandishments to improve IPR enforcement. The application of foreign pressure, always present as a diplomatic tool, has become a defining characteristic of the bilateral relations between the U.S. and China since 1989. The crackdown on June 4 of that year in Beijing and other parts of China, coupled with the concurrent fall of communism in Eastern Europe and the former Soviet Union, changed the very assumptions under which Washington had pursued its relations with Beijing for almost two decades. What had been a largely cooperative and constructive relationship based on a common threat (the USSR) quickly deteriorated once the tanks rolled into Beijing and the Berlin Wall came down. China's image was transformed from what Ronald Reagan had labeled "that 'so-called' communist country" into an archetype of coercive authoritarianism and a political target for a huge spectrum of domestic U.S. interest groups ranging from organized labor to pro-life groups to human rights activists.[4] Whether a reaction to domestic political maneuverings or a measured response to China's actions, U.S. pressure became a constant in its relations with China in the 1990s.

---

3. Interview 98CQ24, August 17, 1998. Because this study relies in large part on extensive fieldwork with sources wishing to remain anonymous, I indicate interviews by code. The first two digits indicate the year, the middle two letters indicate the location ("BJ" for Beijing, "CD" for Chengdu, "CQ" for Chongqing, "GY" for Guiyang, "GZ" for Guangzhou, "KM" for Kunming, "NJ" for Nanjing, "SH" for Shanghai, "US" for the United States, and "XJ" for an unnamed county in Sichuan Province). The last two digits place the interview in the overall interview sequence in a given locale in a particular year. Finally, if there was a sequence of interviews with a particular interviewee in a given location and year, the number of interviews is indicated by the letters A, B, C, etc., at the end of the interview number. Thus, the entry at the top of this note is my twenty-fourth interview conducted (with a source who provided only one interview, as indicated by the absence of a letter following the number "24") in Chongqing in 1998.

4. James H. Mann, *About Face: A History of America's Curious Relationship with China, from Nixon to Clinton* (New York: Alfred A. Knopf, 1999), 146–47.

The question that guides this book is: What has been the impact of external pressure on China's policymaking and implementation processes? Specifically, I focus on China's intellectual property regime to approach this question.[5] A definitive answer has been elusive for several reasons. First, there are strongly held convictions on both sides of the debate: many Chinese officials assert that all IPR-related developments in China occurred independently of external pressure, while foreign commentators argue that foreign pressure was absolutely crucial in getting China to develop its IPR laws.[6] Still others have observed that U.S. pressure has in fact had very little substantive effect:

> Since the criteria for judging the effectiveness of trade pressure include both the extent to which an agreement is signed and the degree to which the signed agreement is implemented to U.S. satisfaction, the close ties between pirate entrepreneurs and officials of both the central and local governments, which account for why the Chinese have repeatedly exacerbated difficulties on the enforcement front, *would have made it difficult to offer a positive evaluation of the effectiveness of U.S. pressure.* [7]

But the reality is not as simple as these arguments suggest. The IPR issue area is inherently complex, and the bureaucratic apparatus charged with managing and enforcing intellectual property in China, particularly at the local level, is correspondingly convoluted and opaque. Wading through these conflicting opinions and conclusions to identify the "footprints" of foreign influence in China's IPR laws and regulations is difficult enough. The task of recognizing the impact of external pressure on local administrative *enforcement* patterns in China is even more daunting. Not surprisingly, given these difficulties, existing analyses of China's IPR policy do not probe very deeply into the country's complex matrix of functional institutions and local political networks.

Yet most often it is here, at the local level, where these forces—external pressure and China's existing administrative systems for managing and enforcing intellectual property—clash head-on. In the summer of 2002, for example, in the Gubei district of Shanghai, I spotted a retail outlet for audio CDs, video compact disks (VCDs), and DVDs. In most respects, the

---

5. William P. Alford, *To Steal a Book is an Elegant Offense: Intellectual Property Law in Chinese Civilization* (Stanford: Stanford University Press, 1995); and Michel C. Oksenberg, Pitman B. Potter, and William B. Abnett, "Advancing Intellectual Property Rights: Information Technologies and the Course of Economic Development in China," *NBR Analysis* 7, no. 4 (November 1996) are the seminal existing works in the study of IPR in China.

6. "The principal engine of IPR development in China . . . has been direct pressure brought about by other countries, chiefly the USA, . . . [which has] essentially set the pace and priorities of China's drive to establish an IPR regime." Economist Intelligence Unit, *China Hand: The Complete Guide to Doing Business in China* (Hong Kong: Economist Intelligence Unit, 1996), 5.

7. Ka Zeng, *Trade Threats, Trade Wars: Bargaining, Retaliation, and American Coercive Diplomacy* (Ann Arbor: University of Michigan Press, 2004), 238 (italics mine).

store was no different from the hundreds that I had surveyed over the previous five years: shelves with the newest releases of motion pictures and
popular music, bargain bins for older disks, and alternately helpful and
sullen staff. I noted the physical layout of the store. Under a notice posted
by the district government about reporting copyright infringement, there
was a homemade sign confirming that the audiovisual products sold in that
section of the store were legitimate (*zhenban*). On the other side of the
shop, clearly divided from the first, there was no corresponding sign, and
it was equally clear—from the packaging, from the selection, and especially
from the price—that the merchandise on this side was pirated (*daoban*).

By dividing the shop into "legitimate" and "pirated" sections, the shop
owners were responding to two directly conflicting forces: a set of formal
laws and regulations forbidding the sale of pirated goods and the tremendous profits that come from selling these same pirated goods. Rather than
fostering tension and insecurity, however, these contradictory signals produced a perverse but relatively stable equilibrium outcome. On the one
hand, the proprietors were signaling to the government that they were in
partial compliance with China's Copyright Law (which, as I argue in chapter 4, is in large part a product of foreign pressure); at the same time, they
were also responding rationally to the fact that local governments lack key
resources to enforce the law to the extent that it would actually threaten
their operations.[8]

These mixed signals are themselves the result of a fragmented institutional structure and reflect some of the inherent contradictions shaping
the entire administrative network in charge of managing and enforcing
intellectual property in China. When foreign pressure and official policy
come into conflict with local incentives, the latter often win out. A store in
Yiwu municipality, Zhejiang province, selling pirated wholesale and retail
video CDs, and housed in a building owned by the municipal traffic police,
provides another case in point. The VCD shop was paying rent in exchange
for use of the site as well as for "protection" against enforcement activity
that, in upholding the laws of the land, would deprive the local proprietors
of their livelihood.

But the same institutions that can hinder effective IPR enforcement
can under certain circumstances also enhance and improve it. In contrast to the frequent claims that there simply is no discernible IPR protection in China or that nothing can be done about it, the reality is far
more subtle. And the impact of foreign pressure on this reality is subtler
still. The application of exogenous pressure toward specific policy goals
does not follow a simple causal pattern in which increased pressure leads

---

8. Unlike previous studies on Chinese law enforcement, I focus on China's functional
administrative enforcement bureaucracies, not its coercive apparatus. On the latter, see Murray
Scot Tanner, *The Politics of Lawmaking in China: Institutions, Processes, and Democratic Prospects* (New
York: Oxford University Press, 1999); and Harold M. Tanner, *Strike Hard: Anti-Crime Campaigns
and Chinese Criminal Justice, 1979–1985* (Ithaca: Cornell East Asia Series, 1999).

Figure 1.1. Retail outlet for pirated VCDs, Yiwu Municipality. Note the government crest in the upper part of the photograph. Photo by author.

directly to better compliance. This is because pressure—even if it leads to formal agreement by the leaders in Beijing, which is then enshrined in official laws and regulations—must pass through China's byzantine network of bureaucracies before it is translated into actual policy outcomes. But by taking these bureaucracies into account, the careful application of external pressure can, in some cases, have very real and lasting effects on policy enforcement. I substantiate these claims through an extensive study of how China negotiates, legislates, and enforces intellectual property rights.

Conceptualizing External Pressure

The argument I make in this book can be summarized as follows: The direction of external pressure and the characteristics of the institutions it is designed to change are crucial to understanding the effects of foreign pressure on policy enforcement outcomes. External pressure has taken on several forms, including threats to impose trade sanctions, to revoke China's most-favored nation status, and to block China's accession to international government organization bodies; it even took the form of dispatching a U.S. carrier group in response to Chinese military maneuvers during the 1996 Taiwan Straits crisis. It can also take more subtle and diffuse forms, as in the case of pressure from individual foreign commercial actors operating in China. How are we to understand international pressure?

It is a truism of international relations theory that deterrence, understood as pressuring an actor to *refrain* from a certain activity, occurs frequently but is difficult to observe because deterrence, successfully applied, results in a nonevent. Compellence, understood as pressuring an actor to engage in a certain activity, is easy to observe but far less frequent. As Robert J. Art writes:

> In contrast to deterrent threats, compellent actions more directly engage the prestige and passion of the put-upon state. . . . A state has publicly committed its prestige and resources to a given line of conduct that it is now asked to give up. . . . Thus, compellence is intrinsically harder to attain than deterrence, not because its objectives are vaguer, but because it demands mere humiliation from the compelled state.[9]

The compellent threat underlying U.S. pressure on China over IPR takes the form of threats of economic sanctions. The conventional wisdom holds that sanctions are generally not very effective or that they are effective only in a small minority of cases. Some take a different view, arguing that sanctions *are* successful about a third of the time, a significantly higher rate than that suggested by the current wisdom.[10] The counterargument runs that this is merely sleight of hand, in which the supposed success of sanctions has more to do with the widening of the *definition* of sanctions than it does with any empirical evidence.[11] My analysis extends beyond the sanctions debate because I am not simply looking at whether economic sanctions are successful per se but rather at how and why the mere threat of sanctions can alter the administrative structure and policy process of the target country.

In order to answer these questions, however, I have had to dispense with a large-n analysis and undertake a more empirically rich qualitative

9. Robert J. Art, "To What Ends Military Power?" *International Security* 4 (Spring 1980): 10.
10. Gary Claude Hufbauer, Jeffrey J. Schott, and Kimberly Ann Elliot, *Economic Sanctions Reconsidered: History and Current Policy*, 2d ed. (Washington, DC: Institute for International Economics, 1990).
11. Robert A. Pape, "Why Economic Sanctions Do Not Work," *International Security* 22, no. 2 (Fall 1997): 90–136.

single-country case study. Lisa Martin argues that such case studies are problematic because

> this type of work suffers from the usual methodological problems inherent in single-case study designs . . . [namely] that we have no way of knowing whether an instance of sanctions resembles in any way a "typical" sanctions episode, or whether the results of any study can be generalized across a wider range of cases.[12]

As far as generalizability claims are concerned, this study can be applied to other cases of international sanctions threats in two ways. First, the mechanisms by which trade issues in general are negotiated and implemented in China are very similar, if not the same, as those documented here. As one official from China's Ministry of Commerce (MOFCOM) asserted, other Sino-U.S. trade negotiations (including the WTO talks) were "exactly like this," that is, the negotiations on IPR. Moreover, when I asked him how MOFCOM might today respond to a hypothetical action by Special 301 (the institutional mechanism for U.S. IPR trade policymaking), the official said that it would respond precisely in the same manner as had its predecessor, MOFTEC (the Ministry of Foreign Trade and Economic Cooperation).[13]

Second, insofar as the various institutions and other mechanisms analyzed in this book are similar to those in other countries, the conclusions are themselves transferable to these other locales. Certainly, the U.S. trade policy agenda-setting process described in chapter 2 remains the same regardless of the country that is targeted. The relationship between the national government and local governments and the ways in which it can undermine the contract fashioned under the shadow of economic sanctions is by no means unique to China. Finally, the presence of foreign commercial actors on the ground in the target country and the relationships they establish with local government agents and other actors occurs all over the world and is increasing in volume and significance.

Martin's reservations also raise the somewhat troublesome notion as to what a "'typical' sanctions episode" actually is. For example, international "audience costs" are central to Martin's analysis, but in her usage they are only relevant in cases of multilateral sanctions, which raises the question of whether it is multilateral or unilateral sanctions that provide a case of "typical" sanctions. In the case examined here, international "audience costs" are at best peripheral to what is a two-state negotiation process governed by bilateral "tit-for-tat" trade sanctions, although domestic audience costs, particularly with regard to the U.S. trade associations discussed in chapter 2, matter considerably.

12. Lisa L. Martin, *Coercive Cooperation: Explaining Multilateral Economic Sanctions* (Princeton: Princeton University Press, 1992), 4–5.
13. Interview 03BJ01B, July 23, 2003.

Drezner also looks at the importance of international audience costs:

> While a robust anticipation of future disputes might make the sender prefer a coercive strategy, it also reduces its ability to obtain concessions. The target's conflict expectations determine the magnitude of concessions. Facing an adversarial sender, the target will be worried about the long-run implications of acquiescing. Because it expects frequent conflicts, the target will be concerned about any concessions in the present undercutting its bargaining position in future interactions. The sender might exploit the material or reputation effects from these concessions in later conflicts. When relative-gains concern [*sic*] is prominent, a concession represents a gain for the coercer and a loss for the coerced. When reputation is important, acquiescence bolsters the sender's credibility as a tough negotiator while weakening the target's reputation. With allies, this concern is less prominent, because the target anticipates fewer zero-sum conflicts. *Ceteris paribus,* targets will concede more to allies than adversaries. Ironically, a sender will obtain the most favorable distribution of payoffs when it cares the least about the relative distribution of gains.[14]

As often happens, the Chinese case confounds this model in part because China is neither an adversary nor an ally of the United States. More important, however, is that although on paper China gave up substantial concessions during the negotiations and ratified them in the legislative processes that followed, the actual administrative enforcement patterns occurred largely independently of these processes. Using Drezner's model, it is unclear whether China gave up significant, moderate, or minor concessions or, indeed, what "part" of China gave up what and why. To get at the actual nature of Chinese concessions, therefore, it is necessary, to go beyond the level of analysis favored by Martin, Drezner, and others and look instead at the institutional structures through which actual substantive, extra-legislative, compliance occurs.

Given the importance of compliance, it is somewhat curious that it has only recently become a central focus of scholarly inquiry[15] and tends to find more traction in environmental politics than it does in trade policy.[16] Analytically, it remains an underdeveloped and slippery concept in international

14. Daniel W. Drezner, *The Sanctions Paradox: Economic Statecraft and International Relations* (New York: Cambridge University Press, 1999), 4–5.

15. Abram Chayes and Antonia Handler Chayes, *The New Sovereignty: Compliance with International Regulatory Agreements* (Cambridge: Harvard University Press, 1995); and Nancy W. Gallagher, *The Politics of Verification* (Baltimore: The Johns Hopkins University Press, 1999).

16. Edith Brown Weiss and Harold K. Jacobson, eds., *Engaging Countries: Strengthening Compliance with International Environmental Accords* (Cambridge: The MIT Press, 1998); David G. Victor, Kal Raustiala, and Eugene B. Skolnikoff, eds., *The Implementation and Effectiveness of International Environmental Commitments: Theory and Practice* (Cambridge: The MIT Press, 1998); and Miranda A. Schreurs and Elizabeth Economy, eds., *The Internationalization of Environmental Protection* (New York: Cambridge University Press, 1997).

relations theory. Many who adopt the two-level games approach often substitute "[formal] ratification" with "compliance."[17] Beth Simmons and Lisa Martin look at the importance of reputational effects—particularly those pertaining to the legal and legislative realms—on future international interaction as an important component of successful compliance.[18] Some, like Michael Ryan, claim that the risk of noncompliance is great in a settlement agreement that is the outcome of power-oriented trade diplomacy.[19] Although these authors look at different aspects of compliance mechanisms, their focus tends not to center on key state institutions and therefore misses some of the important structures and processes that explain state behavior. In the case examined here, for example, the levels of analysis that conform to Graham Allison's organizational process and bureaucratic politics models are at least as important, and often far more important, in explaining outcomes than the executive branch and legislative processes taking place at the national level.[20]

Others, like Checkel, attempt to understand this issue through a constructivist lens, focusing on the role of norms in explaining compliance patterns.[21] Certainly, norms play an important role, and they help explain patterns that a simple structural approach might not, but it is too early to throw the institutional baby out with the legislative bathwater. Institutional structure and organizational incentives are central to understanding compliance outcomes. More to the point, it is difficult to establish a normative framework that captures the variation in enforcement documented here.

What is occurring is a phenomenon described elsewhere as "partial compliance."[22] While I also look at formal compliance at the national level and the official ratification of points argued at the negotiating table, the bulk of the analysis to follow looks at the far less elegant and parsimonious

17. Robert D. Putnam, "Diplomacy and Domestic Politics: The Logic of Two-Level Games," *International Organization* 42, no. 3 (Summer 1988): 427–60; Susanne Lohmann, "Electoral Cycles and International Policy Cooperation," *European Economic Review* 37 (1993): 1373–91; Helen Milner and B. Peter Rosendorff, "Democratic Politics and International Trade Negotiations," *Journal of Conflict Resolution* 41, no. 1 (February 1997): 117–46; and Jongryn Mo, "Domestic Institutions and International Bargaining: The Role of Agent Veto in Two-Level Games," *American Political Science Review* 89, no. 4 (December 1995): 914–24.

18. Beth A. Simmons, "International Law and State Behavior: Commitment and Compliance in International Monetary Affairs," *American Political Science Review* 94, no. 4 (December 2000): 819–35; and Lisa L. Martin, *Democratic Commitments: Legislatures and International Cooperation* (Princeton: Princeton University Press, 2000).

19. Michael P. Ryan, *Playing by the Rules: American Trade Power and Diplomacy in the Pacific* (Washington, DC: Georgetown University Press, 1995), 24.

20. Graham T. Allison, *Essence of Decision: Explaining the Cuban Missile Crisis* (New York: Harper Collins, 1971). To be fair, Simmons and Martin look at democracies in which robust institutions play a large part in bringing about compliance with international agreements. In China, as is arguably the case with many authoritarian and/or developing countries, one cannot assume such a relationship.

21. Jeffrey T. Checkel, "Why Comply? Social Learning and European Identity Change," *International Organization* 55, no. 3 (Summer 2001): 553–88.

22. See Andrew C. Mertha and Robert Pahre, "'Patently Misleading': Partial Implementation and Bargaining Leverage in Sino-American Negotiations on Intellectual Property Rights" *International Organization* 59, no. 3 (Summer 2005).

structures and processes of informal compliance, the norm that governs policy enforcement at the local level. As such, this analysis provides a far more in-depth study than is possible using a large-n research design and, in doing so, opens up brand new avenues of scholarly inquiry.

The Institutional Mechanism of Top-Down External Pressure

In chapter 2, I focus on the type of pressure surrounding the U.S. trade policymaking and negotiation processes: a combination of specific demands, explicit deadlines for agreement, the threat of trade sanctions, and the stigma these impose on the target country. Because chapter 2 focuses on the actual demands leveled during the agenda-setting process for U.S. IPR trade policy as well as describing the institution of Special 301 in detail, my goal in this introduction is simply to illustrate the broad contours of U.S. pressure and the strategies employed by the United States in using pressure to leverage the Chinese side.

Special 301 provides the principal means for actors to compel the U.S. trade representative (USTR) to initiate action against a target country. There are three designations that can be leveled at a country deemed to be violating U.S. intellectual property. The most severe of these is the "priority foreign country" designation, which requires by law the investigation of the target country's intellectual property practices, at the conclusion of which the USTR decides whether the target country warrants "retaliation" in the form of U.S. trade sanctions.[23] Within thirty days of the release of the annual *National Trade Estimates* report, that is, no later than the end of April, the USTR must publicly identify those countries to which it has affixed the label of "priority foreign country" and draw up a preliminary sanctions list.[24] The actual sanctions under which such trade negotiations take place can vary. During the 1991–92 IPR negotiations, the sanctions were set at $1.5 billion. During the 1994–95 intellectual property negotiations, the sanctions were set at $1.1 billion. And during the 1996 IPR negotiations, the sanctions were set at $2 billion.[25]

Of course, these figures represent only a fraction of the actual volume of U.S.-China bilateral trade, so it is reasonable to ask whether such pressure is actually meaningful. Based on the outcomes of the Special 301–led negotiations, the answer is yes. In addition to the direct costs involved in leveling sanctions, there are a number of other, indirect costs that serve to

23. In addition, there are two less stringent rubrics: "priority watch country" and "watch country," described in chapter 2. USTR "Fact Sheet: Special 301 on Intellectual Property," May 25, 1989; and Michael P. Ryan, *Knowledge Diplomacy: Global Competition and the Politics of Intellectual Property* (Washington, DC: Brookings Institution Press, 1998), 80.

24. Ryan, *Knowledge Diplomacy,* 7; and A. Puckett and William Reynolds, "Rules, Sanctions and Enforcement under Section 301: At Odds with the WTO?" *American Journal of International Law* 90, no. 4 (October 1996): 677–79.

25. "China-U.S. Trade Issues," *CRS Brief for Congress,* Congressional Research Service, Library of Congress, March 14, 2002, http://fpc.state.gov/documents/organization/9061.pdf.

add "teeth" to the pressure in question. Uncertainty about looming sanctions can hold back levels of foreign direct investment, which has formed the cornerstone of China's economic development over the last quarter century. It would also have been difficult, if not impossible, to obtain congressional approval to renew China's most-favored nation status if the U.S. were engaged in a trade war involving sanctions and countersanctions with China. Finally, Special 301 places a tremendous stigma on the countries against which it is leveled, sending the message that the country in question is not a responsible trading partner. Even when Hong Kong was designated a "priority watch country," a less serious charge, in 1997, the stigma was so powerful that it led to dramatic internal changes in Hong Kong's enforcement apparatus for combating copyright piracy as well as to the promulgation of a set of new intellectual property laws.

Challenges Facing Top-Down External Pressure

Exogenous pressure does not succeed or fail in a vacuum. It is channeled through various negotiation strategies, it is wrapped around certain substantive demands, it links related issues together to increase leverage, it is backed up by specific threats, and it meets with various forms of resistance. How this pressure is molded into actual strategy and successful negotiated outcomes is a complex and often thorny process.

Exposing China to outside pressure, without adequately taking into account the institutional nexus through which such pressure must pass before it is transformed into actual policy, is almost certainly going to create problems at the policy enforcement stage if not during the policymaking phase. For example, in a 1996 *New Yorker* profile on Charlene Barshefsky, Elsa Walsh writes that "the Chinese bristle, but Barshefsky nevertheless raises human rights concerns whenever she speaks with Chinese officials."[26] But in the compartmentalized world of Chinese bureaucratic politics, the "human rights" portfolio does not appear anywhere within the jurisdiction of Chinese trade officials. The Clinton administration learned this painful lesson early on when it was forced to delink trade and human rights.

The USTR has been more successful when concentrating on issues substantively related to one another. The United States strategically used promises of support for China's bid to become a founding member of the World Trade Organization (WTO) while negotiating the framework of what was to become the 1992 Sino-U.S. Memorandum of Understanding on Intellectual Property Rights. The result, according to a member of the U.S. negotiation team, was that Beijing made deeper commitments on this bilateral agreement than it likely would have under the Trade-Related Aspects of Intellectual Property Rights (TRIPS, the WTO intellectual property regime), to show their good faith.[27]

26. Elsa Walsh, "The Negotiator," *New Yorker*, March 18, 1996, 89.
27. Interview 98HK06, June 24, 1998.

But there are other trade issues can meet with Chinese opposition. During the first Bush administration, USTR Carla Hills studiously kept the issues of IPR and market access separate, while her successor, Mickey Kantor, believed that one issue could be used to leverage the other. From the USTR's perspective, the logic was straightforward: insofar as penetration of the Chinese market by legitimate manufacturers of copyrighted products was blocked, pirates could satisfy consumer demand, which accounted for the nearly 100 percent piracy rates in some of these industries. To the Chinese, however, U.S. demands to open up the market for "cultural products"[28] smacked of "spiritual pollution" (*jingshen wuran*), an attempt to undermine the ideological work of the Chinese Communist Party and government agencies, such as the Ministry of Culture, that focus on "cultural" or "spiritual" products.[29] This introduced a further layer of suspicion into the talks, extending the 1995 negotiations for two more months, and the subsequent implementation of the market access provisions in the final agreement was very poor, improving only slightly in anticipation of China's accession to the WTO some five years later.

Finally, there can be bureaucratic resistance, even defiance, at the national level to changes in the status quo. A case in point is the Ministry of Machinery and Electronics Industry (MMEI).[30] Both former U.S. and retired Chinese negotiators acknowledged that the MMEI was among the most intractable of the Chinese agencies.[31] Given the power that this bureaucracy derived from the lack of copyright protection for software in China—the MMEI was in charge of the "diffusion" of computer software—it is perfectly natural for it to be among the most resistant of the Chinese units during the negotiations, and this intractability was fully embodied in the MMEI representative at the negotiations, Ying Ming. Not only was he unpopular with the U.S. side—at one point he told the U.S. negotiators, "We cannot afford to pay royalties, we don't want to, and what is more, you cannot make us"[32]—some representatives on the Chinese side with whom I spoke opined that Ying and the MMEI were dragging the talks into a direction that served the MMEI but not the rest of the Chinese agencies collectively.[33]

28. "Cultural products" refer to the following categories: amusement/recreation (*yule*), audio/visual products (*yinxiang*), performances (*yanchu*), arts and crafts (*meishu ping*), cultural relics (*wenwu*), cinema (*dianying*), and books/periodicals (*tushu baokan*).

29. Interview 99BJ28, July 27, 1999.

30. The MMEI (*jixie dianzi gongye bu*) was split into the Ministry of Machinery (*jixie bu*) and the Ministry of Electronics Industry (*dianzi gongye bu*) in March 1993. *Zhonghua renmin gongheguo zhengfu jigou wushi nian* [Government Organizations of the People's Republic of China over Fifty Years] (Beijing: *Dangjian duwu chubanshe yu Guojia xingzheng chubanshe*, 2000), 77.

31. Interview 98US09, November 30, 1998; Interview 98US10B, December 4, 1998; Interview 99BJ23, July 19, 1999; and Interview 99BJ28, July 27, 1999.

32. Interview 98US09, November 30, 1998.

33. At this level, the pressure to toe the institutional line is irresistible (Interview 99BJ23, July 19, 1999). Ministry, bureau, and commission representatives, regardless of their own personal views, faced overwhelming pressure to conform to the preferences of the bureaucracy they represented. What is particularly interesting is that the MMEI representative is a respected

Top-Down External Pressure and Eleventh-Hour Agreements

It is therefore noteworthy that, given these dynamics, Sino-U.S. IPR negotiations have consistently resulted in agreements that for the most part conformed to the broad contours of U.S. demands, although there are important exceptions. The Chinese eventually agreed, although reluctantly and with a great deal of foot-dragging (and plenty of fiery rhetoric stating that they were doing nothing of the kind), to many of the U.S. stipulations. Why is this?

First of all, although intellectual property, like many trade-related issues, can be highly complex and sophisticated, the identification of specific instances of intellectual property violations is often straightforward, even as the causes often remain complex.[34] Moreover, there were several high-profile, politically charged, physically identifiable sources of IPR piracy that could be used as an empirical measure of the ability of the United States to get China to move on IPR and of China's credible commitment to intellectual property enforcement. Foremost among these was the continuing operation of thirty or more factories in southern China that were identified as producing pirated compact disks and CD-ROMs. The subsequent 1996–97 "winter action" crackdown on these factories did fundamentally shift the location of production of these pirated goods outside of China (and into Hong Kong, Macau, and Southeast Asia), although it did little to change the systematic shortcomings of China's IPR enforcement regime.[35]

In addition, there was a limit to the damage that could be done if the trade talks had broken down. Unlike a dialogue over strategic issues, a breakdown in IPR talks would not have been catastrophic. Although both sides feared the prospects of a trade war, the United States was prepared to accept this outcome.[36]

Third, for many on the U.S. side, intellectual property was an issue in which China would find it very difficult to defend itself. Although this view was not widely shared on the Chinese side, there was sufficient evidence for U.S. negotiators to demonstrate that China's IPR enforcement was lacking. Assistant U.S. Trade Representative Lee Sands and his staff made numerous trips to China between rounds of formal negotiations to investigate the

---

scholar who has argued in his academic writings for the need to establish a strong copyright protection regime in China, including for computer software (see, for example, Ying Ming, "Jisuanji ruanjian shi shou zhuzuoquan fa baohu de zuopin" [Computer Software is one of the works protected by the Copyright Law], *Zhuzuoquan* [Copyright], November 4, 1991.

34. Interview 99HK04, June 23, 1998.

35. Interview 98SH02, March 19, 1998; and Interview 98US18, December 10, 1998.

36. For example, one former USTR official involved in the negotiations confirmed this by saying that that in February 1995, Deputy U.S. Trade Representative Charlene Barshefsky arrived in Beijing "with sanctions in her pocket" (Interview 99BJ16, March 24, 1999). In the 1991–92 negotiations, the focus moved from "Have the Chinese given us enough?" to "Do we retaliate if China does not give us what we insist upon?" The latter question was ultimately answered in the affirmative (Interview 98US10A, December 3, 1998).

IPR enforcement situation on the ground, and they became increasingly familiar with local experiments in IPR enforcement, particularly those undertaken in Shanghai and Guangdong.[37]

On occasion, U.S. negotiators would show their Chinese counterparts pirated merchandise they had purchased locally. Rhetoric notwithstanding, the Chinese government itself implicitly (and unintentionally) conceded that enforcement levels were unsatisfactory by staging deliberately timed crackdowns on IPR piracy and infringement at critical junctures during the negotiations.[38] Indeed, although this point can be debated, the United States was not asking China to pursue goals to which the Chinese leaders themselves were not committed on paper. The two sides differed on the rate of constructing China's intellectual property regime, on the appearance of China taking orders from the United States, and on the specific details of the U.S. demands.[39]

Finally, several U.S. trade negotiators pointed out that the United States sought substantive outcomes while the Chinese were largely satisfied with symbolic ones. Chinese acquiescence to substantive U.S. demands, and the laws, rules, and regulations that emerged from them, is the subject of chapters 3 through 5. However, U.S. negotiators were willing to give the Chinese symbolic concessions. For example, the U.S. side realized early on that China would be unable to square its incendiary rhetoric with an early resolution of the talks. China would have to hold out until literally the eleventh hour and stonewall as much as possible, utilizing genuine bureaucratic resistance as a negotiation strategy. Such delaying tactics allowed the Chinese side to demonstrate that it would not roll over in the face of U.S. demands—at least not until the very last minute. As a result, the U.S. side was forced to accept this fate and utilized the time before the deadline to try to get as many more concessions as possible (during some of the more excruciating periods, the negotiators would write dirty limericks or engage in other diversions to amuse each other). Even the second agreement, which was an "exchange of letters," was a nod to Chinese sensibilities: to call the 1995 agreement a Memorandum of Understanding (MOU) would imply that the Chinese had failed to implement the 1992 MOU. The Chinese insisted the second agreement not be in the form of an MOU; understanding the semantic significance, the U.S. side complied. Such a trade-off between symbols and substance provided the opportunity for positive-sum outcomes in spite of the heavy-handed accusations and innumerable delays that stretched the negotiations out from days and weeks to months and even years.[40]

37. Interview 98US14, December 8, 1998; Interview 98US15, December 8, 1998; Interview 98US20, December 11, 1998; and Interview 99BJ16, March 24, 1999.

38. Interview 98US09, November 30, 1998; Interview 98US10A/B, December 3 and 4, 1998; and Interview 99BJ16, March 24, 1999).

39. Interview 99BJ28, July 27, 1999; and Interview 99BJ37, August 4, 1999.

40. Interviews 98US10A/B, December 3 and 4, 1998; and Interview 98US15, December 8, 1998.

Local Enforcement and "Lateral" External Pressure

These substantive U.S. demands—and the Chinese acceptance of them—provided the framework for the next sets of IPR-related laws and regulations that China officially adopted, as documented in chapters 3 and 4. However, after all the handshakes, banquets, and toasts of *Moutai* (a prominent Chinese liquor), the far more difficult process of enforcing these agreements and their related legislative and regulatory outcomes had just begun. External pressure may have succeeded in getting Beijing to promulgate satisfactory IPR-related laws and regulations, but the enforcement of intellectual property, as with most policy in China, falls within the domain of China's complex bureaucracies and local government officials. And very often the priorities of these front-line enforcement agencies (or their immediate superiors) compete with, even run counter to, the imperatives of IPR protection.

The chasm that separates policymaking and policy enforcement is the most important political and policy cleavage analyzed in this book. For instance, all of the pressure that the USTR has brought to bear on China from 1991 up through the present day has translated to an astonishingly low degree of copyright enforcement. One could argue that the copyright bureaucracy is so strong that it has been able to withstand the U.S. demands and hold its ground. In fact, the case is exactly the opposite: the copyright bureaucracy is so weak that it has been singularly unable to enforce China's own copyright-related laws and regulations, regardless of whether its representatives want to do so. Its weakness and inertia, not its strength and resistance, explain these outcomes.

One part of the enforcement story is the degree to which a given enforcement bureaucracy is independent of its "host," or superior, bureaucracy. As will be discussed in detail in chapters 3 and 4, both the copyright and the patent administrative enforcement agencies become increasingly absorbed into their superior bureaucracies the farther one goes down China's administrative rungs. For the patent bureaucracy, this superior unit is the science and technology bureaucracy; for copyright, it is the Ministry of Culture's cultural market management bureaucracy. Bread-and-butter issues such as personnel and budgetary matters are managed by these superior bureaucracies, making the copyright and the patent bureaucracies dependent on their "host" units. However, because the latter often have priorities that are more pressing in an organizational sense than patent or copyright protection, the quality of patent and copyright enforcement suffers as a result.

But, while descriptively accurate, this focus on structural embeddedness does not help us understand *variation* in enforcement because another official administrative agency charged with a similar problem that it tackled more effectively, trademark enforcement, was faced with these very same structural problems. It was the presence of two key factors that created an enforcement scenario dramatically different from those pertaining to copyright and patent enforcement. First, the direction of the external pressure differs substantially from that accorded to copyright and patent issues. Since the early 1990s, there has been a striking increase in the presence of foreign companies on the ground in China. In addition to these companies, there has also been a corresponding proliferation of Chinese and foreign private and quasi-private investigation firms operating on Chinese soil. Side payments provided by these foreign companies and the investigative firms on their behalf can take many forms, including solicited "case fees," the allocation of legitimate expenses for enforcement actions, the provision of banquets and other entertainment for local cadres charged with anticounterfeiting enforcement, or even the construction of recreation facilities for individual local government offices. These side payments, or the expectation of them, have served to alter the incentives of the anticounterfeiting bureaucracies toward better enforcement of trademarks.

Second, this pressure succeeded in no small part because it was directed at not one but *two* separate anticounterfeiting bureaucracies—one that was formally charged with trademark enforcement and another that aspired to be—that, unlike their patent- and copyright-related counterparts, are engaged in dynamic competition over their enforcement portfolios. Specifically, the Administration for Industry and Commerce (AIC) and the Quality Technical Supervision Bureau (QTSB) are largely independent agencies that have been competing with one another for the anticounterfeiting portfolio. This combination of competition over tasking and the bureaucratic reach that allows the AIC and the QTSB to extend down to the county level (in the case of the AIC, all the way down to the township level), stands in sharp contrast to the copyright and patent bureaucracies, which have only recently begun to establish a critical mass below the provincial level.

As noted, this set of conditions has provided a particularly auspicious environment for foreign actors to become an active, engaged part of the enforcement process. When allowed to interact with local bureaucracies, foreign actors have been able to establish networks with local enforcement agencies based on trust, mutual respect, and, of course, monetary transfers. These factors have worked to pull these enforcement units away from their previous inertia or cooptation by local governments and transform them into relatively effective enforcement agencies. This "external" pressure from *within* China is critical to explaining such outcomes. More broadly, this process of lateral external pressure can be understood as a particularly localized (and, for some, a not particularly agreeable) example of what Anne-Marie Slaughter calls "the new world order": networks of strange bedfellows united in a common goal but existing parallel to (and rendering irrelevant) formal geographical and jurisdictional state boundaries.[41] Such networks provide a dynamic in which "is born the recursive

---

41. Anne-Marie Slaughter, *A New World Order* (Princeton: Princeton University Press, 2004).

relationship between state and society, the mutually transforming interactions between components of the state and other social forces" in which these latter "forces" are not necessarily indigenous to China.[42]

The Issue Area in Brief: An Introduction to Intellectual Property

Patents

In this book, I use the traditional definition of "intellectual property," which encompasses patents, copyright, and trademarks. Patents provide inventors with the right of exclusion from the use, production, sales, or import of the product or technology in question for a specified period of time, after which use of and other rights over the product or technology become part of the public domain. Patent protection is usually related to technology-intensive innovation, and arguments in favor of patent protection usually center on the various incentives patents create that spur innovative activity. Although patents are not limited to particular industrial sectors or technologies,

> patent protection is seen as particularly critical for capturing returns to basic invention in pharmaceuticals, agricultural and industrial chemicals, and biotechnology. . . . At the same time, IPRs related to drugs, genetic inventions, and seed varieties are precisely the technologies that attract the greatest controversy. There is widespread concern in developing countries over the potential for monopoly pricing and limited distribution of new technologies and products in response to stronger patents.[43]

And, indeed, sometimes these concerns dovetail with strategic national goals and issues that may be excluded from patent protection, namely, national security and public health. In response to these tensions, many developing countries have instituted countermeasures. In some cases, they simply declare that national security and public welfare trump the rights of pharmaceutical companies to set prices or to determine distribution channels. A growing number of developing countries, including Argentina, India, South Africa, Thailand, and China, have challenged the status quo and utilized the Doha Declaration of TRIPS, the World Trade Organization's IPR regime, to relax patent protection in cases of "national emergency."[44] In such cases, it is relatively easy to cross the line between

42. Joel S. Migdal, "The State in Society: An Approach to Struggles for Domination," in *State Power and Social Forces: Domination and Transformation in the Third World,* ed. Joel S. Migdal, Atul Kohli, and Vivienne Shue (New York: Cambridge University Press, 1994), 9.

43. Keith E. Maskus, *Intellectual Property Rights in the Global Economy* (Washington, DC: Institute for International Economics, 2000), 52.

44. The Doha Declaration on TRIPS and Public Health provides flexibility under the international IPR regime for developing countries to authorize local manufacturers to copy a patented

compulsory licensing and "reverse engineering" of patent processes by local pharmaceutical companies in order to develop and manufacture drugs that infringe upon the original patent. Conversely, with regard to genetically engineered foodstuffs and other plant and animal products, many countries simply do not allow imports of such goods, citing the lack of conclusive evidence that these products are *not* harmful, a variant of the national security/public health issue.

The institutions established to manage and administer a given country's domestic patent regime and to harmonize it with international IPR laws and conventions become a part of these controversies when national or international patent-related policies must be administered or enforced. In order to manage these contradictory dynamics effectively, they require a certain degree of autonomy and authority to undertake such coordinating responsibilities. Absent such a mandate and the political authority to back it up, the desire for a normatively just and economically optimal solution is often overwhelmed by an almost Hobbesian world of black-market economics, infringement, and inefficient allocation of the costs and benefits associated with patent protection.

Copyright

Copyright has traditionally been associated with the arts and has generally not been included in discussions over direct industrial applications—until recently. Under copyright, the object under protection is the *expression* of an idea. Copyright protects a literary or artistic work against unauthorized duplication, performance, recording, broadcast, translation, or adaptation, and it also safeguards the integrity of the work by outlawing "prejudicial modification" of the work even after the creator has sold the rights to it. In more recent years, computer software has been included under copyright protection because software is increasingly regarded in international copyright treaties as a "literary work."[45] The goal of copyright protection, like that of patents, is to establish and maintain positive incentives for individuals to continue to create literary works because such works provide social, cultural, and economic benefits to society. The controversies that exist within the subfield of copyright, therefore, occur along economic, social, and cultural fault lines.

---

medicine, under certain circumstances even without the patent owner's consent. Under the agreement, member countries should not prevent others "from taking measures to protect public health [Article 4]." Specifically, this means that "each member has the right to grant compulsory licenses and the freedom to determine the grounds upon which such licenses are granted [Article 5b] . . . [and that] each member has the right to determine what constitutes a national emergency or other circumstances of extreme urgency [Article 5c]."

45. Article 10 of TRIPS on Computer Programs and Compilations of Data states that "computer programs, whether in source or object code, shall be protected as literary works under the Berne Convention (1971)."

These economic, social, and cultural issues become entangled in the issue of piracy of audiovisual products in developing and/or authoritarian regimes. Because the costs of creation are very high but the costs of production are very low, such piracy provides a classic case of "free riding," in which pirates reap profits from manufacturing—and consumers enjoy the savings from purchasing—pirated goods that deny the rightholders their share of remuneration. However, in my conversations with the state agents charged with controlling the sale of these products, the argument they use is a rather curious one: because the legitimate products are too expensive, consumers create the demand for a black market in pirated goods. This is noteworthy because if the task of policing pirated goods were simply a matter of controlling "thought work," market considerations would be irrelevant. It appears that these officials are content to look the other way while such activity takes place for several reasons that combine economic and social/political considerations.

First, although these local government agencies do not support the unregulated production and sales of such "value-laden" products, they recognize their inability to enforce the law in full. Because of resource scarcity, enforcement agents pursue those pirated products that provide a clear threat to social stability and the political status quo. In other words, there is selective enforcement of the "cultural market" of audiovisual products.

Second, state officials may derive economic benefit from such activities. There is no shortage of reports and anecdotes about kickbacks and other bribery schemes involving payouts to local officials that allow the pirates to continue their operations. In the case of Thailand, for example, Susan Sell notes that

> intellectual property protection has placed Thai leaders in a difficult position. In 1987 Prime Minister Prem Tinsulanoud's administration was ousted in a no-confidence motion after attempting to strengthen Thailand's copyright laws. Intellectual property protection is controversial in Thailand because piracy has become a lucrative business there. [Individuals in the government have] a strong interest in protecting the piracy industry that provides jobs in manufacturing as well as in over 12,500 retail shops . . . the domestic political stakes are high.[46]

Sell's account equally well describes what has been occurring all over China in the past decade.

Third, such consumption may actually assist the government in maintaining social stability. Although this point remains somewhat controversial, and outright confirmation of such a statement remains elusive, its logic is powerful. Economic development requires fundamental changes to the social and political fabric of society. As people become increasingly disenchanted with

---

46. Susan K. Sell, *Power and Ideas: North-South Politics of Intellectual Property and Anti-Trust* (Albany: State University of New York Press, 1998), 192.

the changes in the world they live in, they become potential recruits for political activism and social movements. One way to mitigate against this is to allow them to consume cheap audiovisual products, the contemporary equivalent of imperial Rome's "bread and circuses," in order to keep them entertained at home and off the streets—accomplishing this by allowing them to purchase and consume pirated DVDs of the motion picture *Gladiator* is not without its irony.

Finally, as long as black markets are tolerated but not officially sanctioned, they are denied the legitimacy that can threaten state organs charged with censorship. The latter can always institute a campaign against audiovisual piracy under the rubric of "cleansing" society of the negative effects of exogenous "cultural pollution." Thus it is not necessary to change the status quo of censorship that exists. In this way the state can have its cake and eat it too: social stability is maintained by providing the people with some means of escape through watching motion pictures, even if the actual movies are a bit racy at times, while the ultimate authority of the state censorship organs remains intact.

Trademarks

Trademarks are the third leg of the traditional IPR "tripod." Trademark is the protection of a particular name or distinctive mark used to identify a product, company or service (in the case of service marks). Maskus provides a description of the scope of trademarks and the effects of trademark infringement and counterfeiting:

> Like patents and copyrights, trademarks carry legal authority to enforce the exclusive use of an asset created by human thought. In this case the asset is a symbol or other identifier that conveys information to the consumer about the product. If consumers view the mark as a reliable indicator of desirable product characteristics, they would be willing to pay a premium for the good. This premium compensates the firm for the cost of developing and advertising the trademark. If competitors were allowed to duplicate the mark or use a confusingly similar mark these costs might not be recoverable.[47]

Trademarks provide multiple benefits to consumers. First, trademarks convey information on product quality. Second, and related to the first, this creates incentives for these trademark companies to maintain their quality standards. Third, successful trademarks can also provide the incentive for other manufacturers of distinctive products to enter the market, thereby enlarging and deepening it. Finally, trademarks also provide the supply for

47. Maskus, *Intellectual Property Rights in the Global Economy*, 47.

Figure 1.2. Genuine "M&M's" vs. infringing "Sanlian W&W's." Special 301 submission from Mars Incorporated, February 4, 1991, on file at the USTR reading room.

narrower consumer demand on high-end products with "snob appeal." Thus, the success of trademarks lies in their ability to guarantee a generally understood amount of value for the individual (a private benefit) while also contributing to the enlargement and diversification of the market (a public good).

All of these benefits are undermined, however, when trademarks are violated. Trademarks can be counterfeited, wherein the actual mark (and often the entire outer packaging) is simply duplicated. The second form of violation is infringement, in which a very similar mark or outer packaging is used with the intention of confusing the consumer. An example is the packaging of M&M's candies: in the case of the counterfeit, the packaging is more or less indistinguishable from the real one; the trade dress on an infringing package is similar in color and design but the product might be called "W&W's" instead, as was the case with candies produced by China's Sanlian Corporation.

On the other hand, it should also be noted that consumers often purchase certain counterfeit items fully aware that they are fake. Particularly with high-end items, consumers can flaunt the fact that they own such "luxury" items while avoiding the costs of purchasing the real thing, as is the case in places like the Lo Wu Commercial City in Shenzhen, to which 90,000 consumers from Hong Kong daily crossed the border to shop in the late 1990s:

> On a recent Sunday, crowds surged through the mall's maze of corridors, mobbing hundreds of tiny stores selling fake Rolex watches, Gucci shoes, Fendi clothing, Prada bags, and Chanel wallets. While women rummaged through piles of merchandise, their husbands loitered outside, knee-deep in shopping bags. As shoppers elbowed one another aside for coveted items, scuffles broke out . . . [said one Hong Kong resident] "People go up there because they get a great kick out of buying something for a fraction of what it costs in Hong Kong."[48]

Yet sporting a fake Hermès scarf does not incur the same potential risks as consuming knockoff heart medicines or flying in an airplane that uses counterfeit replacement parts.[49] The variation in the type of goods whose marks can be infringed or copied is enormous.

The "So What?" Questions

There are at least two issues that oblige me to underscore the generalizability of this study. The first is Chinese exceptionalism. Many scholars who study a country or area in depth become attracted to and fascinated by the unique aspects of the region. However, this creates a tendency toward exceptionalism and against comparability. Moreover, in the case of China, this tendency is reinforced by two other factors. The first is China's sheer size. Encompassing one-fifth of humankind, the immensity of China makes it relatively easy for the area specialist to dismiss China's comparability by saying, "So what if China is an outlier on dimension $x;$ it is an outlier that is substantively important (i.e., we are justified in studying it in isolation from other cases) purely on the basis of the country's size." The second reinforcing dimension is the ease by which many succumb to the notion

48. John Maggs, "It's Not Hong Kong, but Then It's Not Gucci Either," *New York Times,* February 2, 1999.
49. A somewhat bizarre counterpart in the copyright issue area is the youth culture that has arisen in Hong Kong in which pirated movies are valued precisely *because* they are pirated. The grainier the resolution, the better the movie. Indeed, the B-movie "Bio-Zombie" (*shenghua shoushi*) paid homage to this phenomenon by editing its opening credits with "audience members" finding their way to their seats to make it look as if the movie itself had been pirated. Hsinng-chi Hu, "A 'VCD Generation' or a Lost Generation? The Ambivalence of the Hong Kong VCD Phenomenon," paper presented at "Mapping a New Cultural Geography: Taipei, Hong Kong, and Shanghai as Global Cities," the Sixth Annual Conference on the History and Culture of Taiwan, Washington University, St. Louis, May 4, 2002.

that because China's cultural and historical legacies are unique, China cannot be compared to other states or regions. Such cultural explanations are often deliberately used or unconsciously internalized by Chinese citizens and foreign observers of China alike.[50] Some of the most familiar examples analyze the Chinese negotiation process, arguing that there is a specifically "Chinese" way of doing things. While some of these observations are accurate, these studies tend to understate the role of Chinese institutions in the negotiation process (this structural dimension is analyzed at length in chapter 2).[51] Most cultural explanations tend to obfuscate as much as they illuminate, if not more so.[52] Therefore, I should underscore the fact that even though I focus on the Chinese case, there are important continuities and referents, both explicit and implicit, within this China-grounded study that are applicable to other states, regions, and political systems.

The second issue is that "intellectual property" is considered by many to be an exceedingly narrow issue. I disagree. It is perhaps understandable that until recently IPR remained a third-tier, "technical" issue in the lexicon of U.S. trade policy because it is often articulated in a seemingly arcane discourse that presupposes a considerable degree of specialization and expertise. As a result, much discussion on intellectual property remains somewhat esoteric and inaccessible. Yet people all over the world are perfectly aware of what knockoffs or pirated music, movies, and software are, and they find the topic quite interesting, even compelling, when it is stripped of legalese. Indeed, intellectual property—even if not articulated as such—is a concept that impinges on the everyday lives of billions of people around the globe, not simply on the narrow stratum of intellectual property holders. It is also, as I will argue below, a particularly illustrative and substantively interesting case of U.S. pressure directed abroad and onto the policymaking and enforcement processes in China on any number of other issue areas.

For Those Interested in Intellectual Property but Who Do Not Care about China

The first of two "So what?" questions is: Why China? The Chinese case is instructive because China is similar to many developing and postsocialist

50. A recent example is in a piece by Mayfair Yang: "[Doug] Guthrie did not consider the possibility that, as a Caucasian researcher in China, his interests in *guanxixue* might be interpreted by his subjects as an attempt to dig out the traditional, 'feudal,' irrational, and embarrassing aspects of the Chinese industrial order." This "Caucasian/Chinese" distinction as an impediment to conducting effective research can be interpreted as an example of the cultural relativism that often confounds rather than clarifies. See Mayfair Mei-hui Yang, "The Resilience of *Guanxi* and its New Deployments: A Critique of Some New *Guanxi* Scholarship," *China Quarterly* 170 (June 2002): 462.

51. Richard H. Solomon, *Chinese Negotiating Behavior: Pursuing Interests Through "Old Friends"* (Washington, DC: United States Institute for Peace Press, 1999); and Lucian Pye, *Chinese Commercial Negotiating Style* (Cambridge: Oelgeschlager, Gunn and Hain, 1982).

52. Steven R. Reed, *Making Common Sense of Japan* (Pittsburgh: University of Pittsburgh Press, 1993); and Gerald L. Curtis, *The Logic of Japanese Politics: Leaders, Institutions, and the Limits of Change* (New York: Columbia University Press, 1999) provide excellent critiques of the cultural approach.

countries and, therefore, it is possible to make inferences from the Chinese experience to explain intellectual property development (or the lack thereof) in these other countries. At the root of the problem is the fact that "intellectual property" encompasses two contradictory notions that can easily mobilize interested parties on both sides and quickly lead to conflict. Although lacking the moral resonance of debates over such issues as preemptive war, arms sales to "rogue" nations, or human rights, IPR remains a polarizing issue for many of those involved with it, especially as technological change makes piracy and counterfeiting significantly easier to undertake than was the case just a few years ago.

Generally speaking, "intellectual property" refers to the protection of intangible assets for a specified period of time in order to induce and reward innovation and creativity while at the same time allowing the public to enjoy the benefits of this innovative and creative behavior. These two conflicting goals are resolved by granting what many understand to be a limited-term legal monopoly on the property in question. After a specified period of time, this monopoly right is rescinded and the work in question enters the public domain. The tensions created between *ownership* and *use* claims over intellectual property provide the principal cleavages in the larger social, political, and economic debates over intellectual property between the developed and the developing worlds.

Developed countries often regard the diffusion of IPR without the proper remuneration to the inventor or to the author quite clearly as theft, which in turn leads to the socially negative outcome of stifling innovation and creativity. In developing countries, by contrast, the widespread diffusion of this intellectual property is often regarded as the most effective way to distribute knowledge that will eventually lead to economic development and power. Many developing countries, however, argue that they are too poor to pay for IPR royalties yet should not be forced to curtail development simply because they cannot afford to do so. If such technology is available and can be harnessed without prohibitive royalty payments, the tendency to violate intellectual property becomes irresistible. These states can take moral cover by arguing that criticism from developed countries of their development strategies involving IPR violations is another example of the "Northern hegemony" designed to keep "the South" subordinate, both economically and politically.[53]

Intellectual property in China also suffers from the legacies of socialism. In the socialist system, property was expropriated by the state. In the case of tangible property rights, this meant transferring ownership of the means of production—factories, wholesale and retail outlets,

---

53. In such a context, according to Ryan, the "implication of the strategy for intellectual property policy was that industrial property ought not to receive patent protections and compulsory licensing ought to be demanded of foreign owners of technology." Ryan, *Knowledge Diplomacy*, 127.

research and development facilities—to a state run by a vanguard Party representing "the will and the interests of the people." This debate over the rights of inventors and innovators touches on the set of core assumptions that separate socialist from capitalist systems. In contrast to the West, whereby it is generally accepted that at least some of the inventor's rights are inseparable from the invention itself, that his or her rights are "embedded" within it, the socialist approach to intellectual property is based on the assumption that it is impossible to separate the inventor's activity from the society of which the inventor is a part. The invention is not simply a technical achievement but the logical outcome of the inventor's role as a member of society.[54] Therefore, the rights and obligations granted by a patent, for example, must be weighed against the costs and benefits to society as a whole. The patent holder may have some rights of remuneration and disposal of the patent but cannot govern its use. In other words, the patent is not, nor does it contain elements of, the inventor's private property.[55] The socialist legacy argument helps explain the structural and normative reasons that former Stalinist systems like Russia, the Ukraine, and China have been unable to protect intellectual property. Moreover, these normative predispositions can themselves be reinforced by other historical or cultural legacies of these countries toward intellectual property.[56]

To sum up, there are historical legacies that can contribute to the hostility of the recipient environment in which intellectual property is introduced. "Late developing" countries wish to increase the diffusion of new technologies, innovation, and information through state intervention in order to catch up with the developed world. Socialism adds to this the normative bias against private property, including the limited-term monopoly conferred by IPR. These stand in opposition to many of the western capitalist assumptions that property rights are the very cornerstone of the establishment of a market-based system of economic development. If IPR can be established in China, it is a short leap to the conclusion that intellectual property can take root anywhere.

54. Tao-Tai Hsia and Kathryn A. Haun, "Laws of the People's Republic of China on Industrial and Intellectual Property," *Law and Policy in International Business* 5, no. 3 (1973): 750.

55. Barden Gale, "The Concept of Intellectual Property in China: Inventors and Inventions," *China Quarterly* 74 (June 1978): 338.

56. Some have argued that China also suffers from a third dimension: the difficulty of exporting intellectual property is more regionally specific to East Asian "Confucian" states. As William Alford puts it:

Given the extent to which "interaction with the past is one of the distinctive modes of intellectual and imaginative endeavor in traditional Chinese culture," the replication of particular concrete manifestations of such an endeavor by persons other than those who first gave them form never carried, in the words of the distinguished art historian and curator Wen Fong, the "dark connotations . . . it does in the West." . . . On the contrary, in the Chinese context, such use was at once both more affirmative and more essential. It evidenced the user's comprehension of and devotion to the core of civilization itself.

Alford, *To Steal a Book is an Elegant Offense,* 29.

For Those Interested in China but Who Do Not Care about Intellectual Property

The second "So what?" question is: Why intellectual property? Put simply, IPR provides an excellent window into the policymaking and policy enforcement processes of contemporary China. The legacies discussed in the previous section aside, China's contemporary political system suffers from fragmentation and differing degrees (and trajectories) of institutionalization, making it an even more inhospitable context for IPR to take root. It has been more than three decades since Samuel Huntington famously claimed that "the most important political distinction among countries concerns not their form of government but their degree of government."[57] It follows that any examination of public policies and the political processes in which they are shaped, linked, negotiated, or enforced must take into account the particular political, economic, and social context in which the policy is embedded. If this context is marked by an insufficient degree of institutionalization—an imperfect *degree* of government—as is often the case in developing states, the political process is constrained by a substantial degree of political, institutional, and policy-related fragmentation.

This study follows in the tradition of earlier analyses on China's policymaking and policy implementation institutions.[58] The analysis contained herein builds on the foundations laid by Schurmann, Barnett, and Harding on the challenges of political organization in China; Lampton's scholarship on political bargaining and policy implementation; Lieberthal and Oksenberg's body of work on the structure and process of the Chinese state and the development of the "fragmented authoritarianism" (FA) framework; and Lieberthal and Lampton's extension of the FA framework. As stated in the latter work:

> The fragmented authoritarianism model argues that authority below the very peak of the Chinese political system is fragmented and disjointed. The fragmentation is structurally based and has been enhanced by reform policies regarding procedures. The fragmentation, moreover, grew increasingly pronounced under the reforms beginning in the late 1970s.[59]

57. Samuel P. Huntington, *Political Order in Changing Societies* (New Haven: Yale University Press, 1968), 1.

58. Franz Schurmann, *Ideology and Organization in Communist China* (Berkeley: University of California Press, 1966); A. Doak Barnett, *Cadres, Bureaucracy, and Political Power in Communist China* (New York: Columbia University Press, 1967); Harry Harding, *Organizing China: The Problem of Bureaucracy 1949–1976* (Stanford: Stanford University Press, 1981); David M. Lampton, "Chinese Politics: The Bargaining Treadmill," *Issues and Studies* (March 1987): 11–41 and *Policy Implementation in Post-Mao China* (Berkeley: University of California Press, 1987); Kenneth G. Lieberthal and Michel C. Oksenberg, *Policy Making in China: Leaders, Structures, and Processes* (Princeton: Princeton University Press, 1988), 31.

59. Kenneth G. Lieberthal, "Introduction: The 'Fragmented Authoritarianism' Model and Its Limitations," in *Bureaucracy, Politics, and Decision Making in Post-Mao China*, ed. Lieberthal and Lampton, 8.

No set of Chinese bureaucracies illustrates the basic dynamics of the "fragmented authoritarianism" framework better than those in the service of implementing intellectual property policy. Political fragmentation provides the general context in which many of the inherent conflicts within the intellectual property issue area take place. Incentives that influence behavior are themselves often shaped by a combination of the political structures suggested above (and described in detail throughout the remainder of the book) and certain economic and social costs and benefits specific to patent, copyright, and trademark policy, respectively.

The term "fragmentation" as used in this book can mean a number of different things when applied to the political process. To be sure, any complex bureaucratic system is prone to some degree of fragmentation. The fragmentation I discuss here exists largely along two dimensions. In the first, there are deep jurisdictional cleavages that separate discrete bureaucracies as well as even larger gaps that separate functionally specific clusters of related bureaucracies (*xitong*). The second dimension is based on geography: the relationship between the national government and local governments. These two dimensions can profoundly affect policy formulation because each of the relevant actors, whether due to function or geography, can potentially act as "veto players" and undermine the implementation process, and therefore their preferences must be taken into account during the policymaking stage if the policy is expected to enjoy even a minimum degree of success. In analyzing the effects of pressuring a country to adopt various policies in such an environment, we must identify the broad contours of such fragmentation, both in the larger, more general context and with regard to the specifics of the issue area examined in this book.

More generally, I have chosen to look at the particular issue area of intellectual property—although almost any other policy area would be equally appropriate—in order to map China's complex bureaucratic apparatus from Beijing to the bottom of the administrative hierarchy, and its ability to respond to international pressure—or not respond, as the case may be. I do this in order to get at the relationship between international pressure and policy enforcement in China. Structurally, therefore, this analysis traces the discrete IPR-related bureaucracies from the center of the system, Beijing, down to the township levels along *both* functional and spatial dimensions. As such, it differs from other scholarship that establishes distinct cleavages between center and local at the heart of the analysis.[60] This is not to say

60. Michel C. Oksenberg and James Tong, "The Evolution of Central-Provincial Fiscal relations in China, 1971–1984: The Formal System," *China Quarterly* 125 (March 1991): 1–32; Susan L. Shirk, *The Political Logic of Economic Reform in China* (Berkeley: University of California Press, 1993); Dali L. Yang, "Reform and the Restructuring of Central-Local Relations," in *China Deconstructs: Politics, Trade and Regionalism*, ed. David Goodman and Gerald Segal (London: Routledge, 1994); Wang Shaoguang, "The Rise of the Regions: Fiscal Reform and the Decline of Central State Capacity in China," in *The Waning of the Communist State: Economic Origins of Political Decline in China and Hungary*, ed. Andrew G. Walder (Berkeley: University of California Press, 1995);

that center-local dynamics are not at work here—they most certainly are, as I will argue. Rather than conceptualizing the issues at work through the center-local divide, however, I prefer to look at the vertical hierarchies as an organizational and institutional continuum through which we can see subtle changes and variation that the traditional center-local divide might overlook. I am not arguing that my approach should supplant the traditional center-local framework; rather, the two, when taken together, offer a more complete understanding of this important dynamic than either one could on its own.

With regard to the more specific attributes of the issue area of IPR, the State Intellectual Property Office (SIPO), discussed at length in chapter 3, provides a good illustrative example. SIPO was established deliberately to conform to the traditional notion of "intellectual property" and to institutionalize this traditional grouping into a concrete bureaucratic agency: in theory, SIPO manages and coordinates activities among the discrete patent, copyright, and trademark bureaucracies in their IPR protection and enforcement responsibilities. In reality, SIPO is an organization largely adrift and often disconnected from the actual institutional and political arena in which nonpatent-related IPR protection and enforcement in China take place. Some see SIPO as an organizational fiction established largely for foreign consumption. Indeed, SIPO is supposed to represent officially the configuration of IPR bureaucracies discussed in this book to foreign IPR-related actors. More charitably and possibly more accurately, others see SIPO as an institution that may achieve a lock on real political power commensurate with its official mandate at some unspecified time in the future. At present, however, SIPO lacks the authority to make demands on the IPR protection and enforcement bureaucracies—precisely those institutions it is formally charged with managing.

The intellectual property–related policies that SIPO is charged with implementing are refracted through a fragmented institutional network. The independent bureaucracies in this network have in turn been adapted to meet the parochial organizational goals and have been shaped by the official and unofficial incentives of those directly charged with enforcing these policies. The bureaucracies comprising China's IPR apparatus are not only discrete vertical units themselves; they also belong to distinct bureaucratic clusters, *xitong*, across which member officials have traditionally had very little contact. Patents fall under the science and technology *xitong*, copyright falls under the propaganda and culture *xitong*, while trademarks fall under the finance and economics *xitong*. Thus, the existence of SIPO notwithstanding, grouping patents, copyright, and trademarks together from an *organizational* standpoint makes as much sense as placing molecular physics, pornography, and foreign investment within the same policy

---

and Yasheng Huang, *Inflation and Investment Controls in China: The Political Economy of Central-Local Relations During the Reform Era* (New York: Cambridge University Press, 1996).

area served by a functionally coherent "superbureaucracy." Moreover, considerable fissures exist within the three *xitong* themselves: jurisdictional turf battles, power asymmetries, and competition over scarce resources within these bureaucratic clusters account for much of the variation in the effectiveness of enforcement across these three areas of intellectual property.

As the earlier discussion on compellence and economic sanctions makes clear, however, there is a dimension at work here that previous work on political organization and institutional development in earlier stages of reform-era China has not adequately captured. Not surprisingly, it has been one of the most difficult to conceptualize. This is the role of exogenous pressure—and, increasingly, the participation of foreign political and commercial actors—on the organizational structure and political process in China. It would be inaccurate to say that the role of foreign actors is not documented in the previous scholarship on bureaucratic politics in China. As Lieberthal and Oksenberg have noted, for example, "foreigners may force an issue onto the agenda of the highest level leaders."[61] But such references were largely allusions to national-level policymaking and do not adequately help us understand the far more heterogeneous Chinese state (relative to the mid-1980s) that exists today.[62]

More recently, Gallagher has argued that foreign direct investment as a domestic force has opened up China's economy while helping thwart political reform.[63] Gallagher's focus on exogenous pressure and ownership types helps us understand how external forces have helped shape China's economy, with substantive, albeit indirect, effects on the political system. In this book, by contrast, I look at the direct impact of exogenous pressure on the organizational and institutional structure of the state—that is, without utilizing the evolving Chinese economy as the critical intervening variable between foreign pressure and Chinese political institutions.[64]

Thomas Moore has written eloquently and at length on the literature on external factors that affect domestic politics—"the second image

---

61. Lieberthal and Oksenberg, *Policy Making in China*, 31.

62. Harry Harding, *A Fragile Relationship: The United States and China since 1972* (Washington, DC: Brookings Institution Press, 1992); Robert S. Ross, *Negotiating Cooperation: the United States and China, 1969–1989* (Stanford: Stanford University Press, 1995); Robert L. Suettinger, *The Politics of U.S.-China Relations 1989–2000* (Washington, DC: Brookings Institution Press, 2003); David M. Lampton, *Same Bed, Different Dreams: Managing U.S.-China Relations 1989–2000* (Berkeley: University of California Press, 2001); and Mann, *About Face.*

63. Mary Gallagher, "'Reform and Openness': Why China's Economic Reforms Have Delayed Democracy," *World Politics* 54, no. 3 (April 2002): 338–72.

64. The use of the changing Chinese economy as an intervening variable is a fairly common approach to get at the question of foreign pressure and political/structural change. See Shirk, *How China Opened its Door: the Political Success of the PRC's Foreign Trade and Investment Relations* (Washington, DC: Brookings Institution Press, 1994); Nicholas R. Lardy, *Foreign Trade and Economic Reform in China, 1978–1990* (New York: Cambridge University Press, 1992), *China in the World Economy* (Washington, DC: Institute for International Economics, 1994) and *Integrating China into the Global Economy* (Washington, DC: Brookings Institution Press, 2002); and Margaret M. Pearson, *Joint Ventures in the People's Republic of China* (Princeton: Princeton University Press, 1991). However, as with Gallagher, these analyses do not examine the direct impact of foreign pressure on China's political structure and process.

reversed"—so there is no reason for me to replicate it here.[65] Many people have rightly commended Moore's conceptual approach and his placement of China in the larger global context. However, one of the linkages between international forces and the domestic political process upon which his analysis rests—the administrative stratum of "provincial- and municipal-level [government] officials"—remains tantalizingly underdeveloped as a critical level of analysis, in part due to the methodological limitation of insufficient data.[66] Because this study arguably relies even more on data that only national- and local-level officials can provide, at the core of my research design are extensive interviews with these actors throughout multiple bureaucracies and across various regions in China to get at a similar general research question as that posed by Moore (although in a different policy context): What is the impact on exogenous forces on the workings of the Chinese state?

Finally, David Zweig has written on China's internationalization throughout the reform era.[67] However, Zweig's analysis differs significantly from that offered here because in the cases he examines, China's policymakers have largely set their own terms in choosing the nodes through which domestic and international economic and (thus) political linkages operated. To be sure, there have been many unanticipated consequences that such liberalization has brought to China, including the reshaping and restructuring of state institutions. Nevertheless, unlike the foreign pressure that formed the context of the Sino-U.S. IPR negotiations and the subsequent enforcement, the channels through which China initially pursued its program of internationalization were decided upon in large part by the Chinese themselves. This stands in sharp contrast to the impact that foreign pressure to improve its IPR regime has had on China. This pressure, imposed from the outside, palpably forced its way through the formal labyrinths and informal warrens of preexisting institutions, administrative and jurisdictional fault lines, and, in some cases, political and ideological "forbidden zones." In this case, foreign pressure did not enter on China's terms; indeed, it was often in direct opposition to China's own immediate goals and desires.

The Organization of the Analysis to Follow

This introductory chapter has served to lay out the broad questions and debates over the IPR issue that I will weave throughout the analysis to follow. Chapter 2 provides a summary of the Sino-U.S. IPR negotiations.

65. Thomas G. Moore, *China in the World Market: Chinese Industry and International Sources of Reform in the Post-Mao Era* (New York: Cambridge University Press, 2002), ch. 2. On the second image reversed, see Peter Gourevitch, "The Second Image Reversed: The International Sources of Domestic Politics," *International Organization* 32, no. 4 (Autumn 1978): 881–911.

66. Moore, *China in the World Market*, xviii and 152–58, for example.

67. David Zweig, *Internationalizing China: Domestic Interests and Global Linkages* (Ithaca: Cornell University Press, 2002).

There I will argue that the procedures for establishing international IPR trade policy in the United States involved extensive interaction between the IPR trade associations and the Office of United States Trade Representative under Section 301 ("Special 301") of the 1988 Omnibus Trade and Competitiveness Act. Once the demands had been set, the United States presented them to the Chinese negotiation team, which organized around a strategy of maximum resistance. The demands that Beijing could not withstand provided the substantive framework of the three bilateral Sino-U.S. IPR agreements and, by extension, of the Chinese laws and regulations that emerged from them. This chapter provides a starting point for the discussion of the impact of U.S. pressure on patents, copyright, and trademarks discussed in chapters 3, 4, and 5, respectively.

In Chapter 3, I argue that China's patent regime initially evolved largely independently from foreign pressure, at least until the early 1990s. Although patent issues comprised an important part of the first round of Sino-U.S. IPR negotiations in 1991 and 1992, the 1994–95 negotiations had the greatest impact on the actual structure of the national and local patent bureaucracies. The 1995 Exchange of Letters and Action Plan put an international imprimatur on domestic bureaucratic changes, especially with regard to the patent bureaucracy and the agencies close to it, that had been occurring at around the same time and, in effect, institutionalized them. One important change was the establishment of the IPR Working Conference (IPRWC), an overarching coordination mechanism for patent, copyright, and trademark issues. However, the institutionalization of the IPRWC only served to sustain the fragmented nature of and the disjointed power relations within the discrete bureaucracies charged with managing each of these three IPR subfields. Moreover, China's subsequent IPR super-bureaucracy, the State Intellectual Property Office, modeled itself on the IPRWC, particularly with regard to the consolidation of patent, copyright, and trademark management under a single bureaucratic agency. Yet SIPO contains many of its predecessor's shortcomings, including an inability to manage and control the copyright and trademark bureaucracies effectively. Indeed, at present, such consolidation appears unattainable, given SIPO's organizational weakness and the intense opposition of the copyright and trademark enforcement bureaucracies to a formal merger. Therefore, it remains necessary to examine these other two bureaucracies independently from SIPO, which I do in the next two chapters.

Chapter 4 begins with an analysis of China's legislative and administrative efforts to establish a viable copyright regime. The legislative process that in 1990 led to the enactment of the first copyright law in the People's Republic of China was protracted and difficult. Ultimately, the sway of U.S. pressure accounts for the timing and much of the content of the law and related regulations. In fact, U.S. pressure was so successful that at one point China's copyright regime afforded foreign copyright holders greater protection in China than it did for Chinese citizens. However, the success of foreign pressure in the national legislation of China's copyright laws and regulations stands in stark contrast to the inability of this pressure to translate into meaningful enforcement at the local level. This paradox stems from the fact that China's administrative apparatus for managing and enforcing copyright is hampered by severe personnel and budgetary shortfalls and is embedded within more powerful bureaucracies with organizational goals and priorities that often diverge from copyright enforcement. The chapter concludes with a discussion of possible future copyright enforcement scenarios.

In chapter 5, I shift the focus to trademark issues, specifically anticounterfeiting enforcement. Although the trademark lobby had the least success in pursuing its interests under Special 301, and although its concerns remained severely underrepresented in the three bilateral agreements, trademark enforcement in China ultimately benefited the most from outside pressure. But this pressure to improve China's trademark regime moved in a *lateral* direction from *within* China: it was largely a result of foreign trademark holders with commercial operations in China who took an active and direct role in working together with local Chinese enforcement agencies to protect their trademarks. Interbureaucratic competition by two independent anticounterfeiting bureaucracies facilitated this process, creating chance opportunities for these foreign actors to adapt this competition to their advantage through side payments and other blandishments over and above more direct forms of pressure. Whereas external pressure over copyright and patents focused on legislation and top-down implementation, pressure over trademarks appeared *exo*genous to the formal political system in China, but it was in fact *endo*genous to the social and commercial context in which the political system is inextricably linked. The chapter finishes with a discussion of more recent developments in which these same foreign actors have attempted to move away from administrative enforcement and toward criminal prosecution of counterfeiting.

In chapter 6, I review my argument and pare it down to its essential components. I discuss alternative explanations and, using counterfactual reasoning, argue that these other explanations are far less persuasive than the analysis presented in this book. Finally, I provide a discussion of the interaction between the legal-judicial infrastructure and the administrative bureaucracies analyzed in chapters 3 to 5. The concluding chapter 7 places the results of this analysis in a broader empirical and analytical context.

The analysis in this book provides a new lens through which to understand the confluence of international and domestic politics in China. Many international relations scholars have asserted that "domestic politics matter," while an increasing number of comparativists acknowledge that international forces shape domestic political processes. In very few cases, however, do such analyses actually study the interactions of these international and domestic dynamics in detail. The analysis to follow traces the bilateral trade policymaking, negotiation, and enforcement processes from the Office of the United States Trade Representative to the halls of the Ministry of Foreign Trade and Economic Cooperation to the nexus of enforcement at the provincial level and beyond in China. Moreover, it traces the interaction of foreign and domestic political and commercial actors in two important but distinct environments. On the one hand, it analyzes the formal negotiation process that pits the representatives of the two governments against one another in a largely confrontational milieu. On the other hand, it traces the interaction between local governments and foreign commercial actors in the actual trenches of IPR enforcement. In doing so, it provides an alternative conceptualization of interstate negotiations, one that takes place in the local arena. This analysis also allows us to recast traditional notions of state and society in China as well as more generally by understanding foreign commercial actors as not simply oppressive agents of the state maintaining a status quo that disadvantages society but rather as partners with certain pockets of the state to bring about legal and normative change that arguably benefits society in the long run.

This study also provides an extensive road map of the administrative Leviathan that is responsible for managing IPR. China boasts an enormous bureaucratic apparatus that is charged with, among many other things, IPR enforcement. However, this network, covering dozens of institutions and centering around the four bureaucracies studied at length in this book, is at best opaque to outside observers; very often, it is completely invisible. This is due in part to the somewhat inaccurate expectation that IPR issues are most often handled in China's courts. However, it is also due to the tendency of the Chinese to be extremely guarded with internal information and often extraordinarily reluctant to describe even simple reporting relationships among multiple governmental agencies. As a result, providing a simple but accurate schematic of any individual bureaucracy involves literally dozens of interviews with the government officials who reside within it. So it is not surprising that until now, no such mapping of China's IPR apparatus existed. One of the main empirical contributions of this book is to provide precisely such a record.

The chapters to follow also provide a new way of looking at the contemporary dynamics of bureaucratic competition and policy enforcement in China. This does not simply build on earlier analyses on policymaking and policy implementation in China. The analysis contained herein updates our understanding of the dynamics of policy enforcement in a rapidly changing Chinese context. It traces the relationships between the organizational structure, the jurisdictional reach, and even the institutional culture, on the one hand, and the actual behavior of the key IPR bureaucracies in China. It goes beyond a simple reliance on resource scarcity (which is a necessary but insufficient aspect of the overall explanation) to explain the inertial behavior of some of these bureaucracies. Even in the case of the more sluggish of these enforcement agencies, the explanations for their relative inactivity are far more nuanced and interesting than the conventional wisdom would have us believe (i.e., "they are simply corrupt"). This analysis provides an antidote to simplistic but nonetheless widespread assumptions about policy enforcement in China.

Fourth, it gives us a framework to help anticipate patterns of China's compliance with international legal obligations and treaty commitments. This analysis provides a much-needed corrective to the unfalsifiable conventional wisdom encapsulated by the sentiment that "of course implementation will be a problem, but. . . ." It is important for scholarship on China to fill this lacuna, which will in turn help us anticipate patterns of current and future compliance with China's international agreements. If the devil is in the details, then it is necessary to confront this dimension of implementation and enforcement directly in order to lift the veil of secrecy and often deliberate misinformation to better understand the subject of our scholarly inquiry. Because, as I argue in chapter 2, intellectual property is negotiated and enforced like any other trade issue (albeit with a specific set of bureaucracies charged with implementation), the application of this analysis extends far beyond a narrow focus on intellectual property.

Finally, a note on my approach: because I evaluate intellectual property in a political and organizational framework and not in a legal or judicial one, some may object or at the very least raise an eyebrow over an analysis of intellectual property undertaken through such a perspective.[68] Several Chinese and foreign interviewees in the field initially responded to my questions along the lines of "What you are asking is *political;* I thought we were going to talk about intellectual property." I do not wish to suggest that the legal-judicial dimension is not important in China—it most certainly is. And this study, taken alone, is not sufficient in fully describing the universe of arenas in which IPR adjudication, compliance, and enforcement take place. In order to have a full understanding of the complex environment in China that governs the structure and process of IPR protection, it is necessary to connect this analysis with existing legal-judicial ones. However, because this politico-administrative dimension has received so little attention in the literature to date and because, ironically, this political and administrative focus is precisely the lens through which many foreign and Chinese IPR owners in China themselves view the concept of intellectual property and is the principal means through which they pursue the enforcement of their rights, it is necessary to analyze this critical but hitherto neglected part of the Chinese intellectual property policy community.

---

68. I address these issues in chapter 6.

CHAPTER 2

The Structure and Process of Exogenous Pressure

Domestic Agenda-Setting and the Sino-U.S. Negotiations

All is fair in trade negotiations. At an impasse during one round of Sino-U.S. negotiations over intellectual property, one of the U.S. negotiators placed on the table three homemade signs that he had made. They were the Chinese characters *pingdeng* ("fair/balanced"), *huli* ("mutually beneficial"), and *touming* ("transparent"). After a suitable pause for effect, he placed three more signs, each with the Chinese character *bu* ("not") adjacent to the original three signs, forcing the Chinese to continue the negotiations while staring into a set of Chinese characters accusing them of being "unfair" (*bu pingdeng*), "seeking to undermine mutual benefits" (*bu huli*), and of being "opaque" (*bu touming*). The Chinese were nonplussed. On another occasion, the U.S. team took their Chinese counterparts to the old Cottonwood Café in Washington, D.C., and ordered special dishes for their Chinese guests, including "Snakebites," which consisted of jalapeños stuffed with shrimp and cheese and which caused the delegation members some intestinal distress; this was in response to a Chinese banquet for the U.S. team where the first dish was "a mountain of rice topped with scorpions." During one set of negotiations, a U.S. official who spoke Japanese was greeted by a young Chinese woman outside his hotel room, who attempted (unsuccessfully) to solicit sex *in Japanese* with the likely goal of embarrassing him later on. Many Chinese negotiators recounted how Assistant U.S. Trade Representative Lee Sands would shout at them and insist on stopping the negotiations to pay surprise visits to government ministries in order to prove that they were using pirated software. Indeed, at one point during the negotiations, Sands simply left Beijing unannounced and flew to Hong Kong, effectively ending that round of negotiations. The Chinese were furious.[1]

Their anger is understandable, as is their complaint that they were not being treated with the requisite respect accorded to high-level government

---

1. Interviews with former USTR and Chinese negotiators, 1998 and 1999.

officials. However, trade negotiations should not be confused with diplomacy. In fact, trade negotiations led by the United States Trade Representative have traditionally been characterized by a singular lack of restraint: banging the table, shouting, and engaging in tough talk are all an integral part of the process. Officials in the Department of State complain that the USTR runs roughshod over its painstakingly crafted bilateral relationships with U.S. trading partners, ostensibly for narrow, parochial, domestic business–related goals.[2] Many Chinese concur. Very early on during my interviews for this book, an official in Chongqing asked me, "Why is it that the United States imposes its domestic politics onto China?" At the time, I regarded this largely as a rhetorical question and responded in some polite, noncommittal way. The more I analyzed U.S. trade policy, however, the more this question resonated in my mind, especially after former USTR negotiators would say things like, "The [domestic U.S. trade] associations' goals became the U.S. government's goals." As I studied the institutions through which complaints, demands, and strategies evolve into what eventually becomes U.S. trade policy, the emerging answer to this nagging question was simple but powerful: the United States pursues its domestic politics through its trade policy because that is exactly what the trade policymaking mechanism is designed to do. In a sense, the official's comment aptly summarizes the way in which the IPR issue area evolved and took shape in the United States, and how it was "presented to" (or "forced upon," depending on who is speaking) Beijing under the threat of trade sanctions.

This chapter "unpacks" the notion of external pressure by looking at the process by which the United States sets its trade policy, the structure of the institutions through which it is routed, the actors involved, and, finally, the way these demands were imposed upon the Chinese side during the bilateral Sino-U.S. IPR negotiations. The substance of the demands is itself a product of the structure and the process of U.S. trade policy agenda-setting. The structure is shaped by the institutions of the Special 301 rubric of the 1988 Omnibus Trade and Competitiveness Act, the USTR, and the relevant IPR trade associations. The process consists of interactions among these groups, including the strategies of the associations in putting their concerns front and center on the list of demands that the USTR presented to the Chinese. The structure of the negotiations was shaped by the power relations among the various Chinese ministries, commissions, and bureaus, as well as by the political elites in the State Council, while the process was based on the strategy of closing ranks and resisting as many of the U.S. demands as possible. Those that Beijing was unable to withstand became enshrined in the three bilateral IPR agreements. These agreements, in turn, formed the basis of the formal laws and regulations that followed, although they had little bearing on the actual enforcement patterns that emerged, a theme discussed in chapters 3 through 5.

This chapter proceeds as follows. The first section places the study in the context of U.S. trade policymaking, broadly defined, introduces the Special 301 mechanism of the intellectual property trade policymaking process, and provides a brief summary of the Sino-U.S. IPR negotiations from 1989 to 1996. The second section describes the USTR, the Special 301 process, and the role of IPR trade associations in the agenda-setting process. The final section looks at the structure and process of the Chinese negotiation approach.

Special 301 and Sino-U.S. IPR Negotiations, 1989–96

U.S. trade negotiations with countries engaged in what the United States deems "unfair trade practices" are invoked under Section 301 of the Trade Act of 1974, which requires the USTR to identify and investigate these countries and to impose sanctions where appropriate. Section 301 grants the United States unilateral power to punish countries considered a threat to U.S. trading interests and to enforce U.S. rights under existing bilateral and multilateral trade agreements.[3] It also extends the criteria for the granting or withholding of Generalized System of Tariff status to other countries to include intellectual property protection.[4]

Interestingly, given the salience of the subject matter, there is a dearth of analyses on this process, although the ones that exist, even when they focus on events in the 1980s, nevertheless inform our understanding of what occurs today. The analysis in this chapter owes an intellectual debt to I. M. Destler, Morton Halperin, Michael Ryan, and Ka Zeng, among others, who have looked at this process from different perspectives from that which I employ in this book.[5] Destler and Halperin are by now classics in the fields of IPE and bureaucratic politics, respectively. In the context of this study, their pioneering work reminds us that trade policymaking is a bureaucratic process on the U.S. side every bit as much as trade policy implementation and enforcement is on the Chinese side. When we ignore this, we run the risk of presenting an analysis akin to "the sound of one hand clapping." Understanding the structure and processes of trade policy agenda-setting, therefore, is an integral part of the story.

In *Knowledge Diplomacy* and even more so in his earlier *Playing by the Rules*, Ryan sets out the basic framework by which the USTR pursues U.S.

---

3. A. Puckett and William Reynolds, "Rules, Sanctions and Enforcement under Section 301: At Odds with the WTO?" *American Journal of International Law* 90, no. 4 (October 1996): 676.
4. Susan K. Sell, *Power and Ideas: North-South Politics of Intellectual Property and Antitrust* (Albany: State University of New York Press, 1998), 195.
5. I. M. Destler, *American Trade Politics*, 3d ed. (Washington, DC: Institute for International Economics, 1995); Morton H. Halperin, *Bureaucratic Politics and Foreign Policy* (Washington, DC: Brookings Institution Press, 1974); and Judith Goldstein, *Ideas, Interests, and American Trade Policy* (Ithaca: Cornell University Press, 1993).

trading interests abroad.[6] Because Ryan looks at the Pacific Rim, as distinct from relations across the Atlantic (where the issues covered and power relations are different), his analysis provides a foundation for that presented here. Ryan's characterization of China's "combative counterpunch" strategy remains as relevant today as it did back then, as evidenced by the discussion to follow. Moreover, his overall thesis that the outcome of the Special 301 process depends on the political economy of the target country is certainly supported by the conclusions in this book. But his treatment of China remains rather sketchy in analyzing the processes that explain trade negotiation outcomes, in no small part due to the relative paucity of Section 301 negotiations with China at the time he was conducting his research.

Zeng provides one of the most theoretically grounded and empirically rich analyses on Sino-U.S. trade policy to date.[7] She also illuminates an important part of the trade policy process in the United States that is usually mentioned but not adequately analyzed in existing studies: the role of industry and other lobbying groups. However, I disagree with her conclusions about the impact of the behavior of U.S. industry lobbying groups. Drawing from Coneybeare, Zeng argues that trade complementarity between the United States and China undermines U.S. credibility in threatening trade wars with China because domestic U.S. industry groups, following their narrow economic self-interest, signal their opposition to such action.[8] Although fragmentation or even *factionalism* among industry groups played a large role in determining the parameters of the specific IPR issues to be negotiated, it had an *insignificant* effect on whether or not the USTR would retaliate if the talks broke down.[9] Once the case was made, the issue was effectively "locked in": the USTR was compelled by the statutory requirements of Special 301 to pursue trade negotiations with the target country and, if these talks broke down, to impose sanctions. Industry groups in opposition to this course of action had very little influence at this juncture; they had an opportunity to make their case against sanctions or, more accurately, against sanctions that would hurt *them*, but this always preceded the final rounds of negotiations and ultimately had little if any impact on the decision to impose sanctions if the talks broke down.[10] Nevertheless, Zeng is absolutely right to point out

6. Michael P. Ryan, *Playing by the Rules: American Trade Power and Diplomacy in the Pacific* (Washington, DC: Georgetown University Press, 1995) and *Knowledge Diplomacy: Global Competition and the Politics of Intellectual Property* (Washington, DC: Brookings Institution Press, 1998).

7. Ka Zeng, *Trade Threats, Trade Wars: Bargaining, Retaliation, and American Coercive Diplomacy* (Ann Arbor: University of Michigan Press, 2004), 238.

8. John A. C. Conybeare, *Trade Wars: The Theory and Practice of International Commercial Rivalry* (New York: Columbia University Press, 1987).

9. Andrew C. Mertha, "Pirates, Politics, and Trade Policy: Structuring the Negotiations and Enforcing the Outcomes of the Sino-U.S. Intellectual Property Dialogue, 1991–1999," Ph.D. dissertation, University of Michigan, 2001, especially chapters 2 and 3, and "'Transnational Deterrence' and the U.S. Trade Policy Agenda-Setting Process: The Case of IPR in China, 1991–1997" (working paper).

10. See Mertha and Robert Pahre, "Patently Misleading: Partial Implementation and Bargaining Leverage in Sino-American Negotiations on Intellectual Property Rights" *International Organization* 59, no. 3 (Summer 2005).

that interest groups are an integral part of the agenda-setting process that frames trade issues to be negotiated subsequently.

I build and expand upon each of these dimensions in the analysis to follow.

The Evolution of Special 301

Section 301 originally became law as an amendment to Section 252 of the 1962 Trade Expansion Act; it was intended to give the president increased discretion in limiting imports from countries with "unreasonable" U.S. import restrictions.[11] 301 freed the president's hands by eliminating the requirement to observe international obligations before taking unilateral action. It also provided the president with increased authority in imposing both tariff and nontariff import restrictions. The 1979 amendments to Section 301 instituted specific timelines for both the investigation and the final resolution of trade disputes.

The 1984 Trade and Tariff Act included the "inadequate protection of intellectual property" under the heading of "unreasonable" practices and extended Section 301 provisions to include IPR. Until then, Section 301 measures on intellectual property could only be invoked if a country violated international law. Moreover, international treaties on intellectual property placed weak standards on compliance. The preexisting 301 provisions stated that action was not required if a panel under the General Agreement on Tariffs and Trade (GATT) determined that no unfair practices had taken place; since all GATT members had veto power, it was relatively easy to block decisions made by the panel. In any case, noncompliance with panel decisions usually resulted in no further action. IPR advocacy groups mobilized to close this international loophole.[12] Other amendments at this time included extending the jurisdiction for initiating Section 301 investigations to the USTR.[13]

As far as intellectual property was concerned, the turning point was the 1988 Omnibus Trade and Competitiveness Act (hereafter the 1988 Trade Act), which included statutory mandates for investigations of and the leveling of trade sanctions against countries deemed to be violating U.S. intellectual property. In the 1988 Trade Act, the final decision-making authority in the investigation and enforcement of 301 disputes was transferred from the Oval Office to the United States Trade Representative. Although the president retained some oversight authority, his role was significantly reduced.[14] The Reagan administration and the USTR itself both strongly contested this move, arguing that the president's hands would be unreasonably tied

---

11. For more on Section 301 generally, see Ryan, *Playing by the Rules,* esp. ch. 2.

12. Sell, *Power and Ideas;* Ryan, *Knowledge Diplomacy,* 73; and Puckett and Reynolds, "Rules, Sanctions and Enforcement under Section 301," 687.

13. Puckett and Reynolds, "Rules, Sanctions and Enforcement under Section 301," 677.

14. Ibid., 675–77.

in trade negotiations and that removing direct presidential involvement would weaken the USTR. The USTR argued that only the president is able to weigh the broader national interest against the decision to use Section 301. Nevertheless, frustration in Congress over the president's subordination of trade policy to other strategic interests carried the day, and under the new act final decision-making authority for identification and investigation was moved out of the White House and to the USTR.[15]

The 1988 Trade Act also mandated that the USTR provide Congress with an annual report on unfair trade practices abroad. It institutionalized government-business intellectual property relations by requiring the USTR to post notices in the *Federal Register* soliciting comments on the issue of IPR infringement of U.S. products abroad, including specific evidence of IPR violations and recommendations for action. Most important, it contained the new "priority foreign country" rubric, a designation reserved for countries engaging in

the most onerous and egregious acts, policies, or practices that have the greatest adverse impact on the relevant U.S. products and that are not entering into good faith negotiations or making significant progress in bilateral or multilateral negotiations to provide adequate and effective intellectual property protection.[16]

A "priority foreign country" designation requires by law an investigation of the target country's intellectual property practices, at the conclusion of which the USTR decides whether the target country warrants retaliation in the form of U.S. trade sanctions. Negotiations between the United States and the target country may continue throughout the initial investigation phase as well as after the decision to impose sanctions. As a result of the statutory mandate for investigation and its inherent threat of trade sanctions, the "priority foreign country" designation is an extremely powerful weapon for the United States to use against its trading partners. In fact, in 1988 and 1989, the "priority foreign country" label was considered by many to be excessive, even reckless, and many in Washington deemed its use against strategic allies and trading partners to be irresponsible.

As a response to this political environment, in her first action under Special 301, U.S. Trade Representative Carla Hills chose to create and employ two rubrics not contained in the original 1988 Trade Act: "priority watch country" and "watch country" status.[17] The "priority watch" label

15. Judith Hippler Bello and Alan Holmer, "The Heart of the 1988 Trade Act: A Legislative History of the Amendments to Section 301," in *Aggressive Unilateralism: America's 301 Trade Policy and the World Trading System*, ed. Jagdish N. Bhagwati and Hugh Patrick (Ann Arbor: University of Michigan Press, 1990), 49–89; and Susan C. Schwab, *Trade-Offs: Negotiating the Omnibus Trade and Competitiveness Act* (Cambridge: Harvard Business School Press, 1994), 94–96.

16. Jagdish N. Bhagwati, "Aggressive Unilateralism: An Overview," in *Aggressive Unilateralism*, ed. Bhagwati and Patrick, 44.

17. USTR, "Fact Sheet: Special 301 on Intellectual Property," May 25, 1989.

identifies a foreign country that lacks sufficient intellectual property protection but is not targeted for negotiations and retaliation under a specific deadline.[18] "Watch" countries are identified as providing insufficient intellectual property protection but making "sufficient progress" in ongoing talks with the USTR.[19] Within thirty days of the release of the *National Trade Estimates* report (as stipulated under Special 301), or no later than the end of April, the USTR must publicly identify those countries to which it has affixed the labels of "priority foreign" or "priority watch."[20]

The specific timetable for action depends on whether the 301 action is mandatory or discretionary.[21] The deadline for discretionary action is twelve months from the start of the investigation. In the case of mandatory action, the time limit is eighteen months or one month after the conclusion of dispute settlement proceedings, whichever comes first.[22] A decision to act must be made within thirty days of the designation but may be delayed for up to six months if so requested by the initial petitioner or by U.S. industries, or if the USTR determines that the target country has made "substantial progress."[23]

U.S.-China Special 301 Negotiations 1989–92

The earliest IPR "negotiations" occurred in 1979, when China committed itself to protect foreign patents, copyright, and trademarks in the

18. Ryan, *Knowledge Diplomacy*, 80.

19. The designations "priority watch country" and "watch country" are intended to provide positive incentives to potential "priority foreign countries" to improve their protection of intellectual property, as well as to expand the tools available to the USTR. USTR Press Briefing on Super 301 with Carla Hills, United States Trade Representative, Washington, DC, May 25, 1989. However, the establishment of these rubrics, as well as the decision not to use the "priority foreign country" label in 1989 also appears to have been influenced by the Bush administration's (and Hills's own) unease over using Special 301 against allies like Japan. See Steve Dryden, *The Trade Warriors: USTR and the American Crusade for Free Trade* (New York: Oxford University Press, 1995), 357–60. Another provision, "Section 306 Monitoring," can also be adopted to ensure that other countries comply with the commitments made to the United States under bilateral intellectual property agreements; it states that a country under Special 306 monitoring can be subjected to virtually immediate retaliation under Section 301—without the need to proceed under the timetables of a new Section 301 case—if the country is deemed by the USTR to be in violation of its 301 commitments.

20. Ryan, *Knowledge Diplomacy*, 79. In 1991 and 1994, this decision was moved up to June to prevent complicating the annual debate over renewing China's Most-Favored Nation (MFN) trade status.

21. Action is mandatory if a trade agreement is being violated. It was discretionary if "(1) a GATT panel concludes there is no unfair trade practice; (2) the USTR believes the foreign government is taking steps to solve the problem; (3) the foreign government agrees to provide compensation; (4) the action could adversely affect the American economy disproportionately to the benefit to be achieved; and (5) the national security of the United States could be harmed through action." Puckett and Reynolds, "Rules, Sanctions and Enforcement under Section 301," 677–78.

22. If the dispute extends beyond the deadline, the USTR is required to report to Congress as to the reasons why and on the prospects for future resolution.

23. Puckett and Reynolds, "Rules, Sanctions and Enforcement under Section 301," 679.

U.S.-China Bilateral Trade Agreement of 1979.[24] During the 1980s, China developed its Patent Law (1984), revised its Trademark Law (1982), and joined the Paris Convention on International Trade (1985). However, by 1989, the United States was pressuring the Chinese to fulfill their remaining commitments in the 1979 agreement. Specifically, China had not yet formulated a copyright law, and U.S. copyright trade associations were appealing to the USTR to compel China to do so. On May 19, 1989, following two days of discussions, a Memorandum of Understanding (MOU) was signed between the USTR and China's Ministry of Foreign Economic Relations and Trade (MOFERT).

These events were overshadowed by the June 4 crackdown in and around Tiananmen Square following several months of nationwide student-led protests. One outcome of the worldwide condemnation of the PRC was that "it was impossible to get the USTR to even talk to China between June 1989 and autumn 1990."[25] Domestically, the aftermath of Tiananmen Square saw a campaign of reprisals against various groups that had participated in the protests.

Nevertheless, even if high-profile state-to-state contacts were curtailed, there were efforts to continue developing China's IPR regime during the latter part of 1989. During the fall, the United States, through its representatives at the U.S. Embassy in Beijing, worked with the Chinese to set up bilateral Sino-U.S. working groups on trade and investment as well as intellectual property rights. These meetings involved exchanging information and working together to settle disputes involving U.S. companies as well as more generally to lay the groundwork for a western-style IPR regime in China.[26] At the same time, as we shall see in chapter 4, there were genuine attempts on the Chinese side to establish a copyright law, although there was still a great deal of opposition to the multiple drafts that had circulated up to that point, particularly among conservative elements in the government, some of whom attempted to make copyright infringement a criminal offense as a way of further clamping down on freedom of expression in the wake of Tiananmen Square.

By the end of 1990, the Uruguay Round of GATT had stalled. The United States shifted its focus to taking unilateral action against countries it deemed in violation of U.S. trade laws, including IPR. On May 26, 1991, China was identified under Special 301 as a "priority foreign country" that was failing to protect U.S. intellectual property. On July 10, the House of Representatives voted to revoke China's Most-Favored Nation (MFN) status (now called "Normal Trade Relations," or NTR), citing trade imbalance and China's human rights abuses. The move received enough votes in the House to override a presidential veto. The House also imposed a series of

24. All five agreements (1979, 1989, 1992, 1995, and 1996) are reprinted as appendices in Mertha, "Pirates, Politics, and Trade Policy."
25. Interview 98HK06, June 24, 1998.
26. Reuters, "U.S. to Voice Concern over China's Economic Policy," January 8, 1990.

conditions on any renewal of such benefits the following year. In a calculated move, President George H. W. Bush drafted and distributed a letter in which he vowed that he would take "further action" if the next round of trade talks with China scheduled for August "fail to produce Chinese commitments to take substantial measures to improve market access."[27]

By September 1991, the United States had announced that China's weak IPR enforcement regime was causing substantial losses to U.S. businesses, a claim the Chinese quickly rejected. Later that month, the United States "upped the ante" when the Bush administration announced an investigation into Chinese trade practices under Section 301 of the 1974 Trade Act. China was given a deadline of November 26 to comply with U.S. demands or face a 100 percent tariff increase on exports to the United States.

In late October, a USTR delegation led by Deputy Trade Representative Joseph Massey arrived in China for four days of talks to discuss intellectual property and other trade barriers. Massey called on the Chinese to increase the transparency of their foreign trade regime.[28] The IPR talks took place on the third and fourth days of the delegation's visit and focused on protection for computer software copyright and patents on pharmaceutical and chemical products. The United States also demanded a greater degree of enforcement of China's new copyright law. The talks concluded one month before the November 26 deadline, when U.S. Trade Representative Carla Hills was to make a determination on whether to go ahead with retaliatory action as allowed under Special 301. However, Massey indicated that the USTR could extend this deadline for a further ninety days, postponing the decision until February 26, 1992, although no further extension would be permitted, and sanctions would be introduced one month after the passing of the February deadline if an agreement was not reached.

At the time Massey made two notable public statements. The first was that China's accession to the international copyright conventions, most prominently the Berne Convention and the Universal Copyright Convention, would be necessary but not sufficient to secure the degree of IPR protection demanded by the United States and, by extension, to stave off further U.S. sanctions. The second statement proved to be remarkably apt: Massey noted that by fall 1991, bilateral IPR issues between the United States and China had shifted from the "peripheral to the central."[29] Indeed, they would remain there for the next five years.

Three weeks after the Massey delegation left, Secretary of State James Baker went to China, becoming the highest-ranking U.S. official to visit the PRC publicly since Tiananmen Square. Although the focus of his talks with Foreign Minister Qian Qichen was on arms proliferation and human

27. "U.S. May Be Closer to Sanctions on China," *Los Angeles Times,* August 26, 1991.

28. Ruth Youngblood, "Chinese Trade Minister to U.S.: Don't Threaten Us," United Press International, January 17, 1992.

29. "U.S. and China Said to be Close to Pact on Intellectual Property Protection," *Journal of Commerce,* October 28, 1991.

rights, the talks also touched upon IPR. Meanwhile, IPR negotiations continued. Following an ominous report that a flood of phony Levi's jeans produced in China had entered the U.S. market, the Chinese delegation arrived in Washington for five days of talks over intellectual property, beginning November 21. These talks failed to produce an agreement, and the USTR took appropriate action, publishing a list in the *Federal Register* of the 1.4 billion dollars' worth of Chinese products that could be subject to retaliatory tariffs.[30]

By mid-December, the battle lines were being drawn. Public statements by the USTR asserted that the deadline for the Chinese would not be extended indefinitely. The USTR announcement was also seen in part as an attempt to reassure Bush's trade policy allies in the Senate by reasserting a "get tough" policy with China in order to influence an expected Senate vote on restricting low-tariff rates for Chinese exports to the United States. It was also announced at this time that a delegation of U.S. negotiators, led by Joseph Massey, would travel to Beijing on December 21 and 22 in an attempt to settle the dispute.[31]

This time the Massey delegation met with MOFERT Minister Li Lanqing and senior officials in China's National Copyright Administration and the China Patent Bureau. During this round, the United States had received and promptly rejected a "new text for a proposed agreement on the disputes, presented at the talks by Chinese officials, because the text left out concessions to which China earlier agreed." According to Massey, who spoke with reporters after ten hours of negotiations, the Chinese "did retract some things they earlier agreed to . . . [and because] of the movement backward, the U.S. did not accept the paper"; the United States would insist on returning to the "original version worked out in earlier rounds."[32] Another blow to progress came in December when the proposed GATT rules for global free trade were circulated to the member states. This was seen by many as a way to jumpstart the stalled GATT talks. However, the rules were seen by several lobbying groups as a rollback of their attempts to strengthen international intellectual property protection.[33] Given the fact that Washington's basic negotiating strategy at the time was to use TRIPS

30. John Maggs, "Levi Strauss Plagued by Flood of Phony Jeans from China," *Journal of Commerce*, November 19, 1991.

31. "U.S. Gives China Jan. 16 Deadline in Trade Dispute," *Journal of Commerce*, December 17, 1991.

32. Reuters, "U.S.-China Talks Make Scant progress, Threat of Trade War Looms," December 22, 1991.

33. Pharmaceutical Manufacturers Association (PhRMA) Senior Vice President Harvey E. Bale Jr. asserted that the draft "has such horrendous problems [that] it would be tough to support." Particularly, Bale objected to the proposal that developing nations, including China, would be given as long as twenty years to recognize U.S. patents on pharmaceuticals. Jack Valenti of the Motion Picture Association of America (MPAA), no stranger to hyperbole, summed up industry reaction, when he said that the agreement was "more than unacceptable. . . . It's unthinkable." "Some U.S. Industries Critical Of Draft Trade Rule Changes," *Washington Post*, December 24, 1991.

(the Trade-Related Aspects of Intellectual Property—the WTO IPR regime) as an archetype, this further complicated the IPR talks with China.

The United States and China nevertheless resumed talks in Washington scheduled to end on January 12, 1992. After two days of talks with the Chinese, the USTR volunteered no comment, but a member of the Chinese delegation offered an opinion of "So far, so good." The official added that "we would try our best" to change China's laws in ways that the United States had indicated it might accept.[34] The next day, the Chinese delegation offered a new proposal. The U.S. side conceded that this proposal was better than the one offered by the Chinese in Beijing in late December but added that the new one was still "inferior" to the one the Chinese had made back in November. "Both sides met for most of the day discussing a new Chinese proposal that contains a mix of several more positive elements and many problems," said a U.S. official involved in the negotiations.[35]

On January 12, 1992, after failing to reach an agreement, the U.S. and Chinese negotiators agreed to extend the talks.[36] On January 16, six hours before the deadline (although it would actually take until 1:00 A.M. for all the minutiae to be worked out), the United States and China finally reached an agreement, the Sino-U.S. Memorandum of Understanding on the Protection of Intellectual Property. The most formal of the three bilateral agreements (not counting the 1979 agreement and the 1989 MOU), it is divided into seven articles, starting with the Preamble (Article 1) and ending with a clause calling for the termination of "certain pending U.S. investigations" (Article 7). The first two articles concern patent protection (particularly patents for chemical inventions), a twenty-year term for foreign patents, increased rights for foreign patent holders, nondiscrimination of patent rights with regard to compulsory licensing, provisions for national treatment, and provisions for administrative (or "pipeline") protection. All of these issues were underscored in the 1991 Pharmaceutical Research and Manufacturers of America (PhRMA) Special 301 submission.

Article 3 focuses on copyright, including provisions for China's accession to the Berne Convention for the Protection of Literary and Artistic Works and the Geneva Convention for the Protection of Producers of Phonograms, whereby these conventions would take precedence over Chinese law in the event of an inconsistency—this would become a particular sore point for the Chinese, as we shall see in chapter 4. Article 3 also states China's intention to make amendments to its copyright law (the subsequent Implementing Rules for International Copyright Treaties, promulgated

---

34. Robyn Berry, "U.S., China Open Trade Negotiations; Copyright Protection Seen as Key to Talks," *Washington Post,* January 11, 1992.

35. Keith Bradsher, "U.S. Cool to China Proposal; Dispute on Piracy Continues," *New York Times,* January 11, 1992.

36. "U.S., China Extending Talks on Trade Issues; Negotiators Seek Agreement by Thursday," *Washington Post,* January 13, 1992.

on September 25, 1992) and to recognize computer programs as literary works. These reflected the core concerns of the copyright lobby, as articulated in the Special 301 submissions up to 1992. Article 4, which concerns trade secrets, is brief and somewhat vague, as are Articles 5 and 6, which concern enforcement and consultations, respectively. Particularly noteworthy is the absence of any trademark-specific provisions apart from trade secrets.

U.S.-China Special 301 Negotiations, 1993–95

The remainder of 1992, as well as most of 1993, was relatively quiet as far as the Sino-U.S. dialogue on IPR was concerned. This period saw China implement many of the provisions of the 1992 MOU, as Sino-U.S. trade talks turned to other issues. In October 1992, the United States and China signed another MOU, this one on market access, an issue that the Bush administration treated as separate from IPR.

In April 1993, China joined the World Copyright Convention and the Convention for Recorded Products. At this time, an "Urgent Circular on Augmenting Control over Reproduction of CD and Laser Disk Players" was issued jointly by seven Chinese commissions and ministries, including the State Planning Commission, the National Press and Publications Administration (NPPA), and the National Copyright Administration (NCA). In its wake, Guangdong, Shanghai, and Jiangsu provinces as well as Beijing conducted investigations into the handling of cases of pirated audio and video products. Teams from the NPPA and the NCA were sent to various localities, particularly Guangdong, in order to conduct examinations to register various CD production lines. During this campaign, the authorities closed down four of these production lines, prompting Zhang Yuejiao, deputy director of the Treaty and Law Department at the Ministry of Foreign Trade and Economic Cooperation (MOFTEC),[37] to assert that "as long as there was hard evidence, the Chinese Government will sternly deal with behavior that infringes copyrights."[38]

However, on June 24, 1993, in Washington, during hearings on international trade law, representatives from the Business Software Alliance (BSA) argued that China remained a principal problem with regard to software piracy. These comments were raised in conjunction with the statement that China's placement on the USTR's priority watch list would be deferred until June 30. After initially applauding the 1992 MOU, a BSA representative later argued that in 1993, the U.S. software industry had "direct losses of $322 million in China. . . . Ninety-four percent of all packaged software in use in China is estimated to be pirated, according to

37. The Ministry of Foreign Economic Relations and Trade (MOFERT) was renamed the Ministry of Foreign Trade and Economic Cooperation in March 1993.
38. China News Agency (*Zhongguo tongxun she*), "Beijing Takes Action to Ban Pirated CDs, Laser Discs," October 9, 1994.

BSA research examining the total hardware units sold in comparison with the total software packages sold, and estimated applications in use within that country last year." He went on to say that "sadly, the commitment to enforcement laid out in the [1992] MOU has not been fulfilled. Software piracy remains rampant in China, despite underlying legal protection." He continued:

> We [have] come to recognize that trade pressure from the U.S. may be the only real means we have to see that the Chinese carry out their commitments to enforcement. Just as it took a Priority Foreign Country designation and investigation to cause China to protect foreign works, and accede to Berne, so too have we come to recognize it may take yet another designation to get the Chinese to carry out commitments to enforcement.[39]

This signaled a move on the U.S. side from pressuring Beijing on legal measures to a focus on enforcement.

These concerns over IPR enforcement were reiterated by Assistant United States Trade Representative Charlene Barshefsky a month later, on July 28. At that time, Barshefsky noted several demands made by U.S. industries that formed the outline of what would become the 1995 Exchange of Letters and Action Plan:

> Take immediate, effective action to curb rampant IPR piracy, targeting especially manufacturers and distributors of infringing products, including trademarks; Develop a more effective IPR enforcement regime that has effective deterrents to infringement, eliminates conflicts of interest in the system, creates an effective border regime, and so on; Open China's markets to IP products, including audio-visual and published works.

Actions undertaken by China in the spring and summer of 1994 were not enough to prevent the USTR from moving China from the "watch list" to the "priority watch list" under Special 301 at the end of November. U.S. interests were less than reassured in January 1994 when a Chinese regulatory agency issued a ruling that fined a research institute at Shenzhen University a paltry $260 for counterfeiting Microsoft's trademark. Similarly, in February, a Beijing court ordered a state-run market to pay a scant $1,712 for selling bread under the trademark of the Sino-French joint venture, Vie de France (Beijing), Ltd. These cases, particularly the Microsoft case, were seen by many as a litmus test of China's willingness to provide adequate enforcement and establish a credible deterrent against

39. Testimony of Robert W. Holleyman II, president of the Business Software Alliance, Hearing on Special 301 Trade Remedy Before the International Trade Committee on Finance, United States Senate, Washington, DC, June 24, 1994.

IPR infringement.[40] On June 30, after China's MFN status was approved by Congress, U.S. Trade Representative Mickey Kantor placed China on the Special 301 list.

The negotiations continued over the next several months. During talks held from December 13 to 16, 1993, the U.S. side demanded that China's IPR laws be amended before January 1, 1996, four years earlier than the requirement for developing countries under the Uruguay Round of GATT. The Chinese objected to this deadline, and the Chinese press outlined several of the U.S. demands, which they characterized as "unreasonable."[41] The Chinese side argued that the United States was holding China's accession to the WTO hostage to the ongoing bilateral IPR talks. Moreover, the Chinese asserted that it was wrong for the United States to use Special 301 as the framework for negotiations and that the talks should be based on the framework established by the 1992 MOU. In what would be a recurring theme of these and subsequent talks, there was also bitter conflict over the numbers used by both sides in documenting China's enforcement of IPR.

After an impasse, Deputy U.S. Trade Representative Lee Sands proposed that some of the U.S. demands be incorporated into the Implementation Guidelines formulated by the State Council's newly established IPR Working Conference and that "the talks be concluded in the form of an exchange of documents." The Chinese reportedly agreed to this, with the caveat that market access be handled as a separate issue. The next day, on December 14, the Chinese were taken aback when they saw that the U.S. addendum to the Implementation Guidelines included "all the harsh demands in their original draft of the agreement," and that the Americans were showing "an attitude completely different from that on the previous evening by insisting that agreement on market access must be reached in the IPR talks." The Chinese had set out to work on yet another revised draft, when on December 16 Sands left Beijing without informing the Chinese side. Sands had departed for Geneva for a meeting with the working group in charge of China's application to reenter GATT.[42]

As expected, on December 31, 1994, the United States drew up a preliminary list of trade sanctions, including electronic products, toys, shoes, leather garments, and bicycles, totaling $2.8 billion and gave China thirty days to comply with U.S. demands (and for U.S. industries to comment on the list). The Chinese side responded by drawing up its own list of American imports that would be targeted with similar tariffs. On January 3, 1995, Barshefsky said that the United States had proposed to reopen the IPR

40. "China Fights Trademark Abuse," United Press International, April 12, 1994.

41. "Xinhua Cites 'Legal Experts' on IPR Talks," translated in FBIS-CHI-95–003 Daily Report, January 4, 1995.

42. "Article Views 'Truth' of Sino-U.S. IPR Talks—Part Three," *Hong Kong Wen Wei Po,* January 15, 1995, A1, translated in FBIS-CHI-95–010 Daily Report.

talks with China on January 16, adding that if the talks failed, retaliatory action would be taken on February 4.[43]

On January 18, IPR negotiations resumed in Beijing. Although scheduled to end on January 20, no agreement had been reached by that date.[44] By January 26, however, it appeared that the worst was behind them and that the two sides were close to an agreement. MOFTEC Minister Wu Yi mused about making "a trip to Washington in late January to meet U.S. Trade Representative Kantor, when the two sides will sign the relevant documents."[45] Then the talks suddenly broke down. On January 28, during what one Chinese source colorfully referred to as a "treacherous dinner" (*hongmen yan*), the U.S. side "escalated their bargains, and when the talks were about to end, they raised many new issues totally beyond the scope of intellectual property."[46]

On February 4, the U.S. announced the imposition of 100 percent tariffs on $1.08 billion of Chinese exports to the United States, which would become effective on February 26 if no agreement had been reached. Talks were set to resume in Beijing the following week in a last-ditch attempt to prevent a trade war. In early February, party elder Chen Yun weighed in on the negotiations, arguing that it was imperative for China not to back down in the negotiations. He added that "at worst, we would only have to fight another War To Resist U.S. Aggression and Aid Korea" (*zui duo zai da yici kangmei yuanchao*). Although a Chinese report stated that "it is believed that Chen Yun's speech has already been relayed to the highest levels of the central leadership by the Shanghai officials" and that "Chen Yun's opinion will have considerable effects on decision making in the highest echelon," this turned out to be little more than rhetoric.[47] Meanwhile, the talks continued.

With two days left before the February 26 deadline, Barshefsky reported that progress was "slow," although a Chinese official stated that the differences were "getting narrower." A Chinese report mentioned that the main differences were over "law enforcement by customs authorities and the most effective management of trademarks, patents, and copyrights," noting also that market access "has yet to be discussed." Barshefsky, who by now had taken the role of lead negotiator for the U.S. side, requested meetings with state councilor in charge of IPR affairs, Song Jian, and MOFTEC Minister Wu Yi, possibly to discuss the market access issue before resuming formal negotiations.[48]

43. "Reaction to U.S. Threats of Trade Sanctions—'Cancel' Retaliation To Allow Talks," *Hong Kong Ta Kung Pao*, January 3, 1995, translated in FBIS-CHI-95-001 Daily Report.
44. "Reportage on Sino-U.S. IPR Negotiations—Negotiators Comment on Talks," Beijing Central Television Program One Network, January 20, 1995, FBIS-CHI-95-015 Daily Report.
45. Ibid.
46. New China News Agency, "Reportage on Breakdown of IPR Talks With U.S.—Official Warns Against Sanctions," January 28, 1995, translated in FBIS-CHI-95-019 Daily Report.
47. "Reportage on Intellectual Property Rights Issues—Party Elder Says 'War' an Option," February 11, 1995, FBIS-CHI-95-029 Daily Report.
48. "Reportage on IPR Negotiation Developments—IPR Differences 'Narrowed,'" *Hong Kong Hsin Pao*, February 24, 1995, 7, translated in FBIS-CHI-95-038 Daily Report.

The pro-Beijing Hong Kong newspaper *Wen Wei Po* printed the Chinese version of what occurred during the last several days of negotiations.

On February 23, the Chinese negotiating team grouped the 22 disputes between the two sides into five major categories:

1. The U.S. side demanded that the PRC authorities shut down all 29 production lines involved in piracy, whereas the Chinese side believed that they should be handled with discrimination based on the specific circumstances of their cases;
2. With respect to the judicial issue, the U.S. side held the view that the parties concerned who continued their piracy despite the knowledge that they were infringing upon copyrights, including all pirating activities after July 1994, were illegal in nature;
3. The United States held the view that all U.S. trademarks which had not been registered in China should be protected by China as well as those that had been registered;
4. The U.S. side demanded access to the Chinese market and transparency about import controls; and
5. The issue of founding joint-ventures. The Chinese side agreed to include the judicial issue and market access as well as the founding of joint-ventures in the agreement, but persisted in rejecting the founding of enterprises with U.S. monopoly investment.

The next day, the two sides again exchanged draft agreements; after some more concessions, the two sides finally reached an agreement on February 25, although the comparison and examination of the two texts, numbering some forty pages, dragged the talks into the morning of February 26.[49]

In the "Exchange of Letters" agreed to on February 26, 1995, the Chinese government promised to enforce the "Action Plan" described below as well as to extend its criminal laws to cover intellectual property violations. The substance of the agreement reiterated China's focus on increased enforcement at the manufacturing and retail stages and held that China would allow some revenue-sharing arrangements with U.S. manufacturers of audiovisual products consistent with "measures necessary to protect public morals or to maintain public order . . . consistently and in a non-discriminatory, non-arbitrary manner." It went on to discuss the continuation of bilateral training programs and other consultative exchanges. Finally, it provided that the United States immediately revoke China's Special 301 designation as a "priority foreign country."

The enforcement-based "Action Plan" was divided into two broad sections. The first focused on China's IPR enforcement structure, and the

---

49. "Paper Reveals 'Inside Story' of IPR Talks," *Hong Kong Wen Wei Po*, March 3, 1995, A2, translated in FBIS-CHI-95–044 Daily Report.

second provided for "information dissemination and training, and improving the environment for intellectual laws." The first section institutionalized the formation of China's Intellectual Property Rights Working Conference at the national and subnational levels as well as a series of IPR "task forces" to enhance the enforcement of intellectual property in China. It also outlined a "special enforcement period," in which extensive resources would be brought to bear on increasing the enforcement of IPR throughout China. Twelve pages of the "Action Plan" were devoted to copyright-related administrative enforcement, including specific enforcement efforts targeting pirated audiovisual products, motion pictures, and computer software, as well as books, periodicals, and other printed works. These included the expansion of the role of China's General Administration of Customs, as well as the establishment of several title-verification programs. Trademarks, by contrast, merited less than three pages which covered the narrow but important issue of "well-known" trademark protection and included an ambiguous clause on trademark registration as well as a promise from China to "intensify efforts" to protect trademarks from unfair competition.[50]

In the 1995 "Action Plan," specific patent concerns were notably absent. Moreover, even though there were some specific references made to increased trademark enforcement and some vague stipulations to protect "intellectual property" in general, the 1995 "Exchange of Letters" and "Action Plan" focused overwhelmingly on copyright-related issues.

The "Action Plan" is particularly significant because it illustrates a trend away from international negotiations strictly bound by national sovereignty. It contained numerous provisions pertaining to structural changes in the Chinese political system, an area that China, extremely sensitive about its long and unfortunate history with western encroachment of its borders, has traditionally considered off-limits to foreign interference. One of the most important of these for the discussion to follow was the "U.S. stamp of approval" for the Intellectual Property Rights Working Conference, the establishment of which did as much to preserve the fragmentation of China's discrete IPR bureaucracies as it did to remedy it. This is discussed in the next chapter.

U.S.-China IPR Negotiations 1995–96

The agreement was signed with great fanfare, but the goodwill engendered by reaching this agreement was remarkably short-lived. Less than a year later, the Americans were back at the negotiation table essentially to

---

50. "Well-known" trademarks are those that enjoy protection in a country even if they are not registered in that country on the basis of the fame and renown of the trademark (i.e., Coca-Cola). The concept of well-known trademarks is somewhat vague and remains unresolved in a number of international trademark settings. Not surprisingly, this continues to be a contentious issue in China up to the present day.

force the Chinese to comply with the 1995 agreement. Charges and counter-charges flew as the two sides positioned themselves for battle. In January 1996, the United States announced another set of trade sanctions against China if an agreement could not be reached. Although the rhetoric was extremely heated on the Chinese side, an agreement was brokered on June 16, 1996.

The June agreement was weighted even more heavily in the direction of copyright than the 1992 Memorandum of Understanding. The 1996 agreement was in the form of a Report on Chinese Enforcement Actions under the 1995 IPR Agreement, focusing on actions to stop piracy in compact disk factories, including factory and wholesale market closures, equipment seizures, and continuing investigation and punishment. It went on to articulate the new provisions for copyright verification and authorized production of copyrighted products, as well as clarifying rightholder participation for copyright-related matters. It also underscored China's commitment to extending intellectual property violations under China's Criminal Law and to enhance its border enforcement. Finally, the annex of "other measures" focused exclusively on copyright issues.

The Chinese promised to step up enforcement of the 1995 agreement and the Action Plan. In part because they feared that the Sino-U.S. IPR talks would, like the debate in Congress about renewing China's MFN status, become an annual event, the Chinese launched a series of large-scale and largely effective enforcement campaigns against the targets of U.S. demands (described in chapter 4).

After 1996, the tenor departed from the highly charged confrontational bilateral negotiations that existed from 1991 through the middle of 1996. Since then, there have been regular IPR "consultations" at least twice a year. In 1997 and 1998, the talks were mostly over the status of the implementation of the 1995 and 1996 agreements. One participant described these talks as being dominated by USTR representatives presenting documents that showed China's commitments and demanding to know the progress that had been made. In 1999 and 2000, these talks became much more relaxed, and there was less tension between the two sides. These latter sets of talks could be described as "exchanges of information" and even as "seminars"; they were certainly more cooperative and consultative, and they exhibited little of the confrontational tone of the previous negotiations.[51]

Structure and Process of Agenda-Setting: the USTR, Special 301, and the IPR Lobby

The Office of the United States Trade Representative is the key U.S. government agency charged with pursuing U.S. trade policy. It originated

---

51. Interview 03BJ01A, July 21, 2003.

with the 1962 Trade Expansion Act, in which Congress established the Special Representative for Trade Negotiations as a way of moving the jurisdiction for trade policy out of the Department of State and into the White House while simultaneously bringing Congress directly into the trade policy loop.[52]

Ryan summarizes the USTR mission as "serving a president who has been at once chief policymaker, intergovernmental competitor with Congress for policy leadership, and domestic politician in need of interest group allies himself."[53] However, its role has shifted over time, across administrations, and with regard to specific trade issues, and its relationship with Congress is very close and important. In the view of one former trade negotiator, the USTR in any administration is always regarded as "a suspect child" because it is widely seen as an extension of Congress—"the USTR essentially puts the Congress inside the Cabinet."[54] Another former official agreed that the USTR is "extremely closely aligned" with Congress, noting that the USTR reports to more congressional committees than does any other agency in the executive branch.[55] As a result of these links with Congress, the specific trade agenda of the USTR overwhelmingly reflects domestic interests, often at the expense of expansive bilateral and multilateral issues.[56]

Both the uneasy role of the USTR as a conduit between the White House and Capitol Hill and the impact of Congress on USTR behavior are illustrated by the controversy surrounding the first use of Special 301. Complicating President George H. W. Bush's own free-trade proclivities was the growing pressure on the Hill to take corresponding action against Japan's "unfair" trade practices in the late 1980s. At the confirmation hearings of Carla Hills as U.S. Trade Representative, Senators Lloyd Bentsen and John Danforth, the latter a key player in the creation of Special 301, expressed anxiety over a possible retreat by the Bush administration in aggressively utilizing Special 301. Many in the administration, including White House Economic Adviser Michael Boskin, made no secret of their opposition to Special 301. Nevertheless, Hills decided that, despite her own misgivings, she needed to establish her credibility with Congress early on and reluctantly agreed to use Special 301. Ultimately, Bush supported her decision.[57]

52. Schwab, *Trade-Offs*, 37; and Dryden, *The Trade Warriors*, 6. The Department of State was accused by Congress of focusing on strategic and broader bilateral issues at the expense of trade policy. Interview 98US13, December 7, 1998.

53. Ryan, *Knowledge Diplomacy*, 10.

54. My source went on to characterize the USTR as an "offspring," rather than as an "agent," of Congress. Interview 98US10B, December 4, 1998.

55. Interview 98US13, December 7, 1998.

56. This has been, to some extent, institutionalized within the USTR itself, as intellectual property issues and matters regarding the World Trade Organization are handled by two different offices, increasing the leverage of the USTR over bilateral IPR negotiations by separating them from concurrent bilateral WTO negotiations with China. Interview 98US15, December 8, 1998; and Interview 98US16, December 9, 1998.

57. Dryden, *The Trade Warriors*, 357–59.

The Department of State (DOS), the Department of Treasury (DOT), and even the Department of Commerce (DOC) all have higher cabinet rankings than the United States Trade Representative.[58] However, the USTR has an important set of resources that compensate for this seeming weakness. Foremost among these is the close relationship with Congress that gives the USTR a degree of leverage not enjoyed by other cabinet offices. In particular, the USTR maintains close contact with two important congressional committees, the Trade Subcommittee of the House Ways and Means Committee and the Senate Finance Committee on International Trade, both of which have tended to be nonpartisan, especially under the Reagan and George H. W. Bush administrations.

Second, although the USTR represents a cluster of very powerful constituent groups, it is widely seen—in Washington, at least—as not having been co-opted by them. Therefore, while it is clearly an advocate for the interests of U.S. industry, the USTR is, ironically, regarded as less of an agent for commercial interests than, for example, the Department of Commerce. Third, the USTR has very few political appointees. Rather, it is staffed by a group of knowledgeable professional negotiators (as opposed to career civil servants). This helps make the USTR an aggressive and proactive body. Fourth, the USTR deliberately uses the media to maintain a much higher profile than does the Department of Commerce or the Department of Treasury, and this contributes to the USTR's appearance of power.[59]

Trade with China only began to emerge as an important policy portfolio in the late 1980s. From 1982 to 1985, most U.S.-China trade issues were handled by the DOC-led Joint Committee on Commerce and Trade (JCCT), which met alternatively in Washington and Beijing, performing an information-exchange function and outlining specific trade concerns.[60] The USTR's handling of China was very much an "afterthought" throughout this period, and the Chinese affairs portfolio remained scattered throughout the agency.

Before 1988, international IPR treaties had been the responsibility of the U.S. Copyright Office and the U.S. Patent and Trademark Office, depending on the specific issues to be covered. The first time that IPR was set within the context of international trade was when the USTR joined with the U.S. Patent and Trademark Office to form a U.S.-Japan IPR Working Group, co-chaired by the Deputy U.S. Trade Representative and the Associate Commissioner of Patents.[61] By early 1986, the White House had charged the

58. During the Nixon administration, the Department of Commerce under Maurice Stans had attempted, unsuccessfully, to absorb the USTR.

59. Interview 98US10A/B, December 3 and 4, 1998.

60. The JCCT retains its function as the most systematic and regularized bilateral forum on broad trade issues between the United States and China. The lack of authority of the JCCT is implied in the remark from a DOC official in describing JCCT meetings as "a Commerce-driven little event." Interview 98US14, December 8, 1998.

61. Interview 98US10A/B, December 3 and 4, 1998.

USTR Director of Chinese Affairs to draft a list of the most "unfair" trade practices in which China was engaging at that time—the issues on this list would form the basis for future presidential-initiated 301s worldwide. One of the most egregious practices at the time was China's failure to comply with the terms of the 1979 Sino-U.S. Bilateral Trade Agreement, especially in the area of copyright protection. The subsequent brief submitted to the president by USTR Director for Chinese Affairs William Abnett became the first 301 threat to be leveled against China. Abnett had the thankless task of introducing Super 301 and other similar trade policy terms during a JCCT "working group" session in Beijing that same November.

Even as late as the end of 1986, the Joint Committee on Commerce and Trade still provided the institutional basis for managing U.S.-China trade issues, although that had started to change in 1985. Abnett wrote the first "China Chapter" of the "303 Report," which would eventually become the basis of the annual *National Trade Estimates* report. This was circulated to all the trade agencies for their comments and "clearance." These events contributed to the growing demand in Washington for the establishment or, at the very least, for the empowerment of a proactive trade-related agency that would aggressively pursue U.S. trade interests in the growing commercial relationship with China. Even in 1985, it seemed only a matter of time before the USTR would assume "its rightful role" as the administration's trade policy coordinator and lead negotiator.[62] Within two years, the responsibility for trade negotiations with China was transferred to the USTR—after a brief and "nonantagonistic" turf battle with the Department of Commerce—and the role of the USTR as the final decision-making agency for negotiating intellectual property trade issues with foreign countries was institutionalized in the 1988 Omnibus Trade and Competitiveness Act described at the beginning of the chapter.[63]

The Office of the United States Trade Representative derives a curious advantage from its small size of around two hundred people. In addition, the tenure of many of the key players at the USTR is relatively short, thus providing them with a very effective springboard to lucrative careers in law and business. As a result of its small size and high turnover rate, the USTR is better able to respond to its constituencies; since the USTR does not have the organizational depth to monitor in detail every single trade issue in every U.S. trading partner, it relies more than other government agencies on external, nongovernmental sources for country-specific information,[64]

---

62. Interview 00US01, March 13, 2000.

63. Interview 98US10A, December 3, 1998.

64. Individuals in the USTR have knowledge about the countries with which they are negotiating, but it is impossible for them to track the volume of changes that take place within these countries with regard to the trade issues that are on the table. Thus, in shaping USTR policy and taking action, they must rely considerably on information that is provided by business actors who are directly exposed to these issues. The relative lack of depth in regional expertise also has the consequence of strengthening the USTR's bargaining position with China,

and its lead negotiators are relatively unencumbered by a deep sense of organizational culture.[65]

Because it lacks country-specific investigation teams, the USTR must rely upon submissions from interested parties with legitimate grievances in analyzing a country's performance, shaping specific negotiating platforms and deciding to take action against the target country. This is the most important part of the overall process. Once these submissions are received, the USTR considers possible actions it will take and outlines a list of Chinese exports targeted for sanctions. The U.S. commercial interests affected, in turn, submit petitions or "comments" to argue for or against a specific sector's inclusion in the sanctions package. The first step is targeting Chinese industries that fulfill one of two sometimes conflicting criteria: they should be those most likely to hurt China, and they should be located in regions housing the worst IPR offenders (i.e., Guangdong in 1995 and 1996). The list is compiled by the chairman and the individual members of the 301 Committee, the Trade Policy Staff Committee, as well as individuals and offices at the cabinet and subcabinet levels.

The original list is always larger than the final version and is subsequently pruned down to approximate the calculated losses to piracy. One USTR source said that the Chinese will always assume that the final list will be whittled down from the original and that the debate U.S. industry and the USTR has over the lists will have some bearing on the negotiations. This process is very complex, and it is extremely difficult to predict the outcome; moreover, it is a daunting task to maximize the impact of sanctions against China while limiting their negative effects on U.S. industries: "it is very difficult to surgically inflict pain," said one source.[66]

This approach is suboptimal at best, and unbiased information is often difficult to obtain. Moreover, national policy, as well as the situation on the ground in the target country, is often in flux. As a result, USTR action against a country's trade practices requires—indeed, depends upon—the provision of clear, concise, and compelling information by the various business interests hurt by these practices. As one former negotiator put it, "informing, explaining become persuading."[67]

Moreover, Special 301 institutionalizes this informational requirement: it compels the USTR to act in response to the information—and, more importantly, to the recommendations—it receives from interested actors in the business community. The establishment of Special 301 was an

as there is little temptation or tendency to regard China as a "special case," as occurs in other agencies. Interview 98US15, December 8, 1998.

65. This gives individuals in the USTR a wide berth in pursuing their own strategies, both at the negotiating table and in providing other U.S. government agencies with scarce information. Interview 98US16, December 9, 1998.

66. Interview 98US20, December 11, 1998; Interview 98US13, December 7, 1998.

67. Interview 98US10A, December 3, 1998.

exceptionally successful strategy by the IPR associations. They were able to institute a set of statutory constraints on the conduct of the U.S. trade policy that enhanced the position and the power of the IPR associations themselves. Access to the USTR for these associations was institutionalized, and the USTR was compelled to respond.[68]

It is therefore not surprising that the IPR associations played a major role in the development of Special 301. Beginning in the early 1970s, Pfizer and IBM sought to improve international IPR protection to bring it in line with American standards for intellectual property protection. Pfizer focused its efforts at improving the Paris Convention for the Protection of Industrial Property, while IBM fought to extend the Berne Convention for the Protection of Literary and Artistic Works to include copyright protection for software. These two companies used the forum of GATT's Advisory Committee on Trade Policy and Negotiation to pursue their strategy of multilateral negotiations. This committee broadened its focus to include educating members of Congress, the White House, and the USTR about the link between intellectual property protection and investment abroad. This paid off when the USTR utilized a considerable amount of diplomatic capital to include IPR concerns in the Uruguay Round of GATT (1986–94). When GATT negotiations resumed under the Uruguay Round, Pfizer and IBM established the Intellectual Property Committee as a conduit to press for their goals during the negotiations.[69]

While these multilateral negotiations were taking place, a group of copyright-intensive firms and associations established the International Intellectual Property Alliance (IIPA) to strengthen international copyright laws. While the IIPA's broader goals were similar to those of the Intellectual Property Committee in terms of extending the Berne Convention to protect copyrighted software as well as strengthening enforcement of copyright more generally in developing countries, the IIPA's methods were aggressively and unabashedly unilateral in form.

The establishment of the IIPA in 1984 was not a matter of chance. The timing reflected the role of the IIPA as an advocate of U.S. copyright industries in pressing the USTR to utilize its intellectual property mandate under Section 301 of the 1984 Trade Act (and later under Special 301 of the 1988 Omnibus Trade and Competitiveness Act). The IIPA drew inspiration from previous successes of the Motion Picture Association of America, in particular its successful lobbying to amend the Caribbean Basin Initiative to deny lower tariffs under the Generalized System of Preferences to governments that tolerated violations of U.S. copyright. Subsequently, American book publishers sought to use the Caribbean Basin Initiative against the Dominican Republic in exactly the same way. Partly as a result of their lobbying

68. Ibid.
69. Members include Pfizer, IBM, Merck, General Electric, DuPont, Warner Communications, Hewlett-Packard, Bristol-Myers, FMC Corporation, General Motors, Johnson and Johnson, and Rockwell International. Ryan, *Knowledge Diplomacy*, 67–69.

efforts, "unfair trade practices" was extended to include "inadequate IPR protection" and was thus written into the 1984 amendments.[70]

However, it was clear to the IIPA that it would need to mount an ongoing campaign to educate U.S. policymakers on the importance of intellectual property protection abroad. In 1985, the IIPA submitted a white paper entitled "U.S. Government Trade Policy: Views of the Copyright Industry" and a report called *Piracy of U.S. Copyrighted Works in Ten Selected Countries*. Both were submitted to the USTR and recommended an aggressive unilateral negotiating strategy based on Section 301 as well as the prospect of using sanctions.[71] These recommendations ultimately became institutionalized in the Special 301 provisions of the 1988 Trade Act, and the documents also became a model for subsequent Special 301 submissions to the USTR in the 1990s.

One former USTR official was straightforward with regard to the selection criteria for those industries for which the USTR "went to bat":

> U.S. trade policy is biased toward the "squeaky wheel": those industries that complain the most, influence USTR the most. In our negotiations with the PRC, we would claim to represent the entire U.S. industry, but in reality, we were only responsive to those with the most effective lobbying or PR or information dissemination efforts.[72]

It is therefore necessary to determine exactly what shape and form this "squeaky wheel" takes during the Special 301 process. This analysis, like the USTR itself, places its principal focus on the trade associations. With few exceptions (such as the justifiably pugnacious Nintendo of America, Inc.), individual firms, partly as a result of fear of retaliation against their operations in China by the Chinese government, keep a low profile in the Special 301 process, preferring to hide behind the anonymity provided by the trade associations. The following quotation from a U.S. executive in Shanghai is representative of this widespread tendency:

> [We do] not get too directly involved with the Chinese government in complaining about the trademark issue. First of all, [we need] to maintain good relations with the Chinese government. The rules are always changing and the government can announce an "audit" if [we rub] them the wrong way. [We] also [have] expansion plans and will certainly need the Chinese government to be on [our] side in undertaking such a plan. There are also tax issues. In short, [we do] not want to put [ourselves] on any Chinese governmental "black list."[73]

---

70. Ibid., 70–72; and Interview 98US17, December 9, 1998.
71. Ibid.
72. Interview 00US01, March 13, 2000.
73. Interview 99SH01, April 5, 1999. This interviewee, as far as investigative work is concerned, outsources to private investigation firms in order to guarantee the safety of his staff, noting that in several instances investigators hired by his company were threatened and even physically assaulted.

This makes the trade associations critically important players in the trade policy negotiation process.

Trade associations also bring more gravitas to their IPR recommendations than do individual firms. The IPR associations can petition the government with the same force as if they had unleashed thousands of companies in a massive letter-writing campaign.[74] To underscore this, these associations almost always include aggregate lists of their membership: during the 1990s, the International Intellectual Property Alliance (IIPA) represented 1,350 members, the Software Publishers Association (SPA) represented 1,200 members, the International Trademark Association (INTA) represented 2,500 members, and the International Anti-Counterfeiting Coalition (IACC) represented 160 members. The Pharmaceutical Research and Manufacturers Association (PhRMA) represented over 100 research-based companies, including 40 leading U.S. biotechnology firms.

This type of aggregation also demonstrates the importance of the member bases of these associations to the U.S. economy. In 1996, the International Intellectual Property Alliance indicated that its "core" membership accounted for $278.4 billion in value added, or 3.65 percent of the U.S. GDP, while "total" copyright industries (defined as the "core" membership "plus those that, under 'conservative' assumptions, distribute such products or other products that depend wholly or principally on copyright materials") accounted for $433.9 billion in value added, or 5.68 percent of the U.S. GDP.[75] The Pharmaceutical Manufacturers and Research Association argued that its members accounted for 17 percent of U.S. exports.[76] The International Anti-Counterfeiting Coalition maintained that its members accounted for $500 billion in sales, or 10 percent of U.S. GNP.[77]

74. It is tempting to argue that the size of these associations implies a connection between U.S. electoral politics and trade policy outcomes. Indeed, this is accepted by many as the conventional wisdom. However, all former and current USTR officials interviewed for this book rejected this argument. Some pointed to the fact that both the Bush and Clinton administrations pursued the same USTR-led IPR policy toward China, thereby rendering the "campaign contributions" argument indeterminate at best. Interview 98US15, December 8, 1998; Interview 98US20, December 11, 1998; and Interview 99BJ16, March 24, 1999. Politics did play a role, but in a different way than is often assumed. Because of the high-profile political fallout in the wake of linking (and ultimately de-linking) MFN with human rights in 1993 and 1994. Coupled with the countervailing force of the U.S. industries' push for increased trade with China, Washington sought an issue that would satisfy political opponents of engagement with China (showing that the executive branch could "get tough" with Beijing) while not holding all of U.S. industry hostage to such a policy, IPR provided the perfect political balance between these two motivations. Thus MFN and IPR should not be considered independent, discrete cases, as they were in fact tied together in a strategic calculus.

75. IIPA, Special 301 Submission, February 13, 1995, U.S. Trade Representative Reading Room (Doc.Special.301; 1995).

76. PhRMA, Special 301 Submission, February 9, 1993, U.S. Trade Representative Reading Room (Doc.Special.301; 1993); and Special 301 Submission, February 18, 1994, U.S. Trade Representative Reading Room (Doc.Special.301; 1994).

77. IACC, Special 301 Submission, February 18, 1994, U.S. Trade Representative Reading Room (Doc.Special.301; 1994); Special 301 Submission, February 1995, U.S. Trade Representative Reading Room (Doc.Special.301; 1995); Special 301 Submission, February 1996, U.S. Trade

Finally, associations were able to aggregate the dollar amounts for IPR-related losses in China that firms were unwilling to do on an individual basis for proprietary and other reasons. The IIPA listed losses that ranged from $415 million in 1992 to $2.79 billion in 1997.[78] PhRMA indicated losses estimated at $340 million in 1993.[79] The Software Publishers Association noted losses of $987 million in 1997. The trademark-based IACC was noteworthy in quantifying the losses of *copyright*-related industries while remaining silent on the corresponding losses regarding trademarks.

Because of the dominant role of the copyright trade associations in the creation of Special 301, it is perhaps not surprising that, as an institution, Special 301 seemed to enshrine the priorities, strategies, and approaches to pursuing trade policy abroad of the copyright trade associations. These priorities, strategies, and approaches were in many ways at odds with those of the trademark trade associations, as is illustrated by the trade policy negotiation process and as is reflected in the submissions of these associations under the Special 301 process. These converged around a set of indicators—specificity, credibility of commitment, timing, and form and content—that provided precisely the type of "squeaky wheel" sought by the USTR and that ultimately separated the successful trade associations from the unsuccessful ones.

Specificity

An important distinction separating submissions that were acted upon from those that received less attention was the inclusion of specific recommendations for action. Specific recommendations were crucial for two reasons. First, under 301, such recommendations (in particular, the "priority foreign country" designation) gave the USTR a powerful and effective legal mandate for action.[80] Second, a set of specific recommendations, including a clear designation of the target country under one of the three rubrics afforded by Special 301, provided a clear baseline to measure progress during negotiations with the target country.

The copyright trade associations, such as the IIPA, gave specific recommendations reflecting conclusions based on data often also included

Representative Reading Room (Doc.Special.301; 1996); Special 301 Submission, February 18, 1997, U.S. Trade Representative Reading Room (Doc.Special.301; 1997).

78. IIPA, Special 301 Submission, February 12, 1993, U.S. Trade Representative Reading Room (Doc.Special.301; 1993); and Special 301 Submission, February 23, 1998, U.S. Trade Representative Reading Room (Doc.Special.301; 1998).

79. PhRMA, Special 301 Submission, February 18, 1994, U.S. Trade Representative Reading Room (Doc.Special.301; 1994).

80. Only the "priority foreign country" designation mandates an investigation into the target country's IPR protection regime and subsequent economic sanctions. In other words, the "priority watch" and "watch" labels do not represent a substantive shift away from the status quo toward a more confrontational engagement framework; even the shift from "watch country" to "priority watch country" status reflects a change in tone and not a change in policy. All things being equal, a "priority foreign country" designation enhances the credibility of a given submission (and the petitioning firm or association).

in the submission. The trademark trade associations, by contrast, simply "dumped" the data on the USTR and expected the USTR to draw its own conclusions, which were assumed to be the same as those the trademark associations drew. The International Trademark Association, for example, consistently provided the USTR with reams of information, but only once in its four submissions during the high tide of Sino-U.S. IPR negotiations did it make a specific recommendation—in 1993, INTA, then the U.S. Trademark Association, requested that China remain under Section 306 monitoring status—and even this instance was cited by an INTA official as being highly uncharacteristic of the association.[81]

Credibility of Commitment

An unwritten rule is the expectation that the petitioner demonstrate its credibility, both in terms of the issues at stake and the petitioner's commitment to Special 301 beyond the short term; this is a crucial determinant in the USTR's willingness to "go to bat" on behalf of a petitioner.[82] In the words of one trade association leader, Charlene Barshefsky would use the "shouting and screaming" approach ("industry is shouting and screaming, and we have to reach an agreement to calm them down") as a way of demonstrating the credible constraints to the USTR's bargaining decision.[83] Because of its reliance on outside sources for information, the USTR's own credibility is inexorably linked with the reliability of the submissions themselves. The USTR is wary of firms and associations that might pull out or "defect" before or even during the USTR's confrontation with the target country.

This dynamic is illustrated in the following example surrounding the VCD phenomenon in China. VCDs (video compact disks) look exactly like audio compact disks and use similar technology, but they contain motion pictures.[84] By 1998, China had become so inundated with pirated VCDs that they replaced computer software as the new paradigm of IPR piracy in China. The quality of pirated VCDs is mixed, although people accept the risk of shoddy quality, since the cost of a movie is often under two dollars.

In early 1998, an article in the *New York Times* highlighted the widespread sale of illegal VCDs in China. The article also mentioned that the regional MPAA representatives were largely unaware of the problem:

Michael Connors, the Motion Picture Association's chief representative in Asia, said he had not complained because he was unaware

---

81. The source attributed this to the fact that Robin Rolfe came over to INTA after working at the copyright lobby and had a strategy profile that represented the modus operandi of copyright advocates. Interview 99US01, November 15, 1999.

82. Interview 99SH10, May 12, 1999; Interview 99GZ02, May 31, 1999.

83. Interview 98US17, December 9, 1998.

84. Interview 98HK03B, June 25, 1998.

that the availability of pirated films had become so open. The Motion Picture Association, Mr. Connors said, has recently focused its efforts on helping Chinese customs officials detect smugglers, even though recent seizures of millions of disks represent a small fraction of what is smuggled into China each month. *"We don't have any complaints,"* said Mr. Connors, who is based in Singapore but spoke from Beijing, which he visits regularly. The Motion Picture Association says that pirated movies are a problem throughout the world and it recently set up a team of investigators in New York City to crack down on the problem there.[85]

Individuals on the ground in China monitoring this phenomenon were bewildered by this statement. Even some Chinese officials conceded that the VCD problem was all but intractable.[86] This situation was further complicated by MPAA CEO Jack Valenti's response to the New York Times article. In a letter to the editor dated April 3, Valenti appeared to defend the Chinese position: "'China Turns Blind Eye to Pirated Disks' paints a picture of piracy run rampant in China. In fact, China has accomplished what no other country has achieved."[87] Both the original article and Valenti's response took the USTR completely by surprise, as anticipated in the original article:

> Joe Papovich, assistant United States trade representative in Washington, said he was unaware of the wide availability of pirated movies in China. . . . The United States trade representative office, he said, depends on industry sources for information, and the Motion Picture Association, which is supposed to track movie piracy on behalf of Hollywood's major studios, has not made any complaints about it.[88]

The USTR found this particularly galling, as it directly raised the issue of the MPAA's credibility and by extension the credibility of the USTR. In this case, the MPAA's denial of such a widespread phenomenon could understandably be interpreted in China as a shift toward a more benign "don't ask, don't tell" U.S.-China IPR policy. In responding to this question, one USTR official was straightforward: "U.S. industry is part of the problem on this one."[89]

85. Seth Faison, "China Turns Blind Eye to Pirated Disks," *New York Times,* March 28, 1998; and Interview 98SH05, May 11, 1998 (italics mine).

86. Ibid.

87. Jack Valenti, "China's Pirated Disks," letter to the editor, *New York Times,* April 3, 1998. Valenti's motives are unclear, but the MPAA has on several occasions put market access ahead of its copyright concerns in its dialogue with China. At the time of the Faison-Valenti "exchange," Disney was negotiating the opening of a theme park in southern China, and Hollywood was seeking to limit the damage arising from its distribution of the "three anti-Chinese movies" (*Kundun, Seven Years in Tibet,* and *Red Corner*) all of which Beijing regarded as being "anti-China."

88. Faison, "China Turns Blind Eye to Pirated Disks."

89. Interview 98US19, December 11, 1998.

One way to counteract USTR suspicion of possible defection on the part of IPR advocacy groups and to demonstrate a degree of credible commitment to the Special 301 process was to file Special 301 submissions on an annual basis and to engage the USTR on a full-time, year-round basis. In addition to demonstrating their reliability to the USTR and their willingness to "fight it out" for the long haul, such groups provided critical information that added credibility by reflecting changes over time (or the lack thereof) in the target country. The International Intellectual Property Alliance has the strongest track record on this dimension; it is the only association that has submitted a China-specific petition every year since the establishment of Special 301 in 1988. Similarly, even after it was able to obtain its goal of administrative (or "pipeline") protection for patents in 1992, the Pharmaceutical Manufacturers Association continued to reinforce its commitment to the Special 301 process by submitting annual 301 petitions.[90]

Timing

Timing is also critical in explaining success in the agenda-setting process. The most important timing consideration is the submission of the necessary information to the USTR within the timeline dictated by Special 301. Although the process of keeping the USTR informed of developments in a given target country is ongoing, a critical part of this is to have a Special 301 submission "on the books" by the deadline set in the *Federal Register* of a given year. Failure to submit a petition by the February due date makes it exceedingly difficult for the USTR to give full consideration to the IPR advocacy group or individual firm or to mobilize the requisite political support on its behalf.[91]

For example, in its 1994 submission, the International Trademark Association outlined the ongoing efforts of its Special Trade Barriers Task Force, which was engaged in analyzing trademark problems in Brazil, South Korea, and China. In concluding its submission, INTA conceded

90. "Pipeline protection" refers to administrative protection for U.S. patents not covered in the original 1984 Patent Law of China. Such protection allows for a "grandfathering" of coverage for products invented as early as 1984, with patents granted on or after January 1, 1986. Pipeline products had seven and a half years of marketing exclusivity for applicable products through the end of June 2000.

91. This was mitigated somewhat by the timetable in the 1995 and 1996 negotiations, in which the final agreements were made after the February Special 301 submission deadline, therefore giving the IPR advocacy groups an opportunity to influence the process at a later stage, as well as providing the USTR with crucial leverage in concluding the negotiations with China. This should be understood in conjunction with Lee Sands's approach with regard to leveling demands at China, which stands in sharp contrast to that of his predecessor and former boss, Joseph Massey. While Massey made sure to compile his list of demands before the start of the negotiations, the agenda-setting approach under Sands—while taking the formal 301 submissions as its cornerstone—could be characterized as a "work in progress," much to the chagrin of his Chinese counterparts (Interview 98US10A/B, December 3 and 4, 1998; and Interview 99BJ16, March 24, 1999).

that its country-specific information on China was incomplete and that its task force would make its report available two months later, in April. This left the USTR with very little time to incorporate the report into its own Special 301 engagement strategy with China, as required by law.

The 1994 IACC submission highlights this inability to work within the USTR timeline even more starkly:

> The IACC understands that this year the International Intellectual Property Alliance . . . representing the copyright industry, will be urging the USTR to designate the PRC as a Priority Foreign Country. We are aware of the monumental losses suffered by every sector of the copyright industry attributable to piracy in China. While we believe that the losses due to patent, trademark and trade secret theft in China are just as staggering, *information is not yet available to fully support a recommendation, at this time, that China be designated a Priority Foreign Country* on these bases alone.[92]

This was a particularly important lost opportunity because the most extensive and wide-ranging negotiations that would transpire between the U.S. and China took place in 1994 and 1995, and INTA and the IACC each missed its chance to influence the agenda-setting process in a substantial way at this critical stage.[93]

The timing dimension also refers to the ability to anticipate and exploit events in the target country in order to present a plan of action that is *ex ante* in nature. For example, given the lawmaking process in China, which is often as protracted and contentious as it is opaque, it is far more desirable for a foreign actor to attempt to influence the process *before* the promulgation of the law. This is at best an undertaking with uncertain outcomes. The lawmaking process in China requires the expenditure of considerable political capital on the part of the interested domestic actors, and once a compromise is reached in the form of the final law, attempting to revise this agreement in the short term is a practical impossibility, as we shall see in the exogenous attempts to tinker with the 1990 Copyright Law of China.

For example, the 1994 Special 301 submission from the International Trademark Association, which was widely seen as a request that the USTR demand that China "re-revise" its recently revised July 1993 Trademark Law, was a serious tactical error and betrayed INTA's general disdain for the Special 301 process. INTA listed the revisions in China's revised 1993 Trademark Law and Implementing Regulations, noting that "not all . . .

---

92. IACC, Special 301 Submission, February 18, 1994, U.S. Trade Representative Reading Room (Doc.Special.301; 1994); italics mine.

93. Similarly, in its 1996 submission, INTA stated that 1995—a critical year in the ongoing Sino-U.S. IPR dialogue—was an "off year" for INTA's membership survey concerning trademark-related trade barriers abroad. INTA, Special 301 Submission, February 20, 1996, U.S. Trade Representative Reading Room (Doc.Special.301; 1996).

were improvements." INTA also noted specific enforcement problems inherent in the new regulations.

This submission points to INTA's mistake in making its first Special 301 submission in 1993, one year *after* the first Sino-U.S. Memorandum of Understanding on Intellectual Property Rights, in which the copyright-led advocacy groups, along with the patent-directed pharmaceutical lobby, PhRMA, mobilized the USTR and were able to secure important agreements from China to include their demands in relevant laws and regulations that were then being formulated in China. By abstaining from the agenda-setting process that led to the 1992 MOU, the trademark lobby missed a critical opportunity to influence the process that eventually produced the 1993 revised Trademark Law of the People's Republic of China. Perhaps as a realization that it had missed the boat by abstaining from the agenda-setting process of the 1991–92 negotiations and the 1993 Trademark Law, both the International Anti-Counterfeiting Coalition and INTA submitted regular Special 301 petitions (although INTA again abstained in the critical 1995 301 cycle), but their emphasis on changing China's legal regime was already out of sync with the shift in the USTR's (and the copyright lobby's) growing preoccupation with *enforcement* of IPR in China.

Form and Content

A final consideration in the effectiveness of an individual submission is its form and content. The more successful submissions included easily digestible explanations of events in the target country and illustrations of the laws and international treaties that were being violated. These more successful submissions avoided overly legalistic language and confusing data dumps, instead placing the problems in a commercial context in an easily understandable way.[94] Some provided descriptive statistics that clearly highlighted the problems. The more successful submissions provided country-specific overviews highlighting the IPR problem. This was enhanced considerably if the petitioner was willing "to name names" and identify specific problems encountered by a firm that was willing to go on the record in documenting its grievances by citing specific Chinese violators.[95]

One crucial element of "content" is the feasibility of the recommended actions, as well as the absence of contradictory goals within a set of policy prescriptions. The copyright lobby, particularly the International Intellectual Property Alliance, presented a relatively small list of coherent and ordered goals, which could be separated from the universe of "ideal solutions" contained in the copyright-based submissions. In the earlier stages of the dialogue in 1991 and 1992, these centered on the concurrent developments in China's promulgation of relevant copyright laws and regulations and on pushing China to accede to the relevant international IPR

94. Interview 98US10A, December 3, 1998.
95. Ibid.; Interview 98US20, December 11, 1998.

conventions. After 1992, these concerns shifted to cracking down on illegal manufacturing and export operations in China. As the focus settled on enforcement, priorities gravitated toward the closure of three dozen compact disk– and CD-ROM–producing factories in southern China as well as, less successfully, on market access for audiovisual products. Although the copyright lobby did include a host of other issues, it was clear to the USTR, and subsequently to Beijing, that closure of these pirate factories constituted the critical mass of their demands.

Similarly, the Pharmaceutical Research and Manufacturers Association provides an example of alternating successful and unsuccessful goal articulation. PhRMA was extremely successful in obtaining its early demand for administrative, or "pipeline," protection for U.S. patents not covered under China's 1984 Patent Law. However, after 1992, PhRMA's Special 301 submissions began to include a barrage of goals, many of which were only indirectly related to intellectual property. As a result, PhRMA was never able to replicate its success in 1992, although it was able to maintain the focus on China's implementation of "pipeline" protection.

Clearly articulated submissions with a manageable set of goals went beyond being simple petitions: they provided information, "which was easily converted into influence."[96] By contrast, submissions that did not fit this model had very little impact on the substance of the negotiations. The wealth of information provided by the International Trademark Association and the International Anti-Counterfeiting Coalition was difficult to transform into a coherent set of trademark-intensive demands. The INTA and IACC submissions were often in the form of a "laundry list" of IPR problems in China, without a clearly ranked ordering of principal trademark concerns. This also helps account for the trademark lobby's ineffectiveness in shaping U.S. IPR demands.

In sum, the substantive content of the U.S. demands were overwhelmingly driven by domestic U.S. industries. Rather than reflect a balanced picture, in this case of intellectual property as a legal and commercial issue in the United States, the trade policy agenda-setting process can distort the parameters of the issue area by favoring some IPR subfields (copyright) over others (trademarks). Moreover, the success of one group over another has at least as much to do with the groups' varying abilities and their willingness to master the political process as it does to the actual salience of the issue area subfield in question. For these reasons, U.S. trade policy often does not accurately represent the full range of interested domestic actors in a given issue area policy community, let alone those of the foreign country with which it is negotiating. Although U.S. pressure successfully framed the issues that were negotiated and ultimately adopted in Chinese laws and regulations, subsequent chapters will show that this does not automatically translate into effective policy implementation and enforcement.

96. Interview 98US10B, December 4, 1998.

Structure and Process of the Chinese Negotiation *Modus Operandi*

How were these demands presented to Beijing, and how were they handled during the negotiations?[97] The following is a composite of the various sets of IPR negotiations, which can be extended to describe other trade negotiations from that time up to the present day. The argument of this section is that China added little to the set of demands that arose through the Special 301 process and were transmitted to Beijing. Although the Chinese side did issue some counterdemands, specifically in the form of technical and other assistance from the United States, for the most part China simply hoped to minimize the number of demands that would ultimately end up in the bilateral agreements at the end of the negotiations.[98] Thus, the substance of the negotiations was largely that which arose in the United States. At the end of the day, the resulting agreements would fall far short of embracing a comprehensive and consistent IPR policy package, or even one that accurately reflected the situation on the ground in China, let alone the preferences of the Chinese leadership and interested parties on the Chinese side.

As noted, the actual transfer of the domestic trade agenda into a policy that is then negotiated and subsequently implemented in China is a decidedly one-sided affair. There was little that the Chinese brought to the negotiating table aside from a desire to move as little as possible from the status quo. In most cases, the negotiations began with China receiving a set of demands by the USTR. Once the USTR presented these to China's Ministry of Foreign Trade and Economic Cooperation (*duiwai maoyi jingji hezuo bu*, or MOFTEC), the process of initial bilateral consultations began. Before meeting with the U.S. delegation, MOFTEC disseminated these demands for review and comment among the government units to participate in the negotiations. It is at this stage that a critical step of the negotiation process occurred. MOFTEC convened a discussion attended by these units, in which the specific Chinese negotiation strategies were discussed.[99] These

97. This section draws from interviews with former U.S. and Chinese negotiators conducted in the United States and China in 1998, 1999, 2002, and 2003. See also A. Doak Barnett, *The Making of Foreign Policy in China: Structure and Process*, SAIS Papers in International Affairs, vol. 9 (Boulder: Westview Press, 1985); and David M. Lampton, ed., *The Making of Chinese Foreign and Security Policy in the Era of Reform* (Stanford: Stanford University Press, 2001).

98. The Chinese approach with their counterdemands was along the lines of, "OK, if you want to impose your demands on us, then there are a few that we would like you to meet as well." Interview 03BJ01B, July 23, 2003.

99. The individuals representing these units are either the directors general (*sizhang* or *juzhang*), the deputy directors general (*fu sizhang* or *fu juzhang*), or directors (*chuzhang*), which report the progress of these meetings to the vice minister (*fu buzhang*) with the portfolio over the issue being discussed at MOFTEC. The minister (*buzhang*) does not participate, but, of course, he will ultimately sign off on the unit's position vis-à-vis the negotiations. There is often frenzied activity among the people involved in the meetings and their leaders back in the units, with secretaries running to and from the meeting to report progress and to communicate orders from the unit. There has to be consensus at this level before a submission is sent to the State Council.

meetings were substantive in scope and the attending units were particularly frank in discussions with their counterparts. During this discussion stage, MOFTEC outlined possible negotiation outcomes and demanded that each unit present a "worst-case" scenario i.e., the maximum concessions that it would be able to give up.

MOFTEC would collect this information and use it to create its own general "bargaining space"—what the Chinese side can or cannot concede in the negotiations. This was MOFTEC's principal reference with regard to how far it could move away from its "ideal point." The outcome of these meetings among the participating units and the agreement on the Chinese "bargaining space" were summarized in a brief report submitted to the State Council. These reports included the list of U.S. demands, possible Chinese concessions, and the proposed strategies as discussed in the above meetings. The General Secretary of the Working Office of the State Council read the report, adding comments and highlighting important talking points. This memo was then sent to a state councilor or a vice premier and, in the case of particularly important and/or high-profile negotiations, to the Premier himself, each of whom indicated that he had read it, sometimes adding additional comments. Approval of the memo at this level indicated official approval for this "bargaining space."[100]

The State Council would generally approve these submissions as a matter of course, although there could be "general principles" invoked by the top leadership (i.e., broad-based political considerations) that required some alteration of the initial submission.[101] However, significant changes in the initial submission were rare, partly because the subordinate units were familiar with these "general principles" and built them into their negotiation strategies and their own individual "bargaining spaces." If a "general principle" or some other preference of the top leadership is expressed or

100. During times when the Sino-U.S. IPR dialogue is less politically charged than in the years from 1991 to 1996, the USTR generally presents MOFTEC with its agenda. MOFTEC then drafts a memo to be circulated among the various relevant bureaucratic agencies before sending the revised draft to the MOFTEC Minister for comment; the memo generally does not go up to the State Council. This is the document that delineates what MOFTEC can and cannot do during the negotiations.

101. An example of such a "general principle" is the refusal to allow unregulated access in the audiovisual market. It has gotten to the point where even the USTR recognizes the importance of these "general principles" to the Chinese side and does not try to make forays into these "forbidden areas." The USTR demands to MOFTEC would regularly include market access for audiovisual products, but Assistant USTR Joe Papovich did not make a habit of bringing up the subject during the JCCT meetings.

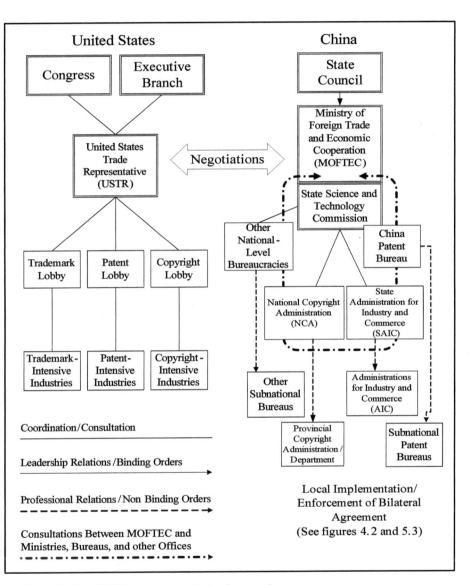

Figure 2.1. The U.S.-China trade negotiation framework

tacitly understood (regardless of how strange it may appear to MOFTEC), it is followed without question. In such an instance, technical issues are trumped by political considerations.

The "Working Level"

Once the bilateral talks began, there were two dimensions within which the negotiations took place: a "working" level and a "political" level. During the first of these, the "working level," the representatives of each of the units involved would go over technical issues among themselves and with the U.S. side. At the time of the Sino-U.S. IPR negotiations, this "working level" configuration was led by MOFTEC's Director General of the Department of Treaties and Laws, while the delegation consisted of directors general, deputy directors general, and directors of the various commissions, ministries, and bureaus that made up the Chinese delegation.

This forum also provided the stage for domestic bureaucratic political wrangling. This was sometimes divided further into two subsets of negotiations. The first has to do with technical issues that require professional expertise. Once these were tentatively agreed upon by the two sides (or if the Chinese side felt that these would satisfy the United States), they were handed over to the "responsible people" of the unit in question (the officials, as opposed to the technical experts, within the functional administrative units), who then made a decision whether or not the compromises were possible. Once the negotiations started again in 1993, these two procedures were collapsed into one configuration of "working level" negotiations.

The substantive issues discussed in this forum can be divided, according to one Chinese official involved in the negotiations, into "secular" matters, on the one hand, and those concerns that did not have an agreed-upon precedent or had political overtones and were thus more problematic, on the other. Most of the issues that were negotiated fit into the first category. For example, the term of validity for customs recordal was one of the issues that were negotiated in 1995.[102] The United States wanted a term of ten years, China a term of five. The two sides compromised on a mutually acceptable term of seven years. However, issues that did not have a clear-cut precedent or were seen as providing an undue burden on the Chinese side placed the Chinese negotiators in a difficult position. Signing off on such an issue could be held against the negotiator by his superiors or by his colleagues in the administrative unit which he or she represented. Such deadlocks were broken only after intervention by the top leadership.

Other issues were more difficult because of their spillover into larger political concerns or because they were seen as unfair to the Chinese side—which made them extremely difficult for the Chinese negotiators to

102. Recordal of ownership of the intellectual property right with Chinese Customs is a prerequisite to invoking Customs IPR protection. It is renewable for another seven years or until the term of validity of the owner's intellectual property rights.

agree to, particularly when those negotiators had an eye on the politics of subsequent implementation. One such issue had to do with the broad jurisdiction of the General Administration of Customs in China (GACC). The U.S. side demanded that the GACC handle investigations of imports as well as exports. However, the U.S. Customs Service generally does not handle the inspection of exports, so the Chinese were being asked to adhere to a standard to which the United States itself did not subscribe.[103]

Yet another issue had to do with the scope of discretion of the GACC over confiscation for exports. The GACC preference was for a set of flexible options, including withdrawal of the goods from export, release of the goods after removing the offending counterfeit trademark, and confiscation. The United States demanded that the GACC limit its scope of action to the most stringent of these actions—confiscation. This posed a dilemma for the GACC: in the fairly common event that a state-run import/export company unwittingly arranged the sale and shipment of counterfeit goods, the goods would still have to be confiscated and the import/export company would be left without payment. This would place an undue financial burden on China's commercial units and would be in contravention to the "general principles" of maximizing economic development, a standard that in the context of these negotiations could only be relaxed by the top leadership. The stalemate was resolved once the GACC was informed by its "superiors" to accede to the U.S. demands. This absolved the GACC of the responsibility of giving up a substantial concession, although this decision was particularly unpopular within the GACC bureaucracy.[104]

In other cases, participating units linked the negotiations with a possible future erosion of their own administrative power, which made them particularly intractable during the talks. In the 1991–92 negotiations, one of the most contentious issues was the designation of computer software as a "literary work." The then Ministry of Machinery and Electronics Industry (MMEI) was responsible for the registration of computer software. However, the MMEI regarded software as a "tool" and was engaged in widespread dissemination of software throughout China's extensive network of State-Owned Enterprises (SOEs), maintaining a network of relationships that gave the MMEI considerable power. As a result of such widespread dissemination, one U.S. negotiator labeled the MMEI as the "biggest pirater of copyrighted products" in China. The MMEI justified its position on the grounds that at that time computer software was not considered a "literary work" and was therefore not covered by copyright protection; thus MMEI dissemination of software was not illegal, which, technically, it wasn't—at

---

103. The Chinese eventually agreed to this. The argument that made this final agreement possible was that a given country's customs bureaucracy handling investigations of both imports and exports is increasingly an international trend. Rather than seeing China as being held to a more rigid standard than the United States, the argument was framed in terms of China joining an international trend, with the United States in the role of the holdout. China was not the outlier—went the argument—the United States was (and is). Interview 99BJ37, August 4, 1999.

104. Ibid.

the time.[105] To break the impasse, the top leadership again intervened and the responsibility for the majority of computer software registration was eventually transferred to the National Copyright Administration (NCA).

Finally, some issues, even at the "working level," went beyond secular trade issues and extended into the far more taboo area of the foreign manufacture and distribution of "cultural" and "value-laden" products within China. In the 1991–92 negotiations, the Chinese "refused to budge" on market access for motion pictures.[106] There was some movement in the 1994–95 and 1996 negotiations, but deep resistance on the Chinese side continued. Although officials at the Ministry of Culture recognized the economic gains for China in allowing an increased foreign presence in developing the "cultural" market, for the most part political and ideological considerations trumped economic ones. Ultimately, although the Chinese side did allow for the licensing of cultural products, the import of products from abroad had to pass a stringent test of scrutiny both sufficiently expansive and ambiguous to give the Chinese side ample leeway in deciding on any particular good being imported. For imports—especially cinema showings, but also mass-market VCDs, LDs, CDs, and cassettes—this framework acted as a gatekeeper. However, it is far more difficult to control this industry/cultural market if foreign companies are allowed into China to produce their own materials and recruit their own talent. This is why China was so insistent on making sure that any foreign company engaged in such activity must do so with a Chinese joint venture partner. This calculation was not so much economic as ideological. The market access issue for "cultural" products was reserved for the final rounds of the 1994–95 negotiations, and it was the most troublesome issue covered in the talks, taking up much of the last six weeks of the process.

The "Political Level"

In contrast to the "working level," the "political level," involves officials from the very highest levels of the Chinese government. It is characterized not so much by the formulation of policy but rather by choosing the option most consistent with the overall political considerations of the top leadership from a small set of policy options presented by MOFTEC, which were the result of lower-level interagency bargaining.[107] In short, the top leadership does not propose as much as it disposes.

105. According to this source, the MMEI and the Ministry of Chemical Industry were the two most intractable units during the 1991–92 negotiations, and MOFERT, the predecessor of MOFTEC, had a difficult time reining them in. Interview 98US10B, December 4, 1998. MMEI officials told the United States that whether those below the MMEI violate copyright or not should not be of concern to the MMEI or the United States; it is an internal affair and not under the jurisdiction of the United States. Interview 98US09, November 30, 1998.

106. Interview 98US09, November 30, 1998.

107. The top leadership was never presented with a report and attached policy options that it would be forced to reject within the formal Sino-U.S. IPR dialogue from 1991 to 1996. This

At the conclusion of these "working level" meetings, MOFTEC would submit a report to the State Council.[108] These reports generally indicated two sets of issues: what had been resolved to date, and what outstanding issues remained. It concluded with a set of "suggestions" as well as solicitations for advice. This report had to be acceptable to all the units involved in the "working" (or interagency bargaining) level and approved by the MOFTEC Minister, who usually agreed with the outcome of the interagency bargaining and sent it upward. Agreement by the MOFTEC Minister is generally understood as the probable outcome, since the minister generally defers to his or her subordinates' more detailed knowledge of the intricate procedural details. These same subordinates would anticipate this, and they took pains to ensure that the report did not undermine the credibility of MOFTEC or the MOFTEC Minister or otherwise embarrass the minister in front of the State Council.[109]

This report was then submitted to the State Council Working Office and reviewed by the General Secretary or the Deputy General Secretary of the office with authority over MOFTEC. If the report was deemed acceptable, it would be sent to the State Council with an attachment stating that the official in question had reviewed this report and believed it to be satisfactory. At the bottom of this attachment, he would type the names of the premier and vice premiers, all of whom had read the report, and indicate their agreement and approval by drawing a circle next to their names and by offering comment where appropriate.[110] Then, this was

---

has to do with the "screening" process in which subordinate officials ensure that the reports they submit to their superiors do not put the latter in a position that would compromise their authority.

108. This report is also circulated to other parts of MOFTEC that have an interest in the larger bilateral relations or in other aspects not necessarily related to IPR but upon which the IPR negotiations can have an impact. One example is the Office for American and Oceanic Affairs. If the other units agree, they affix their stamp, and thus a "coordinated signature" (*huiqian*) by MOFTEC is submitted to the State Council, but via the MOFTEC Minister. If they disagree with it, they write their opinions on the document and follow up with consultations with the MOFTEC office issuing the report. Once they agree, it is sent upwards.

109. With the caveat mentioned above, this also has the sometimes unintended consequences of giving the lower-ranking MOFTEC officials an ability to frame the agenda-setting process that surpasses their formal administrative rank. This tends to be relatively infrequent (and not necessarily deliberate) and is only done with great care.

110. The highest-ranking name on these attachments to the MOFTEC reports is that of the premier, in this case Li Peng. The highest-ranking leader's name comes first, followed by the other names in descending hierarchical order. During the IPR negotiations, Li Peng's name came first, followed by Li Lanqing, Song Jian, and others. The chronological order of the signatures is also not random: they are also in descending order of rank. The highest-ranking leader signs off on it first, which makes it easier for the others to sign, knowing that their higher-ranking colleagues (beginning with Li Peng) have endorsed it. However, if Li is not there, one of his secretaries signed on his behalf. In such a case, the highest-ranking subordinate looks at the information extremely carefully, because he must anticipate the premier's own views on the matter. This has the effect of extending the negotiations, which can move very slowly if there is no impending "crisis." Once such a "crisis" looms, however, things move very quickly. In noncrisis periods Responses to submissions on the part of the State Council can take months. During

handed down to the relevant units and MOFTEC in the form of a simple memo attached to the initial submission and the State Council Working Office's note.[111]

This process occurred a number of times throughout a given round of negotiations. In 1996, for example, there were five such transmissions between MOFTEC and the State Council in the three-week period leading up to the June 27 agreement alone, during a time in which the negotiations were at their most intense. The first four followed the pattern outlined above. The final one—which was composed when the negotiations were approaching some sort of a resolution, if not necessarily a conclusion—put together all the issues discussed and summarized them in a set of (usually) three options, of which MOFTEC's preferred option was clearly specified.[112] Once the Premier and the State Council approve a particular option and add their opinions about the "political" issues,[113] this message was transmitted to the MOFTEC Minister.[114] Several people close to the negotiations mentioned that the top Chinese leadership, having had reviewed a report on the positive impact of increased IPR protection to China's economy in December 1994, informed the negotiators in mid-January that they wanted the negotiators to reach an agreement with the United States, while adding that "we must do it our way" and that the negotiators should not give up any unnecessary concessions.

It is interesting to note that, in contrast to the "working level," the "political level" was characterized not so much by the formulation of policy (i.e., the Chinese negotiating position) but rather by selecting the option most consistent with the overall political considerations of the top leadership from a small set of policy prescriptions presented by MOFTEC, although it always retained the option to alter the proceedings if they deviated substantially from the "general principles" at a particular time. Whether disposing of a particular negotiating point or breaking a deadlock, the top leadership's intervention into the negotiation process was essential for it to

---

the actual negotiations, such communication is put on a fast track, and the turnaround time is around twenty-four hours.

111. In exceptional circumstances, the MOFTEC senior negotiator may actually sign off on some parts of the agreement without clearing it with the State Council. An example of this was when the Chinese side agreed to an extension of patent protection from fifteen to twenty years during the WTO negotiations. This, however, is exceedingly rare.

112. It should be noted that MOFTEC does not include too many options in their submissions: although it is important to allow the leaders some flexibility in making their choice—assuming flexibility is possible—but not so many choices that the leaders have to expend too much time deciding their preferred options.

113. One source was informed that Deng Xiaoping himself gave his assent to the 1992 MOU by way of his daughter. Interview 98US15, December 8, 1998.

114. Each government unit participating in the negotiations is copied on all communications to and from the State Council, including the MOFTEC–State Council dialogue on the initial USTR demands, all subsequent reports, and the final agreement. Moreover, all reports sent to the State Council are cosigned by the relevant units. If one is missing, and the State Council feels that this unit has a certain jurisdiction over the issue, then the State Council demands that the other units be included in the process.

move forward, although this also had the effect of undermining the credibility of China's domestic constraints.

This chapter has illustrated the structure and process by which U.S. demands are transformed into policy and the ways in which this policy is negotiated between Washington and Beijing. It also described the basic strategy of the Chinese negotiation process: withstand as many U.S. demands as possible without endangering the talks themselves. The transformation of the demands that China was unable to withstand—i.e., what China was forced to accept—into policy and the impact of external pressure on the Chinese policy compliance and enforcement institutions and processes—as distinct from policymaking—provide the subject for the remainder of this book.

Before moving on to the domestic context in China, however, it is important to ask whether the foregoing analysis is relevant now that China has joined the WTO and now that MOFTEC has been reorganized into the Ministry of Commerce (*shangwu bu*), or MOFCOM. The answer is that the above analysis of the Chinese negotiation process is as accurate a description of today's MOFCOM as it is of MOFTEC in the 1990s. When I asked a MOFCOM official how MOFCOM would respond to a Special 301 action today, he stated unequivocally that the response would be "exactly the same" as that described in this chapter. Moreover, he pointed out that this description of the Chinese negotiation process also extends to other trade issue areas and is in no way specific to intellectual property. For example, he said that the WTO negotiations up until but not including the final stages in 1999 were "exactly like this."[115]

Indeed, Special 301 has not been supplanted by the accession of China or any other country to the WTO. The framework leading up to the initiation of an investigation—that is, the framework under Special 301—is exactly the same under WTO rules.[116] What is different is that if these

---

115. The final stages of the WTO negotiations differed from the description above in three ways. First, President Jiang Zemin intervened and personally gave instructions to MOFTEC Minister Shi Guangsheng. Second, at some point, Premier Zhu Rongji actually came over to MOFTEC to take part in the negotiations. Third, Premier Zhu called a "principal-force meeting" (*zhuli bangong huiyi*), in which he met in a closed-door session with the ministers of the ministries involved in this stage of the negotiations in order to find out what they would be able to concede in the final run up to an agreement with the United States. Interview 03BJ01B, July 23, 2003.

116. At least two legal arguments support this assessment. First, in 2002, there was a WTO Dispute Settlement Body (DSB) ruling upholding the validity of Sections 301 to 310 of the U.S. Trade Act of 1974. Second, Section 313 of the Uruguay Round Agreement Act of 1994 (URAA) makes it clear that the TRIPS Agreement standards are considered only as a threshold, not the ceiling. Therefore, the United States will continue to pursue what it considers the worst offenders around the world through this unilateral/bilateral approach. While other countries clearly do not agree with this position, it is questionable exactly how many options they have to prevent the United States from doing so. Note that the URAA defers to the WTO/DSB proceedings but reserves the final say on whether the United States will take unilateral action against a given state.

concerns fall under the WTO's own IPR regime, Trade Related Aspects of Intellectual Property (TRIPS), they can be pursued under the WTO's dispute settlement mechanism. The Chinese case is no different than those of other WTO member countries against whom the United States has initiated and continues to initiate Special 301 actions. Moreover, for issues falling outside TRIPS, the WTO dispute settlement mechanism is not used. Knowing this, the domestic IPR trade associations in the United States may strategically frame their concerns in such a way that they bypass the WTO dispute mechanism, thus ensuring unilateral USTR action under Special 301.[117]

At the end of the day, whether before or after China's accession to the WTO, that which becomes policy to be implemented locally in China does not begin at the negotiating table. Rather, it is formed in the United States through the interaction of the relevant IPR associations, which, in turn, takes place under the institutional framework of a domestic U.S. law, specifically Special 301. The role that Beijing has taken on in this process has been to resist as many of these demands as possible. Those that Beijing ultimately accepts become national policy, which is then implemented throughout the country. The next three chapters look at how these demands have been subsequently transformed into national policy in China and the specific institutional settings in which these policies are implemented and enforced. Put another way, they examine how challenges impede the attempt to impose a fragmented issue area onto an equally fragmented political system.

---

117. Interview 02US01, April 5, 2002.

CHAPTER 3

Patents and *Faux* Consolidation of China's Administrative Patent Regime

A full decade before the United States and China became embroiled in the IPR negotiations described in chapter 2, China was taking tentative steps toward establishing its own intellectual property regime. On December 10, 1984, Vice Premier Li Peng and other national leaders were present at the groundbreaking ceremony for the National Patent Bureau (*Guojia zhuanli ju*). Located far from the center of Beijing on what would become the third ring road, the Patent Bureau was strategically close to Beijing University, Qinghua University, and the Zhongguancun district, which would later blossom into what became known as "China's Silicon Valley." In charting the "natural evolution" of intellectual property in China, I focus on the Patent Bureau, and the institutional legacies it inherited and passed on to its successor organization (the State Intellectual Property Office, SIPO), starting with the evolution of China's 1984 Patent Law, which went into effect only a few months after the opening ceremonies at the National Patent Bureau on April 1, 1985. The glowing speeches, the bright red and white propaganda banners, and the barrage of firecrackers that draped the surrounding streets in a sea of red paper all belied the notion that China was embarking on a long and tortuous path to establishing its nascent intellectual property regime. Nobody anticipated that in less than ten years, IPR would become a lightning rod for Sino-U.S. trade conflict, which would in turn shape China's intellectual property trajectory in unforeseen ways and send it in unexpected directions.

I make three claims in this chapter. First, I suggest that the first ten years in the development of China's patent regime provide a window into the natural evolution of IPR in China, at least until the early 1990s. Second, I argue that this evolution was overtaken by events when the United States engaged China under Special 301 with the goal of strongarming Beijing to establish an IPR regime compliant with international norms and U.S. objectives. Third, this exogenous pressure, combined with the efforts of certain interested parties in China, sought to impose the idea of a consolidated IPR regime combining patents, copyright, and trademarks under an umbrella organization, the State Intellectual Property Office (the successor organization to the China Patent Bureau), onto the preexisting bureaucratic landscape. The result has been an institutionalization of the tensions among and across the bureaucracies representing discrete IPR subfields, which has made effective coordinated enforcement impossible. This is because power and jurisdictional considerations were never fully taken into account.

Empirically, this chapter provides a political history-based overview of the patent system in China. I trace the debate that provides the context for the legislative history of China's first Patent Law. I map the organizational structure and jurisdictional terrain of China's administrative patent system at the national and local levels. Finally, I discuss the heretofore unsuccessful morphing of China's patent system into a coordinating agency for intellectual property in China, the State Intellectual Property Office. In doing so, I set the stage for a discussion of the copyright and trademark bureaucracies in chapters 4 and 5, respectively.

The "Natural" Evolution of China's Patent Law

By the middle of the 1980s, there appeared to be considerable momentum in China for intellectual property rights—or, more accurately, patents.[1] As early as November 1973, after the Chinese delegation to the World Intellectual Property Organization (WIPO) returned to Beijing, delegation leader Ren Jiaxin, who would later become Chief Justice of China's Supreme Court, proposed the establishment of a patent system in China. According to the *People's Daily,*

This was the first time that New China has sent representatives to an international conference related to intellectual property rights. At that time, many people in China found the term "Intellectual Property" rather unfamiliar. The [China Council for the Promotion of International Trade] had rendered it, for the first time, into the Chinese equivalent, *zhishi chanquan.*[2]

However, the first substantive moves in this direction were not taken until after the death of Mao Zedong in September 1976, the arrest of the

1. The term "intellectual property" (*zhishi chanquan*), was not widely used at that time. At the time, the preferred term was "industrial property" (*gongye chanquan*). In the late 1980s, copyright barely registered on the IPR radar—it would take five more years and considerable exogenous pressure from the United States and others before the PRC adopted its first copyright law—and trademarks fared only slightly better.
2. *People's Daily,* September 4, 1995.

Gang of Four a month later, and the rise of the reform coalition two years after that. By 1979, it was clear to many of the top leaders that the continued existence of the Chinese Communist Party depended on the success of modernization and economic development. One of the tactics used by Deng Xiaoping to make his case for reform was to sponsor trips for China's leaders to visit Japan and other Asian countries that over the previous twenty-five years had prospered economically as China had stagnated. These leaders were genuinely shocked by what they saw and profoundly shaken by the degree to which China had fallen behind. China's reform leadership understood that China was generations behind in terms of scientific knowledge and technological expertise and recognized that a viable patent regime was essential to attracting technology transfers from abroad as well as for fostering China's own domestic scientific and technical development.

At the same time, however, the notion of intellectual property was in many ways inconsistent with both the basic assumptions of socialism and those embraced by developing states more generally. These assumptions had a profound impact on the character of the modern Chinese state and on the evolution of the PRC's efforts to protect the rights of invention. Indeed, it took no less than thirty-five years from the founding of the People's Republic until the first Patent Law of the PRC saw the light of day.[3]

The Mao Era (1949–76)

Much of the debate leading up to the promulgation of the 1984 Patent Law was framed and informed by developments that occurred during the era of Mao Zedong. Flush with victory in 1949, the Chinese communists sought to break with the past. In establishing a framework to encourage innovation, China's new leaders did not look to their Nationalist predecessors (or to those Nationalists who remained within the legal apparatus after 1949) as much as to the Soviet Union. William Alford argues that the most important reason for this is that the values and assumptions underlying the Soviet approach to invention and innovation dovetailed with traditional Chinese attitudes toward intellectual property.[4] This was most clearly reflected in the belief that creation and invention are social activities that draw from a repository of knowledge that belongs to all members of society.

Put differently, innovative activity was understood to be a public good, and any attempts to control it for profit were considered a form of rent-seeking—rational from the point of view of the individual patent holders

---

3. China's first Patent Law was promulgated by the Qing in 1889. It was followed by the first Republican Patent Law in 1912. The Patent Law of 1944, promulgated by the Nationalists, is still in effect in Taiwan, although it has been subject to many changes since then. Interview 99BJ27, July 23, 1999.

4. William P. Alford, *To Steal a Book is an Elegant Offense: Intellectual Property Law in Chinese Civilization* (Stanford: Stanford University Press, 1995), 56–57.

but inefficient from a social good perspective. Because socialism held the social good to be paramount, this was not simply an academic debate; it had important negative political overtones as well. Moreover, the Soviet and traditional Chinese approaches to innovative activity were also similar regarding the dissemination of ideas, that "it was wholly appropriate, indeed necessary, to control the flow of ideas to the populace. Moreover, each believed that this control was to be exercised by a very small group of persons for the benefit of society as a whole."[5] These ideas provided the foundation of China's award-based system that emerged during the Mao era.

On August 11, 1950, the Government Administration Council (GAC), the highest government body in the PRC, approved the "Decision of the Government Administration Council on Awards and Inventions, Technological Improvements, and Rationalization Proposals Relating to Production." Six days later, on August 17, the GAC approved the "Provisional Regulations on the Protection of the Invention Right and Patent Right." In these regulations, the state acknowledged patent rights, but it appeared to be preparing for a shift to an awards scheme. The regulations contained an option for inventors to donate their ideas to the state in exchange for a reward (the course preferred by the state); the state retained as much discretion as possible. However, in these early regulations, the power of the state still trumped that of the inventor. Article 14 of the 1950 Provisional Regulations stipulated that

> if after already awarding the patent certificate, the central principal organ (the Central Bureau of Technological Management) thinks it necessary that the invention's use and management revert to the state, it may negotiate with the patentee, requesting assignment to the state; if the negotiations do not eventuate in agreement, the Government Administration Council may make the final decision, changing the patent right to the invention right and granting a specified amount of monetary award.[6]

Article 12 provided what some considered a veiled threat: it stipulated that it was a criminal offense to usurp the state's right to exploit or manage an invention. Moreover, if the invention took place within the scope of the inventor's official capacity in a state factory, the inventor was automatically ineligible for a patent award.[7]

On May 6, 1954, the GAC approved the "Provisional Regulations on Awards for Inventions, Technical Improvements, and Rationalization Proposals Relating to Production," in which China formally adopted the Soviet

5. Alford, *To Steal a Book is an Elegant Offense*, 57.
6. Tao-Tai Hsia and Kathryn Houn, "Laws of the People's Republic of China on Industrial and Intellectual Property," *Law and Policy in International Business* 5, no. 3 (1973): 754–55.
7. Ibid., 755.

institution of inventor's certificates (*faming zhengshu*) while phasing out the remnants of patent rights from the pre-1949 era. These developments were overtaken by events as the Anti-Rightist Campaign of 1957–58 picked up steam, a development in which the intellectual community arguably suffered the most. Even before then, however, out of only a dozen applications for inventor's certificates from the mid-1950s to the mid-1960s, only *four* were issued.[8] Things only got worse during the Cultural Revolution (1966–77) by which time intellectuals were saddled with the moniker, *chou lao jiu* ("the stinking ninth category"). Indeed, three years earlier, in 1963, incentives for innovative activity were sharply curtailed in the environment that arose around Mao's recent exhortation to "never forget class struggle."[9]

On November 3, 1963, the State Council (the successor of the GAC) issued the "Regulations to Encourage Inventions and the Regulations to Encourage Improvements in Technology." Individual achievement was deleted from the legislative intent, and patents were no longer issued; for that matter, the same was true for inventor's certificates.[10] Article 23 of the 1963 "Regulations on Awards for Inventions and the Regulations on Awards for Technical Improvements" asserted that "all inventions are the property of the State, and no person or unit may claim monopoly over them. . . . All units throughout the country (including collectively owned units) may make use of the inventions essential to them." Provisions were established for recognition of the inventor's achievement through the award of one of five classes of certificates, each with an associated lump-sum cash bonus ranging from 10,000 yuan for a first-class invention to 500 yuan for a fifth-class invention. This represented a significant curtailing of the potential financial rewards for innovative work as stipulated in the 1950 and 1954 regulations.

Given the gargantuan political, economic, and social challenges facing China's leaders in the power vacuum left by Mao Zedong's death in the early fall of 1976, the establishment of a viable patent framework would have to await the consolidation of China's post-Mao leadership and their orientation toward reform at the Third Plenum of the Eleventh Central Committee in December 1978.

Initial Steps after the Third Plenum

In 1978, on the eve of reform, the State Council charged the State Science and Technology Commission (SSTC) with developing a patent system for China. In March 1979, the drafting group of the Chinese Patent Law was established. On October 17 of the same year, the formal request for the establishment of a patent system in China was submitted to the State Council by the SSTC. On January 14, 1980, the State Council approved the

8. Interview 99BJ27, July 23, 1999.
9. Mao Zedong Speech at Central Work Conference, August 9, 1962.
10. Barden Gale, "The Concept of Intellectual Property in China: Inventors and Inventions," *China Quarterly* 74 (June 1978): 348.

request, and on March 3, China became a member of the World Intellectual Property Organization.

In anticipation of the PRC's first-ever Patent Law, there was a flurry of training workshops, propaganda campaigns, and liaisons with the relevant government agencies sponsored by the SSTC. In this environment, there was considerable debate over the scope and content of what would become China's Patent Law. However, it would still be a tortuous five years before the first Patent Law of the People's Republic of China would come into force.

In its October 1979 submission to the State Council, entitled "Solicitations and Instructions for the Establishment of a Patent System for the Country," the drafting group concluded that China must establish a patent system and offered suggestions on how this might be accomplished. Their recommendations were based on several principles. The first had to do with maintaining and incorporating some aspects of the inventor's certificates into China's new patent regime. This consideration rested on the assumption that positive incentives were necessary to spur innovation while remaining ambiguous on the issue of diffusion. This was an attempt for China to have its cake and eat it too.

The second issue concerned inventors' rights with regard to the manufacture, sale, and use of inventions. For those employed by their work units (*danwei*), the patent rights of the inventor were to be handled by their own work units, while other work units could also make use of the invention; however, the latter had to make a payment for such use to the original work unit. This was one way to reach the goal; since the inventor did not have private monopoly rights on the invention, and since they were directly controlled by their work units, it was possible to encourage support for the collective and the good of the country. Foodstuffs, medicines, chemicals, and substances relating to nuclear fission, however, remained squarely in the public domain (i.e., monopoly rights were *not* conferred).

Perhaps in anticipation of the smooth evolution of a patent regime, months before the State Council's approval of this report, in June 1979, Beijing established the National Patent Bureau. The responsibilities of the drafting group were now transferred to the Patent Bureau, which began to work on the draft protocol of the Patent Law of China. However, even though these trends suggested an important step toward the institutionalization of a patent system in China, ideological and jurisdictional battles and institutional growing pains lay ahead.[11]

Controversy and Debate in the Drafting of China's 1984 Patent Law

There were several dozen people directly involved in the drafting process, representing the Patent Bureau, the SSTC, and the State Economics

11. Tang Zongshun, "*Huiyi zhuanli fa de qicao*" [Recollections about the Drafting of the Patent Law], in *Zhongguo zhishi chanquan ershi nian* [Twenty Years of Intellectual Property in China], ed. Liu Chuntian (Beijing: *Zhuanli chubanshe*, 1998), 95–96.

Commission (*Guojia jingji weiyuanhui*, SEC), among other offices. A group of these people, primarily scholars, was sent overseas at the time to learn first-hand about patent systems in other countries. The first director of the China Patent Bureau, Wu Heng, had been the director of the International Affairs Office of the SSTC and had a keen appreciation for this sort of exchange of knowledge with more developed countries.[12] These included the United States, Canada, France, Japan, and especially Germany. Upon their return to China, these experts met and compared notes to decide which system, or which elements of these many systems, would be the most beneficial to China.[13]

Despite the wealth of insight that this group of experts represented, two major problems in the legislative history of any given law or regulation in China presented themselves. First, many competing interests are represented during the drafting sessions, with the result that the eventual legislation reflects a political compromise that is either substantively little different from the status quo or that is so ambiguous or downright confusing that it can be easily manipulated. The second problem, particularly in the period under review here, is that while there were quite a few "internal" consultations with functionally related bureaucracies, there were precious few discussions with outside parties who would actually utilize the law, parties that could have made many valuable suggestions and other contributions. Although this has changed dramatically in recent years, this tendency was particularly acute in the early 1980s.[14]

A few months into the deliberations, in August 1980, an official from the Ministry of Machinery wrote a letter to paramount leader Deng Xiaoping. The official asserted that some administrative offices were somewhat carelessly going about constructing a patent system and were drawing from mistaken and erroneous assumptions. Realistically, the official argued, China needed "know-how" (*zhuanyou jishu*) and not patents per se.[15] The buyers of patents are simply receiving a license to *use* those patents, went this line of reasoning; it is not the same as buying technology. He pointed to "many United Nations officials having advised him that 'there is no advantage to [having] patents.'"[16] He opined that China should not be anxious to establish this type of patent system; indeed, it could actually put China's development strategy at a disadvantage.

In October 1980, Vice Premier of the State Council Tian Fangyi presided over a meeting attended by the leaders of the relevant administrative offices and experts to discuss the utility of establishing a formal patent system, at the same time that the SSTC and the Patent Bureau were holding "comparatively well-attended" meetings to discuss the Patent Law. The

12. Interview 99KM04, June 17, 1999.
13. Interview 99SH05, April 28, 1999.
14. Interview 98BJ10, July 13, 1998.
15. Tang, "*Huiyi zhuanli fa de qicao*," 96.
16. Although the source cites that in fact it was a *single* Indian United Nations official. Ibid.

consideration of the majority of the attendees in these two sets of meetings was that China should pursue a patent regime, although there remained a minority view that China should not be overly anxious to establish a patent system. In response, Wu Heng issued a letter of opinion stating that building the national economy depended on science and technology, which in turn required institutions to encourage inventors to produce new technologies—in short, a patent system. This report indicated that it was not necessary to copy foreign production methods. Rather, the Patent Law should take into consideration the special needs of China with the principal goal of benefiting the good of the country.

After the discussions in these two meetings had run their course, officials within the Patent Bureau concluded that it would be best to continue to revise the draft protocol of the Patent Law. By March 1981, the SSTC and the Patent Bureau passed on a revised draft of the Patent Law to the State Council for consideration. The view of the State Council was based on political considerations: at the time there were too many differing opinions on the part of too many government offices. As a result, the draft protocol was returned for further revision. Despite the momentum of the previous two meetings and the majority view favorable to a patent regime, it was clear that it was going to be impossible to ignore the strong misgivings on the part of the sizable minority of individuals and agencies regarding the establishment of a patent system.[17]

At this time, there were several prevailing counterarguments to the establishment of the patent regime. The first was based on the traditional socialist view that patents represented an economy and a society governed by private ownership and specifically that the monopoly rights granted to the patent holder were in opposition to socialist norms of ownership and production. This political question was addressed by the other side in the debate by the contention that, for practical reasons, the Soviet Union and Eastern Europe at that time both had patent systems. There were several reasons for this. Apart from the fact that a patent system can encourage innovation and facilitate the introduction of new technologies, in socialist planned economies information on production is poorly managed and is not readily available. In trying to accommodate a patent regime and an economic system made up of socialist communal enterprises, the socialist countries in Europe had undertaken an experiment that China would be wise to follow or at least to utilize as a blueprint.

The second counterargument against establishing a formal patent regime was the time-honored "stage of development" argument: China is a developing country, the level of science and technology is low, and innovative production is small. A corollary ran that any patent system would only serve to protect the inventions of foreigners. This, in turn, would allow foreigners to monopolize China's markets and undermine

17. Tang, "*Huiyi zhuanli fa de qicao*," 97.

the development of China's national economy. Some in China's emerging patent regime policy community argued that this thinking was flawed. First of all, by "letting foreigners in" (i.e., in allowing foreigners to patent their inventions in China), China could draw on foreigners' prior technological achievements to advance China's own scientific knowledge base (presumably by paying for it, although the specific terms of this admittedly critical dimension were left ambiguous). Moreover, argued the patent advocates, only in the United States and Japan do domestic patent holders outnumber foreign patents. In all other countries, this ratio is reversed, in some cases dramatically so. Therefore, simply looking at the ratio of patents issued domestically and those granted to foreign entities is misleading. Indeed, with the passage of time, the patent policy community argued, the absolute number of patents issued to domestic actors in China could not possibly remain small.

The third counterargument was straightforward, even starkly frank in its honesty: an admission that copying foreign technologies has been an important component in national development, a practice that the adoption of a patent regime would make it impossible to continue. Those in the patent policy community responded that copying is not an appropriate method of developing a national economy; while it was important to use foreign technological achievement as a base, it was necessary for China to undertake its own innovative activities.[18] Copying and reverse engineering are trial-and-error processes that can take a very long time to achieve results. Moreover, they argued, production that arises from this type of copying is very often of poor quality and performance and in any case cannot be exported to countries in which that patent is protected.[19]

Perhaps the most dire and contentious issue, however, had to do with national security concerns, particularly with regard to chemical and pharmaceutical patents. Although these categories were included in the revised 1993 Patent Law (in part because of U.S. pressure), they were deliberately excluded from the original Patent Law. Chinese leaders were afraid of being held hostage to foreign patent holders for products indispensable for maintaining public health, which would make China vulnerable to exogenous forces in the event of a downturn in political relationships with the advanced West. This was a somewhat dramatic scenario, but it was continually brought up by officials in the patent hierarchy. Regarding chemicals, relevant Chinese actors were powerful political players and saw things in a particularly zero-sum light: the gain of foreign chemical companies was a loss for China. In any case, there was a fairly widespread fear among officials familiar with the patent issue that China could find itself forced along a development trajectory that represented the interests of the advanced industrial countries and that might actually

18. Ibid., 98.
19. Ibid., 98–99.

undermine China's own interests.[20] This "national interest" argument was one that was repeated over and over again across the negotiating table in the early 1990s.[21]

As these battle lines were being drawn, it was becoming increasingly clear that there were several administrative offices that were not only opposed to the establishment of a patent regime but were also hostile to the very notion of patent rights, particularly the notion of monopoly rights, which constitutes the foundation of patent protection. One of the original drafters of the 1984 Patent Law identified the Ministry of Chemical Industry and the Ministry of Electronics as being particularly opposed to a shift away from the Soviet model with its inventors' certificates.[22] However, it would not be long until the pro-patent forces would find momentum to be on their side and ultimately prevail.

Wu Heng retired in 1982. He was getting on in years and felt that he did not have the energy for the activism necessary to put the National Patent Bureau on the political map. His replacement, Huang Kunyi, lost no time in pushing for the Patent Law. Taking into account both the ideological and pragmatic opposition to the establishment of a patent regime, in a report to the State Council Standing Committee, Huang used *Marxism* as a foundation upon which to argue for the establishment of a patent regime in China:

> Inventors' productive accomplishments not only need human intellect and labor, they also need instruments and equipment (which are also the product of labor) so that inventor's production is also the result of labor and is of value. With the inventor's effort applied to production this can be translated into production for livelihood, production for technology, production for the economy, or production to benefit society. Therefore, inventive activity also takes on value. Since innovative activity takes on [intrinsic] value and practical value, it takes on commodity-like property attributes, it can mobilize people and turn into a form of commodity itself. As a result, it is impossible not to desire a law to protect this as a form of property. If China does not protect innovative production, it would confuse and dampen the enthusiasm of inventors, and impede the production and exchange of technology-based goods. So, without reference to whether this system is capitalism or socialism, as long as it requires the manufacture and exchange of technology-intensive goods, it requires the establishment of a patent system. It is for this reason that [we need a patent system].[23]

20. Interview 99SH05, April 28, 1998.
21. Interview 98BJ10, July 13, 1998.
22. Interview 98SH05, April 28, 1998.
23. Tang, "*Huiyi zhuanli fa de qicao,*" 99–100.

After the basic agreement that China should have a patent system, the Patent Bureau again revised the draft protocol of the Patent Law, giving it to the State Council for review; in August 1983 it passed the Standing Committee of the State Council. At this point, the Patent Bureau again made revisions, particularly with regard to the State Council's "suggestions" that foreigners should not be encumbered by too many designations and that compulsory licensing prescriptions regarding expropriation should be deleted, in order to put foreign patent applicants at ease. By 1983, the momentum for establishing a patent regime was gaining considerable support; it had become a question of *when* and not *if:* even Deng Xiaoping himself signaled his support for establishing a patent system for China.[24]

On March 12, 1984, the Patent Law of the People's Republic of China was adopted at the Fourth Session of the Sixth National People's Congress to much fanfare, and it was put into force a little over a year later, on April 1, 1985. Ultimately, the dissemination of the law and the establishment of an effective patent infrastructure required the creation of a strong bureaucracy to guide it and to enforce patent rights. This responsibility was placed within the Patent Bureau.

Organizational Evolution of China's Patent Administrative System

Institutions are, to borrow a phrase from Edward Steinfeld, "living museums" that represent decisions made a generation or more ago, forks in the evolutionary road that were crossed in the past, and exogenous shocks that shaped these organizations in earlier times.[25] This path-dependent development continues to influence the current operation of the Chinese state, even if the policies have changed and the institutions restructured. The organizational history of China's patent administrative system demonstrates that power considerations have ultimately stunted the effectiveness of the patent bureaucracy as an autonomous administrative agency. Although this bureaucracy boasts an impressive technological infrastructure, it lacks the requisite political power necessary to be a major player in national politics. This would not be a problem if it had existed only as a technical agency. But this was not the case. By the late 1990s, the Patent Bureau was slated to become, and is thought by many actually to have become, the principal coordinating agency between the other two major IPR subfields in China. This is largely a fiction, albeit a well-disguised one. To understand the current weakness of the State Intellectual Property system at the national and local levels, one must go back in time to identify and evaluate its antecedent bureaucracy, the China Patent Bureau.

24. Interview 98SH05, April 28, 1998.
25. Edward S. Steinfeld, *Forging Reform in China: the Fate of State-Owned Industry* (New York: Cambridge University Press, 1998).

The China Patent Bureau

On January 14, 1980, the State Council approved the SSTC's "Report on Instructions Regarding the Establishment of the Country's Patent System" and paved the way for the establishment of the China Patent Bureau as the principal administrative organ charged with enforcing patent rights once they are codified in law. The chief responsibility of this new office was to examine and approve patent applications from China and from abroad. Although the Patent Bureau was a directly administered office of the State Council, it was to be managed (*daiguan*) by the SSTC because of the strong association at the time between patents and China's scientific and technological development.[26]

In 1982, the Patent Bureau was transferred out of the SSTC and placed under the control of the State Economics Commission (SEC), which had binding leadership authority relations over (giving it the power to issue binding orders to) the Patent Bureau.[27] This transfer reflected the shift in the association of China's patent regime from scientific and technological goals to economic ones.[28] It was at this time that the directorship of the bureau passed from Wu Heng to Huang Kunyi. On September 24 of that same year, the Office of the State Council issued a circular entitled "Decision Regarding the Resolution of the Standing Committee of the National People's Congress and the State Council." The Patent Bureau, which was originally a directly administered unit of the State Council and concurrently subjected to the SEC, was now to be named the *China* Patent Bureau (Zhongguo *zhuanli ju*) in order to better meet its domestic and international responsibilities and obligations.[29] Future premier Zhu Rongji headed the SEC at that time and had already established a close relationship with the individual who would run the China Patent Bureau from 1987 to 1988 and again from 1989 until 1998, Gao Lulin.

During the 1988 restructuring of the government following the Seventh National People's Congress, which coincided with Zhu Rongji's departure from the SEC and relocation to Shanghai, the Patent Bureau was removed from under the SEC. In accordance with the August 13, 1988, circular "Regarding State Council Establishment of Organizations," the Patent Bureau was again placed at the level of a centrally administered office under the State Council. At the same time, however, it was also directly administered by its original "host" bureaucracy, the SSTC. On September 10, 1988, the National Committee on the Composition of Government Offices (CCGO, or *Guojia jigou bianzhi weiyuanhui*) reaffirmed this in its approval of the "Blueprint for the 'Three Fixes' [*san ding*] for the China

---

26. *Zhonghua renmin gongheguo zhengfu jigou wushi nian* [Government Organizations of the People's Republic of China over Fifty Years] (Beijing: *Dangjian duwu chubanshe yu Guojia xingzheng chubanshe*, 2000), 156. Interview 99BJ27, July 23, 1999.

27. Interview 99BJ02, March 5, 1999.

28. Interview 99BJ27, July 23, 1999.

29. *Zhonghua renmin gongheguo zhengfu jigou wushi nian*, 156.

Patent Bureau." This stated that the China Patent Bureau was the principal administrative organ for executing China's Patent Law and that it was
in charge of all functional organs involved in patent work, that is to say,
responsible for simultaneously managing and executing the law under the
direct leadership of the SSTC.[30]

In March 1993, after yet another round of State Council restructuring,
the Patent Bureau became a centrally administered independent organization of the State Council in the form of an "undertaking unit," or *shiye
danwei*.[31] It was authorized by the State Council to continue to carry out
its government functions of managing the administration of China's patent system, but, unlike before, it was able to do so by engaging in profit-
generating services, such as processing patent applications, establishing
training programs, and the like. This is reflected in the organizational
structure of the Patent Bureau, which, unlike the relationship between the
Patent Bureau itself and its alternating immediate superior organizations,
remained fairly stable over time.[32]

By 1993, like other bureaus and ministries, the Patent Bureau contained a general office, responsible for day-to-day administrative matters
and issues between other offices within the Patent Bureau, and a Party
committee. In addition, there was a general planning section, a statutes
and laws section, a patent work management section, a personnel and
education section, and an international cooperation section. There were
several divisions with more technical functions, including the examination services management section, the first trial and technical process
management section, the patent documents section, the patent review
committee, and the supervision office. Finally, there were six separate
examination sections responsible for engineering, electronics, physics,
chemistry, new utility, and external design. The overall personnel allocations for the China Patent Bureau numbered 1,260 (with a proviso not
to exceed 20 percent of this number) and a *nomenklatura* list numbering
fifty-seven.[33] This figure, which was quite high, was possible because, as an
"undertaking unit," the China Patent Bureau's personnel allocations were
not straightforward administrative personnel allocations (*xingzheng bianzhi*), but the easier-to-secure personnel allocations for undertaking units

30. Ibid.
31. Even though at the national level the China Patent Bureau was taken out from under
the direct leadership control of the SSTC, provincial-level patent bureaus remained under the
provincial STCs. I discuss the local-level patent bureaus below.
32. Among the top leadership by the late 1990s, Li Lanqing was the highest-ranking official
for copyright, Wu Bangguo was the highest-ranking official for patents, and Wu Yi was the highest-ranking official for trademarks. Interview 98CQ27, September 17, 1998.
33. *Zhongyang zhengfu zuzhi jigou* [Central Government Organizations] (Beijing: *Gaige chubanshe,* 1999), 437–41. By 1996, there were several service-related organizations (*zhishu danwei*)
directly administered by the China Patent Bureau itself, including the Patent Documents Publishing House (*zhuanli wenxian chubanshe*), the *China Patent News* Bureau (*Zhongguo zhuanli bao
she*), the China Patent Information Center (*Zhongguo zhuanli xinxi zhongxin*), and the China
Intellectual Property Training Center (*Zhongguo zhishi chanquan peixun zhongxin*).

TABLE 3.1.
Organizational evolution of the China Patent Bureau

Years	Superior or "host" organization
1980–1982	State Science and Technology Commission (*kexuejishu weiyuanhui*)
1982–1988	State Economics Commission (*jingji weiyuanhui*)
1988–1993	State Council/State Science and Technology Commission
1993–1998	State Council

(*shiye bianzhi*).[34] Given the service orientation of the China Patent Bureau by this time, these numbers should be understood as a function of the sophistication of the China Patent Bureau's scientific functions, not as a proxy for its political prowess.

The foregoing suggests that by the end of the 1990s the China Patent Bureau's technical functions had grown quite sophisticated. At the same time, however, the China Patent Bureau remained institutionally adrift and, as a consequence, politically weak. This was largely because the Patent Bureau was constantly being transferred from one administrative "host" unit to another during its relatively brief lifetime—from the SSTC to the SEC to the SSTC to the State Council, all in the space of thirteen years. The China Patent Bureau never had the opportunity to establish its roots and stabilize its own independent power and authority. By the time the China Patent Bureau was renamed the State Intellectual Property Office, its technical abilities were quite well-established but its political base was shaky. The China Patent Bureau/SIPO had been unable to develop the minimum power needed to compete with, let alone issue binding orders to, related agencies. Moreover, at the provincial level and below, this political weakness, particularly continued dependence on the Science and Technology bureaucracy (which after 1993 was no longer the case at the national level) was even more pronounced and has continued to be so up to the present day.

Subnational Patent Bureaus

In speaking with Chinese officials, one is often told that national-level ministries and bureaus are replicated at the provincial level and below. But these same officials will, with only a little prodding, qualify such statements by describing the "specific conditions" of their own region and the need to adapt the national model to local circumstances. As a result, as far as the structure and function of these local-level counterparts of national organs

34. *Shiye bianzhi* were easier to obtain because the personnel allocation included only a partial budgetary allocation. Unlike in the case of an administrative *bianzhi*, decisions to allocate *shiye bianzhi* were premised on the idea that the undertaking units' profits would make up the difference. Interview 99CD06, July 1, 1999; Interview 02CD03, July 12, 2002; Interview 03GY01 and 03GY02, July 19, 2003.

are concerned, there is continuity along some dimensions and variation in others. In short, one must be skeptical of the notion that national government offices are fully replicated at the local level. This variation does represent adaptations to local conditions, but it also provides the fissures along which institutional tensions can—and do—arise.

Provincial-level patent management offices (*zhuanli guanli chu*) were officially established in late 1984 with the promulgation of China's Patent Law. Given the centralization of the patent process, the notion of "local" patent bureaus is somewhat curious. Although the actual responsibilities of these local counterparts to the China Patent Bureau are described in more detail below, the regional patent bureaus served several general functions. First, local patent bureaus served an educational/propaganda function, as many inventors, and certainly the common citizen, were generally unfamiliar with the notion of patents, let alone the intricacies of the new patent process. Second, patent bureaus served as regional clearinghouses for local inventors sending their patent applications up to Beijing for review. Third, local patent bureaus served as an administrative arena for the mediation of patent-related disputes.

Even before the Patent Law was finalized, patent offices (*zhuanli bangong shi*) were established in some regions in the beginning of 1984 to recruit and train new staff for patent-related work (including patent agents), as well as to develop and disseminate propaganda in anticipation of, and to coincide with, the promulgation the Patent Law.[35] These were formally reconfigured as patent departments (*zhuanli chu*) beginning in 1984. Some science and technology commissions (STCs) at the prefecture level (*di zhou shi*) had some sort of patent office. By the beginning of 1999, of the twenty-one prefectures in Sichuan province, seventeen had established administrative patent management organs.[36] That said, an official in the patent bureaucracy cautioned that one must be careful in making generalizations about the patent bureaucracy below the provincial level.[37]

Much of local patent work at this time focused on propaganda to educate the general public about the new Patent Law and to persuade inventors to patent their inventions. This often meant traveling to universities, research institutes, and other enterprises to provide such training. The expectation at the time was that people receiving such training would then pass this information along to colleagues in their own work units. Other measures at the time included newspaper articles, bulletins, and lectures relating to patent work to educate the wider public as well as to inform people in the patent system.[38] The emphasis on propaganda at this time

35. Interview 98GY08A, August 21, 1998.
36. *Sichuan Zhuanli* [Sichuan Patents], Sichuan Provincial Patent Bureau, January 5, 1999, 11.
37. Interview 98GY08A, August 21, 1998.
38. The Sichuan Provincial Patent Bureau provided monthly mimeographed updates of events through the internal publication *Sichuan Zhuanli*. Any given issue was divided into the following sections: study and reflection (*xuexi sikao*), work and planning (*gongzuo jihua*), information exchange (*xinxi jiaoliu*), fields of expertise (*zhishi yuandi*), municipal and local work (*shi, di*

was due to an almost complete ignorance about patents on the part of the general public. Even among inventors and people with some knowledge about patent issues, the specifics of China's patent regime were unclear and ambiguous, even contradictory. This lack of understanding was particularly severe in China's interior.[39]

In the years to follow, the local patent bureaus would add legislation and mediation to their daily responsibilities. In addition to disseminating patent-related information, these local patent bureaus held a number of other important administrative functions, including formulating patent programs and other plans. Specifically, this involved producing relevant local regulations. Local patent bureaus were also charged with guiding and directing the patent-related work of local industries and enterprises. Another important responsibility had to do with investigating and mediating patent disputes. Finally, local patent bureaus, in conjunction with local patent agents, many of whom were directly administered by the local patent bureaus, provided preliminary consultation and appraisal of patentable inventions.[40]

Beginning in the early 1990s, provincial-level patent bureaus were given an upgrade in administrative rank. The Chongqing Patent Bureau was promoted from a department (*chu*) to a bureau (*ju*) in 1991, although it remained under the authority of the Chongqing STC.[41] In Yunnan, this shift occurred in 1994, while in Guizhou it happened in 1997. Along with this increase in rank, the new patent bureaus, in theory, saw a corresponding increase in enforcement power: as a *ju*, they were able to fine, confiscate, and in general crack down on illegal patent activity.[42] Patent bureaus did not have their own formal enforcement teams, as do some of the other bureaucracies described in subsequent chapters; rather, these bureaus put together a core of staff and, with the assistance of the local Administration

---

gongzuo), and statistical materials (*tongji ziliao*). Other provincial-level patent bureaus also issue their own similar internal publications (*Chongqing Zhuanli, Yunnan Zhuanli Tongxun,* etc.).

39. Interview 98GY08A, August 21, 1998.

40. Interview 98CQ02A, March 24, 1998. With some variation, the provincial patent bureaus were generally divided into the following departments. Like many administrative offices in China, there was a comprehensive management office, which managed patent agents, controlled and distributed information (i.e., statistics), and handled the day-to-day work of the Patent Bureau. In addition, there was a legal services office or a law and regulations office to investigate patent disputes and mediate patent-related arbitration. Finally, in some cases, there was a patent implementation office, which handled the implementation and dissemination of patents directly into the workplace to enforce the economic development of the area under its jurisdiction. Essentially, this refers to the operationalization of patents ("translating theory into practice"). This office also handled issues relating to remuneration to the patent holder. In some cases, the tasks of this office were handled by a more general-sounding management department.

41. Interview 98CQ02A, March 24, 1998. There is some confusion regarding the relationship of some third-tier patent bureaus and the STC. In the case of Guizhou, the Patent Bureau was "under" and not "within" the STC (it is a *xiashu danwei* of the STC). Interview 98GY08A, August 21, 1998.

42. The Guizhou Patent Bureau and others, for example, had investigation brigades (*jicha dui*) to examine cases of patent infringement, although the actual makeup of these brigades is somewhat unclear. Interview 99GY04, June 15, 1999.

of Industry and Commerce (discussed at length in chapter 5), undertook periodic campaigns against illegal patent-related activity.[43]

However, as far as these new responsibilities were concerned, there was a great deal of variation in the political power and administrative effectiveness of individual provincial-level patent bureaus. Some patent bureaus were quite strong, while others were extremely weak, and this had an important impact on how patents were protected and enforced from region to region.[44] Very often, the power and the effectiveness of the local patent bureaus reflected the priorities of local governments. Moreover, this variation did not follow conventional expectations along the coastal-interior dimension of economic and technological development. All these points are illustrated by the following digression, which, in turn, will help illuminate subsequent sections of this chapter.

A Comparison of the Sichuan, Shanghai, and Chongqing Patent Bureaus

Out of the four IPR bureaucracies analyzed in this book, the subnational patent bureaus are the most interesting in terms of the variation in size (specifically, personnel and budgetary allocations, or *bianzhi*), scope of responsibilities, and authority relations with the host unit. This variation makes generalizing problematic, but this difficulty is alleviated somewhat by comparing the three basic types of patent bureaus: those of Sichuan, Shanghai, and Chongqing.[45] It should also be noted that although the formal rank differences upon which this variation was based had been abolished by the end of the 1990s, the structural differences brought about by this variation remain relevant to understanding the effectiveness of these subnational patent bureaus' successor organizations, the local intellectual property offices (IPOs) to be discussed in more detail below.

At this point, another digression is in order. In order to appreciate the subordination of the patent bureaus (and the other bureaucratic actors to be discussed in the chapters to follow), it is necessary to describe briefly the notion of leadership and professional relations. All Chinese administrative units make a distinction between two types of binary political relationships: ones governed by binding orders and those governed by nonbinding instructions.

43. Generally speaking, local patent bureaus have been quite successful at investigating patent violations, but they have much less independence and authority when it comes to conducting raids and imposing punishments than do other agencies, such as the Administration for Industry and Commerce discussed in chapter 5. Economist Intelligence Unit, *China Hand: The Complete Guide to Doing Business in China* (Hong Kong: Economist Intelligence Unit, 1996), 10.

44. For example, by the end of the 1990s, Guangdong Province appeared to have a very proactive and aggressive Patent Bureau. Economist Intelligence Unit, *China Hand: The Complete Guide to Doing Business in China* (Hong Kong: Economist Intelligence Unit, 1999), 59. The same could be said for Shanghai and, as will be discussed below, Sichuan.

45. Each of these is a provincial-level administrative unit: Shanghai and Chongqing (after May 1997) are directly administered provincial-ranking municipalities (*zhixiashi*). There are no discernible differences between the Shanghai and Chongqing and other second- and third-tier patent bureaus, respectively.

Any given political unit in China has the second type of relationship with numerous other units. But it has the first type of relationship with only one, its immediate "superior." A relationship based on such binding orders is referred to as "leadership relations," or *lingdao guanxi,* while the other type is based on nonbinding "professional relations," or *yewu guanxi.* In China's reform-era political system, such leadership relations are often not with administrative superiors (described by the Chinese as "leadership along a line," or *tiaoshang lingdao*), but *with local governments at the same administrative level* (or "leadership across a piece," *kuaishang lingdao*).[46]

Most of China's functional bureaucratic systems (*xitong*) operate under this latter type of decentralized (*kuai*) leadership relations in order to maximize their sensitivity to local conditions when implementing policy. For many of these bureaucratic systems, this was the case even before reform.[47] The difference is that the central government's trump card in the pre-decentralized planned economy, the ability of central-level ministries to withhold valuable production inputs, is now missing from the equation.[48] Local governments since reform provide the same personnel allocations (*bianzhi*) and staffing, budget, and property rights allocations (*rencaiwu*) as they had in the past, only with far less central oversight. This has allowed them to wield more power over these local functional units and to bend the policy stream more effectively in a direction that is consistent with their own preferences.

This first difference between these three classes of provincial-level patent bureaus is based on administrative rank. At the national level, there is a fairly clear distinction between ministries (*bu*), bureaus (*ju*), and offices (*bangong shi*). At the provincial level, however, this tripartite division is far less clear: the provincial-level counterparts of these national administrative rankings are all collapsed into the rank of "bureau," or *ju.* Within the generic administrative rank of *ju,* there are actually three subdivisions. The first is the "first-tier bureau" (*yi ji ju* or *shengji zhengting ju*), which is the provincial-level counterpart to a national ministry. It holds the same administrative rank as a prefecture (*di zhou shi*) government. The second of these is a "second-tier/vice-level bureau" (*er ji ju, futing ji ju,* or *shengji futing ju*), which is one half-step down in rank from the first-tier bureau. The third bureau is a "third-tier bureau," although it is not called this in Chinese; rather, it is referred to as a (*sheng ji*) *xian ji ju,* or "county-level provincial bureau"; these are outranked by the previous two and hold the same administrative rank as a county (*xian*) or urban district (*shiqu*) government. This rank ordering is

46. See Kenneth G. Lieberthal and Michel C. Oksenberg, *Policy Making in China: Leaders, Structures, and Processes* (Princeton: Princeton University Press, 1988), 148–49; and Lieberthal, *Governing China: From Revolution Through Reform,* 2d ed. (New York: Norton, 2004); and Andrew C. Mertha, "China's 'Soft' Centralization: Shifting *Tiao/Kuai* Authority Relations Since 1998," forthcoming in *China Quarterly.*

47. See, for example, *Zhongguo difang zhengfu tizhi gailun* [General Outline of Local Chinese Government Structure] (Beijing: *Zhongguo guangbo dianshi chubanshe,* 1998), 1–22.

48. Steinfeld, *Forging Reform in China,* especially ch. 3.

important, in addition to the differences discussed at length below, because the administrative rankings dictate the ability of these offices to compete with other agencies and the degree to which these agencies are obliged to take the patent bureaus' views into serious consideration.

In 1995, ten years after it was established, the provincial Patent Bureau in Sichuan was upgraded to a first-tier bureau (also referred to as an "equal ranking," or *pingqi ting ji ju,* bureau). This placed the Sichuan Patent Bureau at the same administrative rank as the provincial STC. In other words, this type of bureau did not have authority relations whatsoever with the STC and instead enjoyed direct leadership relations with the provincial government. It follows that a first-tier Patent Bureau was a somewhat curious administrative phenomenon. In, fact, the Sichuan provincial Patent Bureau was the only one to have been placed at the first-tier level.[49]

The Sichuan Patent Bureau differed from all others in China because of its size, its effectiveness in discharging its responsibilities, and its authority relations with its superior administrative unit. With regard to size, the initial personnel allocation (*bianzhi,* upon which the core budgetary allocations are based) was twenty-eight. This jumped to forty-nine when the Sichuan Patent Bureau was upgraded to a first-tier bureau (there was, in addition, a *nomenklatura* list of three, one director and two vice directors). Although the general orientation of its responsibilities remained similar to those of its second- and third-tier counterparts, the increased personnel and budgetary allocations allowed the Sichuan Patent Bureau to undertake them in a more effective way.[50]

The third way in which the Sichuan Patent Bureau was distinguished from its counterparts in other provinces had to do with its authority relations with the Sichuan Science and Technology Commission (STC). Alone among the provincial-level patent bureaus at the time, the Sichuan Patent Bureau had direct leadership relations with its provincial government. It had professional relations with the Sichuan Economics and Trade Commission, the Foreign Economics and Trade Commission, and the STC, as well as with other units. The important point here is that once it became a first-tier bureau, the Sichuan Patent Bureau had no special authority relationship with the STC (although there was a close functional, professional relationship). Its budget came directly from the provincial finance bureau and not through the STC.

So, why was the Sichuan Patent Bureau the only one in the country to be placed on the first tier? What accounts for this anomaly? It is a case of the provincial government deliberately empowering the status of the patent bureau (which, in the case of patent protection at the time, was

---

49. The Sichuan Provincial Patent Bureau was established on January 17, 1985; it was originally a second-tier bureau. It was not until 1995 that the Sichuan Patent Bureau was bumped up to the unique first-tier bureau level. Interview 99CD02, June 28, 1999; Interview 03CD05, July 16, 2003.

50. Interview 99CD02, June 28, 1999.

the exception that proved the rule: provincial governments in general tended to neglect patent bureaus). By the mid-1990s, the Sichuan provincial government was attempting to move the local economy away from its overdependence on agricultural commodities, and it wanted to become a manufacturer and exporter of value-added and technology-intensive goods. In order to foster this environment, the provincial government increased the capacity of the patent bureau to undertake effectively the responsibilities involved in achieving this goal. It was also a deliberate signal to foreign investors and other potential joint venture partners that they could confidently "invest in Sichuan because we take patent/IPR protection seriously."[51]

Moving from the interior of China to the coast, Shanghai illustrates the second organizational, or "second-tier/vice-level," bureau ranking (*er ji ju, futing ji ju,* or *sheng ji futing ju*). In this rank ordering, the patent bureau was placed a half step below the corresponding provincial STC.[52] Because Shanghai enjoys provincial-level rank, and because the patent bureaucracy in Shanghai was not considerably different from that of a typical province (except in terms of the overall geographic distance covered), it provides a good example of a second-tier bureau. The Shanghai Patent Bureau has an interesting history. Initially, there were three offices in Shanghai: the Shanghai Patent Management Bureau (*Shanghai zhuanli guanli ju*), the Shanghai Branch Office of the China Patent Bureau (*Zhongguo zhuanli ju Shanghai fen ju*), and the Shanghai Patent Service Agency (*Shanghai zhuanli shiwusuo*). Sometime in the late 1980s, these three bodies were merged into the Shanghai Patent Bureau.

The personnel and budgetary allocations for the Shanghai Patent Bureau were somewhat more generous than was the case with many of its second-tier counterparts. By the end of the 1990s, it enjoyed a large personnel allocation of forty.[53] This staff was divided into the following sections: the general service section, the legal services department, the propaganda and education section, and a general office.[54] In addition, in 1999, the Shanghai Patent Bureau was one of the first offices to experiment with a pilot project allowing it to get around China's "first-to-file" patent rule. Under this rule, the first person to file—not necessarily the first person to have created the innovation in question—is awarded the

51. Ibid.

52. Second-tier patent bureaus included those of Beijing, Shanghai, and Tianjin municipalities, and Liaoning, Jiangsu, Hebei, Henan, Hubei, Hunan, Guangdong, Hainan, Fujian, Shaanxi, and Shandong provinces. Interview 99KM04, June 17, 1999.

53. In 1999, the Jiangsu Patent Bureau had a staff allocation of thirty. Interview 99NJ02, May 25, 1999.

54. By contrast, the Jiangsu Patent Bureau had, in addition to a regular administrative office, a comprehensive management office, a laws and regulations department, a patent implementation office, and a patent agency section. This gives a sense of the variation in internal subdivisions even in the same functional offices with the same administrative rank, in this case the patent bureaus of Shanghai municipality and neighboring Jiangsu province. Interview 99NJ02, May 25, 1999.

patent. This adds a tremendous amount of pressure to speed up the patent application process. Under this experimental program, the Shanghai Patent Bureau would assess patent applications, issuing an earlier filing date and a temporary filing number on behalf of the China Patent Bureau (under the State Intellectual Property Office, or SIPO). This was run out of a newly established unit, the acronym-defying State Intellectual Property Rights Office/Patent Bureau Representative Office (*Guojia zhishi chanquan zhuanli ju daiban chu*).

In the words of one knowledgeable official, the relationship between the Shanghai Patent Bureau and the Shanghai STC is very complicated (*hen fuza*). Formally, the Shanghai Patent Bureau is not a subordinate unit (*xiashu danwei*) of the Shanghai STC, as is the case among third-tier patent bureaus. These relations are governed by a procedure known as *guikou guanli*, which in this context means that the STC manages the personnel and budgetary allocations for, but is unable to issue binding orders to, the Shanghai Patent Bureau (similarly, in the case of Jiangsu Province, the Jiangsu STC always used to assign the ranking cadres [*ganbu daiguan*] to the Jiangsu Patent Bureau).[55] It is very difficult, added the official, to navigate between the Shanghai STC and the Shanghai municipal government. When two conflicting orders cannot be resolved, the director of the Shanghai Patent Bureau takes his cue from the unit with which the bureau had leadership relations—the Shanghai municipal government.[56]

The third-tier ranking of provincial-level patent bureaus is the lowest, "county-level" (*sheng ji xian ji ju*) ranking.[57] The patent bureaus of the majority of China's provinces were at this level. The Chongqing Patent Bureau was established in November 1984 and, mirroring the political framework in Beijing, was placed within the Chongqing Municipal Science and Technology Commission.[58] However, when the China Patent Bureau was moved out of the SSTC in 1993, provincial-level patent bureaus like the one in Chongqing remained embedded within the provincial STCs. In fact, the director of the Chongqing Patent Bureau (ostensibly a bureau director *juzhang*) only held a degree of power commensurate with a lower-ranked department director (*chuzhang*).[59]

The Chongqing Patent Bureau, housed physically and inserted administratively within the Chongqing STC, had a staff of sixteen, with a correspondingly low budgetary allocation.[60] At the end of the 1990s, the annual

55. Budgets were controlled by the STC finance section. However, the Shanghai Patent Bureau could request extra budgetary funds from the municipal finance bureau. Information on the Jiangstu STC comes from Interview 99NJ02, May 25, 1999.

56. Interview 99SH07, April 29, 1999.

57. One official told me that one never refers to this type of bureau as a "third-tier bureau" (*san ji ju*) unless the aim is to belittle or make fun of the unit in question. Interview 02KM01, July 23, 2002.

58. Interview 98CQ02A, March 24, 1998.

59. Interview 98CQ20A, August 12, 1998.

60. In fact, the Chongqing Patent Bureau was housed inside the STC compound, but in a separate building from the STC itself (both moved after 2000). As of 2003, the Yunnan Patent

budget hovered around 240,000 yuan ($29,000), which was expected to cover both staff salaries and expenses. Moreover, this budget was also expected to cover part of the salaries of the four people working in the attached patent agency (an "undertaking unit," or *shiye jigou*). This money was released monthly to the Patent Bureau by the regulation and finance department (*tiaojie caijing chu*) of the Chongqing STC.[61] Much like the copyright bureau to be analyzed in chapter 4, funds for special projects must be applied for separately.

On the eve of its transformation into the Chongqing Municipal IPR Office, the Chongqing Municipal Patent Bureau consisted of three offices. The first was a comprehensive management office that handled patent issues. Of the three offices within the Chongqing Patent Bureau, this office had the largest staff (eight people). The second office, the legal services office, investigated patent disputes and mediated patent arbitration with a staff of three. Finally, the patent implementation office, also with a staff of three, was charged with implementing and disseminating patents directly into the workforce to help in the economic development of the region. This office also handled issues relating to royalties and remuneration to the patent holder.[62] The Party secretary of the Chongqing Patent Bureau mostly handled personnel-related work and, being an engineer himself, was linked to the work of the Patent Bureau both professionally and politically.[63] Indeed, his weakness is demonstrated by his not having a seat on the STC Party committee; rather, he received his marching orders from the STC Party "core group," or *dangzu* (*kewei dangzu lingdao ta*).[64]

The single most important authority relationship for a third-tier patent bureau is in sharp contrast to that of its first-tier counterpart: third-tier patent bureaus are part of the STC, as a result of which the patent bureau has rather indirect "leadership relations" with the provincial government in its position as an organization within the STC, while having direct leadership relations with the STC.[65] The degree of the Chongqing Patent Bureau's embeddedness within and dependence upon the Chongqing STC was pronounced. One lawyer who dealt extensively with the Chongqing Patent Bureau said that it

Bureau in Kunming is housed in the same building as the STC, with the former having been allotted two floors.

61. Interview 98CQ02D, August 17, 1998.

62. The Guizhou Patent Bureau, by contrast, had an administrative office, a management office, and a laws and regulations office. Interview 99GY04, June 15, 1999. The Yunnan Patent Bureau—like that of Guizhou, also a third-tier bureau—had a legal department, an implementation department, and a comprehensive management department, although individuals were assigned to specific tasks, not to any particular office. Interview 99KM04, June 17, 1999. As was the case with second-tier patent bureaus, there was a great degree of variation in the formal internal organization of their third-tier counterparts.

63. Interview 98CQ02C, August 6, 1998.

64. Interview 98CQ02D, August 17, 1998.

65. Interview 98CQ02C, August 6, 1998 and Interview 98GY07, August 21, 1998. Indeed, this extends all the way down the system. For example, the Patent Office at Shanghai's Fudan University is under the control of the Fudan University Science and Technology Office. Interview 98SH13, May 25, 1998.

First-tier patent bureau   Second-tier patent bureau   Third-tier patent bureau

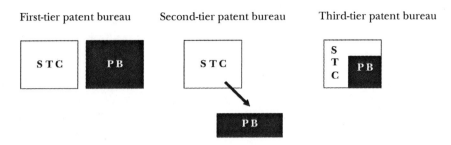

Figure 3.1. Provincial patent bureaus and science and technology commissions

always deferred to the STC. Indeed, the STC often delayed payment to the Chongqing Patent Bureau—already constantly short of money—which undermined the Patent Bureau's ability to perform its responsibilities.[66] These constraints facing the third-tier Chongqing Patent Bureau are important because the majority of provincial patent bureaus throughout the 1990s were third-tier bureaus.

It would be an overstatement to say that the STCs were intentionally undermining the work of the patent bureaus—although such disruptions are not unheard of. Rather, a combination of tensions in the immediate goals of the two agencies, combined with the asymmetrical power relations between the patent bureau and the STC, led to suboptimal outcomes on issues that one would assume to be in the functional interests of both sets of actors. The STC is charged with developing the scientific capacity for the industries and other units under its jurisdiction. At an early stage of economic development, as discussed in chapter 1, it would appear that such goals are better served with the "dissemination" (*puji*) rather than the "protection" (*baohu*) of new technologies. One source summed it up in no uncertain terms: "There is a bias in favor of the market, and away from the inventor, because there is pressure to get the invention out into the open quickly" and to avoid delaying the benefits to the economy that would occur in the lead time toward securing a patent.[67] This is due in part to the organizational legacy of the STC. Established at the national level in the early 1950s and modeled on the Soviet system, the SSTC and its local counterparts had several decades in which to establish bureaucratic standard operating procedures, organizational goals, and power relationships among their various departments—in this case, centering on the distribution and diffusion of technology in order to usher in China's scientific and technological development, as evidenced in the debates surrounding the Patent Law discussed above.[68]

66. Interview 98CQ20A, August 12, 1998.
67. Interview 98SH13, May 25, 1998.
68. Lieberthal and Oksenberg, *Policy Making in China,* 78.

It is within this bureaucratic landscape that the Sino-U.S. IPR negotiations superimposed the notion (or deepened a preexisting one) that the patent bureaucracy—more specifically, the SSTC—should somehow act as a coordination agency for intellectual property in China. Patent issues per se did not make up the bulk of the substance of the negotiations; the key issues were to afford patent protection to "products" as well as "processes" and to ensure "pipeline" protection (*guanxian baohu*). Rather, the patent bureaucracy and the SSTC were central players in structuring the negotiations on the Chinese side in terms of negotiating "technical issues" and, equally important, in coordinating the implementation and enforcement of the agreement once the negotiations were concluded. This would provide the genesis of what would become the State Intellectual Property Office, which, unlike the SSTC, would broaden its formal focus to include copyright and trademark issues, but also unlike the SSTC, lacked—and continues to lack—the requisite power to do so. The institution that links these two stages in the evolution of China's patent/IPR regime is the IPR Working Conference and its administrative office.

Exogenous Influence and the IPR Working Conference/Office

By the early to mid-1990s, both the legal and institutional development of China's patent system and its IPR regime more generally were being shaped by outside pressures at least as much as by "natural" domestic conditions. This was in no small part due to the seemingly endless bilateral IPR negotiations with the United States that continued from 1991 through mid-1996. This is not to say that China placed itself in a cocoon while it developed its IPR laws before 1990. Chinese legal experts often sought advice from experts in the United States and other countries. Ironically, the perceived credibility of such external advice often increased the likelihood that Chinese officials would adopt the recommendations of these legal experts. Paraphrasing one of the U.S. negotiators, Chinese officials, like the director of the China Patent Bureau, Gao Lulin, would say things like, "Thank you very much for your information; we would have never had such progress without you." During this time, the Chinese tended to be more self-critical, and there appeared to be a more relaxed and congenial intellectual and policy-related "meeting of minds" and "free exchange of ideas."[69]

The crackdown on June 4, 1989, changed all that. The events in Beijing, Shanghai, Chengdu, and other parts of the country in the first few days of June altered the trajectory of U.S.-China relations such that more than fifteen years later, they have still not yet returned to what they had been prior to June 1989. Like in so many other policy areas of China, the

---

69. Interview 98US14, December 8, 1998.

carefully cultivated channels of communication over IPR suffered a severe setback, as exchanges became far more politicized on both sides. Nevertheless, issues over trade and particularly intellectual property became the principal way in which the United States could show the new spate of domestic anti-China groups that it was getting tough on China, while at the same time not completely alienating Beijing.

China was not part of GATT, which made it easier to level unilateral sanctions toward the PRC without being accused of violating the broader GATT norms of multilateralism. Moreover, the events of June 1989 isolated China from potential niches of support in the United States—in the early 1990s, very few people were willing to stick their necks out on Beijing's behalf. Third, unlike Japan—another country with which the USTR has had a long and uneasy relationship over trade—China is not a U.S. ally. Finally, President George H. W. Bush needed to demonstrate that he was tough on China so that he could effectively split the opposition to renewing China's Most-Favored Nation trade status in 1992. It was particularly important for Bush to display such tenacity because of his long association with China dating back to the Nixon administration, during which Bush headed the U.S. Liaison Office in Beijing. Before Tiananmen Square, Bush's "friend of China" status was a point of pride. After June 1989, it became a political liability.[70]

The 1992 MOU had a significant impact on the Chinese laws and regulations that were being promulgated and revised, particularly those pertaining to copyright, as is discussed in chapter 4. It was also significant because it bound China to international IPR treaties. But this agreement was largely mute on the issue of enforcement. The 1995 Exchange of Letters, by contrast, had a great impact in shaping China's enforcement apparatus. This shift in focus toward enforcement went beyond accepted notions of sovereignty and was remarkable for what it actually demanded that the Chinese do: change the configuration of their domestic institutional enforcement apparatus. In the words of one former USTR negotiator:

> Most of the GATT/WTO provisions have a bias that strongly favors national regulations on enforcement. So negotiations seek a commitment to enforce, but generally do not enshrine the specific mechanisms to be used in complying with the trade agreement. That is left up to the country to decide. The 1995 agreement was a "post-TRIPS" framework which seemed to be saying, "if you are not going to enforce, we are going to be far more intrusive."[71]

This demand for credible promises to enforce, coupled with the gradual emergence of an informal and untested but potentially powerful

70. Interview 98US10A, December 3, 1998.
71. Interview 98US09, November 30, 1998.

institution in China, the IPR Working Conference, provided a locus of agreement between the two sides in fashioning an enforcement program that both sides could accept.

On paper, the 1995 agreement institutionalized this set of offices, which on the surface appeared to have both the mandate and the ability to coordinate and manage IPR enforcement to a degree that would meet U.S. standards of approval. The IPR Working Conference was presented to the United States during the negotiations and received the USTR "stamp of approval" as the new administrative center of gravity for IPR enforcement in China; its role as a major "player" in IPR enforcement in China was institutionalized in the "Annex/Action Plan for Effective Protection and Enforcement of Intellectual Property Rights" to the 1995 Sino-U.S. IPR Exchange of Letters:

> The State Council has established a Working Conference on Intellectual Property Rights which through forceful measures, centrally organizes and coordinates protection and enforcement of all intellectual property rights throughout the country, and will ensure that effective protection is provided and infringement of intellectual property rights is substantially reduced. For the purposes of this Plan, intellectual property rights include copyright and related rights, trademark, patents, protection against unfair competition, including protection of undisclosed information, and other relevant subject matter.

The IPR Working Conference (*zhishi chanquan bangong huiyi*) or, informally, the "IPR leadership small group" (*zhishi chanquan lingdao xiaozu*) was itself an indigenous development from within China's administrative apparatus.[72] However, this office amassed its power and its influence in part because of the role it played during the Sino-U.S. IPR negotiations. This U.S. preoccupation with consolidation empowered the IPR Working Conference, which enshrined U.S. expectations and Chinese calculations (namely, that the U.S. would refrain from future Special 301–led negotiations), but ultimately it failed on both dimensions. As commanding as it appeared on paper, the IPR Working Conference system suffered from inherent weaknesses that were most apparent at the local level. Although it was quite powerful at the national level, its reach beyond Beijing was far less effective.

The National Level

The IPR Working Conference (IPRWC) was a national coordinating agency directly under the State Council; it was headed by State Councilor

---

72. Variations on the name add to the confusion surrounding this office. In Shanghai, for example, it was referred to as the Shanghai Municipal IPR Coordination Conference, or *Shanghai shi zhishi chanquan lianxi huiyi*. Interview 99SH14, May 28, 1999. Information on the administrative apparatus is also drawn from Interview 98KM01, September 1, 1998.

Song Jian. It was established as a coordinating (*xietiao*) body to bridge the gaps in regular communication and smooth over misunderstandings among the cluster of bureaucracies that have a functional relationship with intellectual property issues. In the words of one local patent official, the IPRWC was less an organization and more of a system (*xitong*): it was extremely fluid and flexible, but, as a coordinating body, it had neither formal leadership (*lingdao*) nor traditional professional (*yewu*) authority relations with any of these agencies.[73] The power of the IPRWC lay in the fact that it was headed by Song. Yet this body only met two or three times a year, and its work consisted mainly of coordinating decisions among the participants, balancing their various concerns, and issuing policy circulars.

The day-to-day responsibilities were undertaken by the IPR Working Conference Office (*zhishi chanquan bangong shi*, hereafter referred to as the IPRWO) of the IPRWC. This office was placed within the SSTC and was headed by Duan Ruichun. The responsibilities of this office included facilitating coordination across bureaucratic lines and resolving issues that arose. The IPRWO would "legitimize" contact among multiple bureaucracies that, outside of their IPR-related interests or concerns, would have little reason to communicate with one another. It also provided a forum to discuss technical matters among these bureaucracies. For example, if a given type of patent right also involved copyright issues, the IPRWO would arrange for the China Patent Bureau and the National Copyright Administration to discuss the intricacies of the issue and find a solution to any problems that might arise. The IPRWO would solicit opinions from its member organizations on the specific IPR issues facing them and bring the parties together for discussion. Finally, the IPRWO was responsible for compiling the policy decisions of the IPRWC and "putting them together for practical use"; in short, to implement these decisions.[74] This last responsibility was especially difficult because, as an office, it was outranked by the commissions, ministries, and bureaus that made up the membership of the IPRWC, so none of its membership was bound by any of the implementation directives that came out of the IPRWO.

The IPRWC gained strength when the Sino-U.S. IPR talks were resumed in 1994. The Ministry of Foreign Trade and Economic Cooperation (MOFTEC), like its predecessor, the Ministry of Foreign Relations and Trade (MOFERT), and not the Ministry of Foreign Affairs, was the lead negotiating agency for these IPR negotiations because they fell under the rubric of "trade relations." MOFTEC was the representative to the United States during the talks (*dui wai*) and was not involved in the implementation of the agreements that it signed. This internal coordination (*dui nei*) fell under the jurisdiction of the SSTC. These agreements involved a number of competing units and were very complex from an administrative

73. Ibid.
74. Ibid.

point of view. The SSTC coordinated the implementation of these agreements through the IPRWO and the relationship between Song Jian and Duan Ruichun. According to one Chinese negotiator, the coordination by the IPRWO was not without its problems; however, many of these were the inevitable outcomes of bureaucratic self-interest on the part of the agencies involved. By and large, however, each of the offices within the IPR community knew what its responsibilities were and what it needed to do, and the "problem wasn't particularly big" (*wenti bu da*).[75]

The "big" problems arose at the local level, as the SSTC attempted to replicate this "internal orientation" at the provincial level and below. Before discussing the factors that gave rise to these problems, I provide a brief description of the IPRWC/IPRWO at the local level.

The Local Level

Starting in 1994, the IPR Working Conference was replicated at the local level, all the way to the municipality (although some appeared, in rare instances, at the county level as well).[76] At the provincial level, a vice governor of the province usually led the provincial IPRWC; at the municipal level, this position would often be filled by a vice mayor, and so on.[77] The actual membership of the local IPRWC included representatives from various IPR-related bureaucracies. The Shanghai IPRWC leadership included the vice director of the Shanghai Administration of Industry and Commerce (representing the trademark subfield), the director of the Shanghai Patent Bureau, the vice director of the Shanghai Press and Publications Administration (the individual in charge of copyright), and the vice director of the Shanghai Economics Commission (the individual with the science and technology portfolio). Local IPRWCs also included representatives from the Bureau of Culture, the Customs Administration, the Bureau of Radio, Film, and Television, the Public Security Bureau, and the courts, among others.[78]

As at the national level, meetings of the local IPRWCs were infrequent, usually about twice a year. According to one official, meetings were organized as a response to one of two dynamics, those from above (*xialai*) and those from below. An example of the former would be a debriefing about a recently concluded bout of IPR negotiations between the United States and China. The National SSTC, through its agent the national IPRWC, would coordinate the enforcement plan and then downshift it to the local levels through the local IPRWC and its own IPR Working Office. A case of the latter would revolve around coordination of a public demolition of IPR-infringing merchandise or a local IPR campaign or crackdown.[79]

75. Interview 99BJ23, July 19, 1999.
76. Interview 99CD05, June 30, 1999.
77. Interview 98KM01, September 1, 1998.
78. Interview 99SH14, May 28, 1999; and Interview 99CD05, June 30, 1999.
79. Interview 99SH14, May 28, 1999.

The local IPRWO was authorized by the local government and empowered to undertake coordination responsibilities among its various member bureaucracies. The director of the local IPRWO, following Beijing's lead, was generally appointed by the Science and Technology Commission (STC), and the IPRWO was placed within the STC. There is some variation with regard to its placement within the STC: some provincial IPRWOs, like those of Yunnan and Shanghai, were placed within the STC's laws and regulations department (*fagui chu*), while others, like that of Chongqing, were placed in the STC's main office.[80]

The local IPRWOs held meetings irregularly, but on average they were held once or twice a month. There was some variation regarding the staff allocations. In Chongqing, for example, the IPRWO did not have a fixed staff; it was not designated a fixed-staff organization (*bianzhi jigou*) but rather a separate "organization in name only" (*xushe jigou*).[81] Salaries and other budgetary outlays ("working finance," or *gongzuo jinfei*) were doled out according to the nature of the specific tasks assigned and undertaken by the IPRWO.[82] However, its counterpart in Jiangsu province had five full-time employees, while the Sichuan IPRWO had five part-time employees drawn from other parts of the STC.[83]

The IPRWO at the local level replicated the functions of its national counterpart, with some local variation. Its chief responsibilities involved coordinating the various offices with jurisdiction over some aspect of intellectual property. For example, the Shanghai IPRWO coordinated enforcement by discussing the boundaries of jurisdictional authority among its member bureaucracies even though it did not have the power to enforce these distinctions. Indeed, the "hotline" for reporting IPR violations in Shanghai was routed through the IPRWO, and then the complaints were channeled by this office to the appropriate enforcement agency. The IPRWO did not meet with the actual enforcement arms of these bureaucracies; rather, it let its member organizations work with their own enforcement units—otherwise, it would get "too messy," according to one source.[84] In Sichuan, by contrast, the IPRWO would occasionally mediate disputes among multiple agencies regarding their official jurisdictions in day-to-day matters, but more often it handled special, large-scale projects that involved participation by its member bureaucracies.[85]

80. Ibid.; Interview 99KM02, June 17, 1999; Interview 98CQ08, April 10, 1998.

81. In some cases, such as in Shanghai and Chongqing, the title, "Intellectual Property Rights Working Office" did not even appear on the officials' business cards, while in other cases, such as in Sichuan, it did.

82. Interview 98CQ08, April 10, 1998.

83. On Jiangsu: Interview 99NJ02, June 25, 1999.

84. Interview 99CD05, June 30, 1999.

85. The Sichuan IPRWO also appeared to take more of an active involvement in copyright enforcement than it did in trademark enforcement. The reasoning behind this was that the Sichuan Copyright Administration was understaffed and the IPRWO saw its role as making up for these personnel shortfalls. Interview 99CD05, June 30, 1999.

Another major task of the local IPRWO was to sponsor IPR-related train-ing programs. Working together with such units as the local bureaus of jus-tice, the IPRWO targeted research organizations, universities, commercial enterprises, and government units at lower administrative levels to edu-cate them on IPR.[86] This particular responsibility became even more pro-nounced after the IPRWO was transformed into local intellectual property rights offices (IPOs). Before going into these developments, however, it is important to analyze the structural weaknesses of the IPRWO system, weak-nesses that persisted into its successor organizations, the local IPR offices.

Problems with Replicating Informal Power Relations

The principal structural problem of the IPRWC/IPRWO system was that at the national level, the power of the IPRWO was concentrated in the personal relationship between the director of that office, Duan Rui-chun, and the state councilor who headed the SSTC, Song Jian. Even if the formal power relations between these two national-level officials could be replicated at the local levels, the same was not true for the complex and nuanced *informal* power relations ultimately required for the success of the national IPRWO.

Insofar as the IPRWO achieved any level of effectiveness (and at the national level, it did), this was due to the power of IPRWC leader Song Jian and IPRWO director Duan Ruichun's ability to skillfully exploit Song's power. According to one particularly well-connected source, if it came to light in a State Council meeting that Song Jian was displeased by the actions of somebody in the IPR policy community, that person was effectively out of a job. Moreover, he said, "everybody knew that Duan spoke for Song."[87] Duan's actual behavior resembled nothing so much as the whip in the U.S. Congress, although he was receptive to concerns from both the bureaucra-cies he was managing and outside parties. If, for example, a foreign com-pany had a concern about IPR infringement, it might send a representative to Duan; if Duan was receptive, he would place calls to the relevant national unit, after which the process would trickle down to the local level. Without Duan's attention, the issue would get lost in the bureaucratic quagmire. When Duan became involved, he would expend considerable energy to forge a solution to the problem at hand. He was not particularly well-liked, but he was respected and sometimes feared even by officials who formally *outranked* him—but who did not outrank Song Jian.[88]

---

86. These efforts included the distribution of publications designed to educate these targets about intellectual property. An example of these publications is *Zhishi chanquan fa jianming jia-ocheng* [Concise Tutorial on Intellectual Property Rights Law] (Chengdu: Sichuan renmin chuban-she, 1999).

87. Interview 99BJ21B, April 1, 1999.

88. In addition to Duan's relationship with Song Jian, the placement of the IPRWO within the SSTC also enhanced Duan's power. Patriarch Deng Xiaoping's daughter, Deng Nan, joined the SSTC after leaving her post at the Chinese Academy of Sciences. Song Jian wisely gave Deng

These informal power relations obscured the fact that the IPRWO was effectively outranked by the ministries and bureaus at the national level and the bureaus and departments at the provincial level that it was charged with managing and coordinating. These seemingly arcane but absolutely critical power considerations were largely glossed over and were not considered in the "Action Plan":

> The State Council Working Conference *will issue directions to* the provincial, directly administered municipalities, autonomous regions and city bodies coordinating and guiding intellectual property rights, to formulate action plans and work programs in their own localities for effective enforcement of the laws on intellectual property rights, as well as plans on providing information and education on intellectual property rights.[89]

Although one could argue that, as a body within the State Council, the IPRWC could press its provincial-level counterparts into action, this turned out not to be the case. The IPRWC met infrequently and the actual follow-up and implementation of IPRWC "directives" was left to the IPRWO, which, as discussed above, lacked the formal power to issue binding orders to its member units and, in effect, was dependent on the willingness of the member units to abide by the IPRWO's recommendations. In the absence of the type of informal power arrangement that existed between Song and Duan in Beijing, in effect this often meant nonimplementation. Indeed, the puzzle is not why the local IPRWOs were not effective but rather why the national IPRWO *was* effective. The answer hinges on the relationship between Song Jian and Duan Ruichun.

In other words, power begat success, but power was based on personal authority and the ability to exploit it, not on the formal authority of the IPRWO as an institution. It is not difficult to replicate the formal structure, but it *is* difficult to replicate the informal power structure that gave the IPRWO its sway. Or, put differently, if intellectual property was not a burning issue in a given locality, the person in charge of the IPRWC would not pay too much attention to it, and the person put in charge of the IPRWO might well be a bureaucratic hack with no expertise or interest in intellectual property. To the leading IPR officials at the China Patent Bureau, particularly its director after 1989, Gao Lulin, the IPRWC/IPRWO system, despite its flaws, provided the core of what would be the next generation of IPR coordinating agencies in China, the State Intellectual Property Office and its local units. Gao's vision was ambitious and expansive, but it remains unclear, years after the fact, as to whether his efforts were as effective as the IPRWO had been.

Nan a great deal of power at the SSTC, and the SSTC benefited in turn. Interview 99BJ17, April 1, 1999.

89. "Annex: Action Plan for Effective Protection and Enforcement of Intellectual Property Rights," February 26, 1995 (italics mine).

Institutionalized Fragmentation? The State Intellectual Property Office

Reading the *China Intellectual Property Yearbook,* one is immediately struck by what seems to be a vast coordinated administrative network to protect intellectual property in China.[90] Standing alongside the State Intellectual Property Office (*Guojia zhishi chanquan ju,* or SIPO) and housed in the same building (the former China Patent Bureau) is the Patent Bureau within SIPO (*Guojia zhishi chanquan ju zhuanli ju*), which has more than a dozen functional departments.[91] Together with the dazzling array of speeches, statistics, and reports on enforcement activity, this leads one to conclude that the IPR bureaucracy, including patent, copyright, and trademark management, is a well-oiled machine spearheaded by SIPO. Indeed, casual observers of China's IPR regime would agree with this sketch of SIPO's role in China's efforts to establish a world-class IPR regime. However, this impression is flawed: although SIPO represents greater technical scope than the China Patent Bureau, in terms of political power there is little to distinguish the two. Indeed, it appears that, at least nationally, the IPRWO under Duan Ruichun and Song Jian had more authority, thanks to the informal authority relations, than does SIPO. Today, at the local level, the provincial IPR offices (*sheng ji zhishi chanquan ju*) appear to have even less responsibility (although a higher bureaucratic rank) than did their antecedent organizations, the local patent bureaus.

SIPO conforms to the U.S. notion (the organizational blueprint of SIPO was the U.S. Patent and Trademark Office) of what an inclusive intellectual property bureaucracy should be, while ignoring or denying the fundamental power differences between the various discrete bureaucratic systems for patents, copyright, and trademarks.[92] It is therefore relatively easy to be swept away by the possibility that China has finally achieved one of the goals driving the Sino-U.S. IPR negotiations: the establishment of an IPR "superbureaucracy" that would effectively manage the discrete bureaucratic systems for patents, copyright, and trademarks and impose discipline upon them to ensure better enforcement in each IPR subfield. This is not to say that IPR protection is not improving in China; it is. But the reasons for this improvement, discussed at length in the next two chapters, has very little to do with SIPO and much to do with local incentives and institutions that are acknowledged by SIPO (but are largely independent from and not controlled by it). For the most part, SIPO remains both a substantive and symbolic monument to the institutional fragmentation of IPR in China.

---

90. *Zhongguo zhishi chanquan nianjian 2000* [China Intellectual Property Yearbook 2000] (Beijing: *Zhishi chanquan chubanshe,* 2001), 44–47.
91. Ibid., 44–54.
92. Interview 02BJ01, August 5, 2002.

Figure 3.2. SIPO's grand opening, April 1998, *China Patent News*

The Genesis of SIPO

Initially, Song Jian was not pleased when Zhu Rongji picked Gao Lulin to head the China Patent Bureau.[93] This was due in part to the bureaucratic rivalries between the SSTC and the Economics Commission; Gao had worked in and Zhu had been a leader in the SEC.[94] Song Jian wanted to install one of his people as the director of the Patent Bureau, so he sent a factotum to direct the Patent Bureau alongside Gao Lulin. Ultimately, however, Song grew to like Gao Lulin and no longer saw him as a threat to the SSTC. Song Jian's factotum quietly disappeared, and Gao again became sole director of the Patent Bureau.

Over time Gao became dissatisfied with the implementation of patent-related issues. First, because of their inherent complexity, many local judges were having trouble understanding the intricacies of patent issues that arose during disputes that were brought to trial. Moreover, Gao was

93. This section draws heavily from extended interviews in 1999 and 2002 with an individual very close to the top officials in the China Patent Bureau and SIPO, particularly Gao Lulin.

94. Recall that the China Patent Bureau had, during various times in its organizational history, been placed under each of these two commissions.

growing increasingly disturbed at "local protectionism" (*difang baohu zhuyi*), particularly because, in his view, the local patent bureaus were under the local STCs and thus had no real enforcement arms to speak of. Gao wanted to establish one strong central IPR coordinating agency. There was a personal interest as well. At this time, Gao was already past the mandatory retirement age, and there was increasing pressure for him to turn over the reins to somebody else. If Gao would be able to make SIPO a *zongju*, or a ministry-level bureau, he would be able to stay on until he was sixty-five or possibly even later.

Gao started lobbying in earnest in late 1997. The goal from the beginning—broached initially over a dumpling dinner attended by the main political players—was to incorporate patents, copyright, and trademarks under one umbrella organization, SIPO. Zhu Rongji himself was initially supportive of the idea. However, the opposition from the bureaucracies that would be transferred to SIPO was intense. Moreover, the political climate made it impossible for Zhu to push for the establishment of SIPO as a *zongju*. At the time, the government was in the process of finalizing regulations that would cut the number of ministries and staff by up to fifty percent. In this climate of downsizing, it would be very difficult to "upgrade" SIPO, especially because of Zhu's well-known ties with Gao Lulin from their days together at the State Economics Commission. This would have left Zhu open to accusations of cronyism at precisely a time when he could least afford it: he needed to appear objective while he was asking the Chinese bureaucracy to make significant sacrifices. Ultimately, Zhu had to tell Gao that it would be impossible to make SIPO a *zongju* at that time.[95]

But the real problem was not simply one of timing; it was one of politics and the struggle over authority relations in the attempt to consolidate the three distinct IPR bureaucracies under the banner of SIPO.

IPR, SIPO, and the Problems of Consolidation

The National Level

SIPO has inherited the responsibilities of the Intellectual Property Rights Working Office, and the IPRWO was indeed moved into SIPO even though it does not appear on the formal organizational chart in the *2000 Intellectual Property Rights Yearbook*. With the "quasi-retirement" of Song Jian and the downgrading of the SSTC to the Ministry of Science and Technology (*kexue jishu bu*), the SSTC no longer held sway over the IPRWO. However, although SIPO is an office directly administered by the State Council, it lacks the personal Song-Duan binary authority relations that once had

---

95. Gao reportedly replied that he felt that this was not a problem as long as SIPO eventually became a *zongju*. In other words, Gao was not necessarily looking for a more powerful position for himself (although he would certainly have taken it if offered) but rather saw SIPO as his legacy and wanted to see it ultimately evolve into a *zongju*. Interview 99BJ17, April 1, 1999.

made the IPRWO as powerful as it was. Not surprisingly, SIPO's first few months were not particularly auspicious.[96] In late 1998, one high-ranking USTR official put it plainly, "We don't know whom to talk to." The U.S. Embassy, he continued,

> is running all over the place trying to figure out who the people with real jurisdiction over IPR really are. The State Council is out of the business of handling IPR issues . . . [while at] the same time, the State Council is in charge of the re-drafting of the trademark and the copyright laws. But nobody knows "who" at the State Council is involved in this. Both MOFTEC and SIPO want to have the full jurisdiction over IPR, but neither one is qualified. Currently the division seems to be the ambiguous-sounding: "MOFTEC is in charge of 'trade-related international IPR issues,' while SIPO is in charge of 'other international IPR issues.'" Nobody has an answer; nobody has a clue as to how SIPO can claim jurisdiction over copyrights and trademarks.[97]

As the dust settled and the lines of authority became somewhat less opaque to those intimately involved with IPR in China, SIPO emerged as little more than the China Patent Bureau with some contested IPRWO responsibilities.[98] As the Economist Intelligence Unit noted in 1999:

> It is not surprising that the major criticism of the bureaucratic regime established to protect intellectual property rights is that it is too fragmented. Since April 1998, the transformed State Intellectual Property Office . . . is supposed to have had a co-ordinating role, though in reality it has little authority over other bodies involved. . . . SIPO is also slated to play a leading role in bilateral talks with the U.S. on IPR issues. However, the USTR has chosen to negotiate with MOFTEC rather than SIPO since the latter's creation, something observers say has undermined SIPO's credibility.[99]

The biggest obstacle facing SIPO's ability to accomplish Gao Lulin's designs has always been, and continues to be, opposition from the two other key bureaucracies that would be subsumed under SIPO's control: the State Administration for Industry and Commerce (SAIC) and the National Copyright Administration (NCA).

96. To be fair, it takes years for a new bureaucratic agency to consolidate its power and carve out a new jurisdictional niche for itself. However, at the time, SIPO was being presented by Chinese officials in the IPR policy community as a better, more effective institutionalized version of the IPRWO.

97. Interview 98US19, December 11, 1998.

98. For example, SIPO is the lead agency in dealing with foreign bodies if IPR is not treated as a trade issue; if it is, SIPO and MOFTEC share the lead agency responsibilities, with SIPO deferring to MOFTEC. Interview 99BJ04A, March 11, 1999.

99. Economist Intelligence Unit, *China Hand: The Complete Guide to Doing Business in China* (Hong Kong: Economist Intelligence Unit, 1999), 9.

SAIC opposition to such a merger is intense, for two principal reasons. First, the Trademark Office (*shangbiao chu*) located within the national SAIC generates a substantial amount of revenue for the SAIC through its function as a clearinghouse for trademark registration (this is akin to patent registration, which can only be done at the national level). Given the status of the Trademark Office as a cash cow for the SAIC, it is highly unlikely that it would hand it over to SIPO without a fight. Moreover, since the SAIC has been elevated to *zongju* status in the past few years—precisely the administrative rank that SIPO unsuccessfully tried to secure for itself— the SAIC can dismiss any requests from SIPO out of hand. SAIC officials do not hide their disgust at the idea of such bureaucratic consolidation. For example, when a U.S. company had a question regarding trademarks in China, its representatives went to SIPO and were given an answer from the SIPO official. On a subsequent meeting with the SAIC, these same representatives of the U.S. company mentioned this to their SAIC interlocutors, who replied with contempt: "We don't care what SIPO says."[100]

There is similar opposition at the local level, but for slightly different reasons. The Administration for Industry and Commerce (AIC) offices at the local level do not have the authority to register trademarks. Rather, they are charged with enforcing registered trademarks, including the right to issue fines to trademark violators. For a number of reasons that will be explored in subsequent chapters, local AICs can derive a substantial amount of income from trademark-related activities, including trademark enforcement. Like their national-level counterpart, they are loath to give up this income-generating activity and are opposed to any attempts to encroach on their jurisdiction. Like the SAIC, the local AICs are first-tier bureaus, meaning they carry a higher bureaucratic rank than SIPO and its second-tier local counterparts. Moreover, the AIC has enjoyed a long bureaucratic history and is a complex and powerful organization that extends into many different areas of economic and commercial activity. In short, it is a formidable opponent in any bureaucratic turf war. As a result, there is very little difference between SIPO's ability, at the local level, to coordinate and manage IPR issues across bureaucratic lines and that of its predecessor, the IPRWO.[101]

The reaction of the National Copyright Administration (NCA) to the prospects of a merger with SIPO has been somewhat less uniform than that of SAIC/AIC. The NCA is a subordinate organization to the National Press and Publications Administration (NPPA). A switch over to SIPO would mean that the NCA retains its subordinate status. At the time that the idea of the merger was being floated, however, the head of the NCA, Shen Ren-gan, who takes an active interest in copyright issues, had two reasons to be favorably disposed to such a consolidation with SIPO. First, Shen enjoyed

---

100. Interview 99BJ17, April 1, 1999.
101. Ibid.; Interview 02BJ01, August 5, 2002.

good relations with Gao Lulin. Second, and more to the point, if SIPO were to become a *zongju,* Shen would automatically become a *zongju fu juzhang,* a promotion in official rank.[102]

Moreover, the NCA does not have a complex vertically integrated network with local offices. If it could break away from the local press and publications bureaus (PPB), it could effectively move its staff over to the local intellectual property offices with arguably much less of a problem than would be the case with trademarks and the AIC. More generally, the local PPBs and copyright administration offices are not as complex, vertically and horizontally integrated, or powerful as the AIC. However, the problem had nothing to do with the NCA; the opposition that quashed the merger came from another source altogether.

Between 1999 and 2001, the issue of SIPO's consolidation percolated all the way up to Premier Zhu Rongji. In discussions about the merger, however, Ding Guan'gen, director of the Chinese Communist Party Propaganda Department, voiced his personal opposition to the proposed spinoff, effectively scuttling the idea. Administrative copyright work falls somewhere in the "shadowy area" between press and publications, culture, and propaganda work. Unlike the other two subfields of intellectual property discussed in this book, copyright is unique because it has a value-laden component, to which a government with a strong preoccupation with managing the opinions of its citizens (through "thought work") is particularly sensitive. The culture/propaganda bureaucracies are extremely resistant to moving their responsibilities to more "secular" administrative systems. For example, the Administration for Industry and Commerce handles the administrative management of all commercial products in China—except cultural products. Cultural products (*wenhua chanpin*) all fall under the jurisdictional purview of the Culture Market Management Office (*wenhua shichang guanli ju*) under the Ministry of Culture. This ideology- and value-tinged opposition, therefore, should not come as a surprise. Ding reportedly had told Zhu Rongji personally that it was a sensitive issue and needed to remain within the propaganda apparatus. Once Ding made his opposition clear, the idea of moving copyright administration offices to SIPO became a "forbidden zone" and has never been mentioned again. One particularly knowledgeable source was probably overstating the case only slightly when he likened SIPO to "the Patent Bureau with a different name."[103]

The Local Level

The situation at the subnational level is somewhat mixed and remains largely in flux. On the one hand, with regard to the handling of patent disputes, the IPR offices (IPOs) have a narrower jurisdiction and fewer

102. Interview 99BJ17, April 1, 1999.
103. Ibid.

responsibilities than they did before, in sharp contrast to the Administration for Industry and Commerce, which on the subject of trademarks now has a larger jurisdiction. Although it is difficult to generalize, the overall trend appears to be that, measured in relative terms, the number of cases going to the courts has increased, while in absolute terms, the number of cases of administrative mediation [*xingzheng tiaojie*] has also risen.[104]

The legal departments (*fazhi chu*) of the IPOs no longer handle issues that are ancillary to patent-related disputes, such as contracts. Rather, they focus on disputes surrounding infringing (*qinfan*) and "passing-off" (*maochong*) or outright counterfeit patents (*jiamao zhuanli*) through civil mediation (*minshi tiaojie chuli*). The second way of dealing with infringement is through administrative investigations (*chachu*), which can take several forms. People can come to the IPOs with their complaints or use a hotline created for that purpose. IPO staff also visit exhibits and product conventions because there is a higher concentration of patent-intensive products at such venues, and it is also more manageable than undertaking market sweeps, especially as IPOs do not generally have formal investigation teams set aside for such activities. Of course, the IPOs cannot actually enforce their rulings. Once a fine is issued, the individual must go to the bank and pay the fine, which is then put in a special account for that purpose. If the party does not pay, the enforcement units of the courts (*sifa bumen*) follow up. If the party still refuses to pay, his goods are seized and auctioned off under the supervision of the *sifa bumen*.[105]

Much of the shift in organizational functions, however, involves an increasing emphasis on education and propaganda. The logic appears to be based on the assumption that many instances of patent infringement and the disputes that result arise because of general ignorance about IPR. Therefore, one of the key roles for the local IPR offices at present is to saturate relevant administrative agencies, commercial enterprises, institutes and schools, and the public with general information about intellectual property.[106]

The other broad trend has been a modest upgrade in administrative rank for the IPO bureaucracy at the provincial level, while the corresponding offices at the sub-provincial level are becoming increasingly institutionalized, so that even though lateral consolidation remains unlikely, vertical functional integration is continuing apace. Indeed, there have been some benefits for the IPOs as a result of these recent administrative changes. Apart from Chongqing, which remains a third-tier bureau, and Sichuan, Guangdong, Heilongjiang, and Shanghai, which are now all first-tier

104. Interview 03KM02, July 25, 2003 and Interview 03CD05, July 16, 2003. See also articles 57 through 59 in the revised Patent Law of China and articles 27 and 28 in the associated Implementing Regulations.

105. However, my source in Chengdu told me that, in Sichuan at least, this has not happened yet. Interview 03CD05, July 16, 2003.

106. Interview 02C01, July 10, 2002; Interview 02CD01, July 11, 2002; and Interview 02KM01, July 23, 2002.

bureaus, the majority of provincial-level IPOs have either maintained their second-tier bureau status or been upgraded to it.[107] The Yunnan Provincial IPO (YIPO) was elevated from its department, or *chu,* status within the STC in 1999 to a genuine bureau, or *ju,* with four internal departments of its own. The personnel and budgetary allocations (*bianzhi*) of the Yunnan IPR Office have been upgraded from that of a third-tier bureau to that of a second-tier bureau, increasing its staff from twelve to twenty-five, and these allocations come directly from the provincial government and not from the STC, which has only functional, professional relations (*guikou guanli*) with the IPR Office, even though they are located in the same building.[108] And the Sichuan IPO (SCIPO) has seen a net increase in its personnel allocations from forty-six to fifty-one, while many corresponding administrative units in other bureaucracies that had higher personnel allocations than SCIPO prior to the administrative downsizing in 1998–99 now have fewer personnel allocations than SCIPO.[109]

Perhaps sensing that there could be no movement on the organizational consolidation issue, provincial IPOs have been concentrating work on institutionalizing their administrative structure at the sub-provincial level. Starting in 2002, the IPOs (or their administrative counterparts) in Yunnan Province's sixteen prefectures have begun to handle their own mediation cases instead of sending them up to the YIPO in the capital of Kunming. Unlike YIPO, which is a directly subordinate unit (*zhishu danwei*) of the provincial government, the sub-provincial IPOs remain under the administrative control of the Science and Technology Bureaus (called STBs; the STCs were downgraded from commissions [*weiyuanhui*] in the administrative restructuring of 1998–99). However, even this relationship varies from prefecture to prefecture and from county to county.[110]

For example, all of Sichuan's prefectures have IPOs, and some counties also have IPOs, or at least they have offices that perform this type of work.[111] Before 1997, only four sub-provincial STCs had "established two sets of signboards" (indicating that the same office and staff were simultaneously an STC and a Patent Bureau), demonstrating that patent management had a growing responsibility. After 1997, all sub-provincial STCs had two sets of signboards. In 2000, they changed their second set of signboards from "Patent Bureau" to "IPR Office" at the prefecture level and in some counties.

Symbolically, this may be important in that it signals that IPR concerns are being extended down into the localities, suggesting a shift in priorities, or at least improved responsiveness to perceived national priorities. Substantively, however, the establishment of "a single organization, two different

107. On Chongqing, Interview 02CQ01, July 10, 2002.
108. Interview 02KM01, July 23, 2002.
109. Interview 03CD05, July 16, 2003.
110. Interview 03XJ01/5, July 17, 2003.
111. Ibid.; Interview 03CD05.

signboards" (*yige jigou liangkuai paizi*) simply means that the STC can also be referred to as the IPR Office; there is no associated upgrade in staff or resources.[112] Moreover, some subnational IPOs are more subordinate to the STBs than are others. For example, there are three types of administrative subrankings at the prefecture level. Of the twenty-one prefectures in Sichuan, only the Deyang Municipal IPO is a first-tier bureau managed directly by the municipal government and administratively independent from, and ranked equally with, the STB. The IPOs of Mianyang, Bazhong, Luzhou, Zigong, Leshan, and Yibing municipalities are all second-tier bureaus under the leadership of the STB. Finally, the rest, including the provincial capital of Chengdu municipality, are third-tier bureaus in which the IPO is a department (*chu*) of the STB in a "single organization, two different signboards" relationship.[113]

In spite of these developments, the prospect of organizational consolidation (*sanjia fangzai yikuai*), in which the various IPO bureaucracy officials with whom I have met remain very interested, now appears to be as unlikely as it ever did. The main coordinating responsibilities lie within the IPRWO, which is now housed in the IPOs.[114] They are charged with coordinating large-scale IPR work that involves two or more IPR-related bureaucracies—that is, essentially the same work as they did when part of the STCs. Although a network of IPRWOs has been established at the prefecture level, all of the problems that plagued the IPRWOs when under the STCs still hold true for them now that they are under the IPOs.[115] The difference is that the IPOs generally rank lower than the STCs did, so that the IPRWOs have actually lost a shade of formal power.

So even when officials from these offices anticipated that SIPO and its local counterparts would secure the management and enforcement responsibilities for copyright and trademarks, they expected this to be a long-term development. Initial changes are more symbolic than substantive. For example, officials at the Sichuan IPR Office have interpreted the renaming of the Sichuan Patent Bureau to SCIPO as a first step in this regard.[116] Yunnan IPR Office officials were also hopeful but cautioned that it would take some time (*yi bu yi bu zou*) before this goal will become reality.[117] As of 2003, the prospects for such a merger seem increasingly slim, and these same officials appear to have grown correspondingly fatalistic.[118]

112. Interview 02CD01, July 11, 2002. This is also the case in Yunnan. Interview 02KM01, July 23, 2002. The practice of *yige jigou liangkuai paizi* is a common one throughout the Chinese bureaucracy, and the IPR bureaucracy is no exception, as we shall see in the next two chapters.
113. Interview 03CD05, July 16, 2003.
114. Its leader, the head of the IPR leadership small group (or IPRWC) at the provincial level, is the vice governor with portfolio for intellectual property.
115. Interview 03CD05, July 16, 2003.
116. Interview 02CD01, July 11, 2002.
117. Interview 02KM01, July 23, 2002.
118. Interview 03KM02, July 15, 2003.

The argument of this chapter is that domestic institutional fragmentation combined with exogenous shocks (mostly by the United States) have shaped the Patent Bureau–cum–IPR Office to what it is today: a technically proficient but relatively weak bureaucratic agency with a goal, consolidation, that cannot be realized at the present time. Insofar as recent changes within the IPO bureaucracy have served further to institutionalize the importance of IPR, this is a step forward. However, it seems very unlikely that the initial goal of SIPO and its provincial-level counterparts, the consolidation of patents, copyright, and trademark management and enforcement under one "superbureaucracy," will be met any time in the short- or even medium-term future. SIPO and the local IPOs face tremendous hostility to these plans by the two other bureaucracies that would be transferred into the SIPO system. These bureaucracies—and the bureaucratic clusters in which they are embedded—are the subject of the next two chapters. Chapters 4 and 5 will analyze the complicated organizational structure of the copyright and anticounterfeiting bureaucracies, respectively, and underscore just how difficult it will be for SIPO to realize its goal of bureaucratic consolidation over IPR in China. The chapters also focus on the relationship between foreign pressure and local enforcement.

CHAPTER 4

The Copyright Problem

One day in 1999, I was interviewing a local government official who worked in the Office of the Education, Science, Culture and Public Health Committee of the Provincial People's Congress in one of China's more economically developed regions. We spent the whole afternoon discussing many of the intricacies of intellectual property rights law, the philosophies that provide its foundation, and the advances that China had made during the preceding several years in establishing its own IPR regime. At the conclusion of our conversation, I mentioned in passing that I had seen an advertisement for a CD-ROM set of China's national and local laws and regulations. I had wanted to purchase it, but even at the discounted price the cost was more than $1,000. Almost before I could finish my sentence, my interviewee promptly hailed a taxi and took me to a part of town where pirated audiovisual equipment and computer software were sold openly. My source not only located a pirated version of the CD-ROM, the official even negotiated the price down to half of the three dollars initially quoted by the seller. And this was done without a trace of self-consciousness or hypocrisy.

This chapter focuses on the bureaucratic politics of copyright management and the enforcement institutions in China to explain the overall lack of success in managing copyright in an institutional setting in which the deck is stacked against such an outcome. In addition to filling such analytical and empirical lacunae, an understanding of China's administrative copyright management and enforcement apparatus allows us to reevaluate the seemingly contradictory behavior of a wide array of actors in China, from the official described above to the hundreds of millions of consumers who purchase pirated goods and understand such behavior as perfectly reasonable responses to a fragmented regulatory environment.

In this chapter, I make three claims. First, even more than the Patent Law, China's first copyright law was shaped by foreign pressure, with the result that foreigners enjoyed greater legal protection under China's Copyright Law than China's own citizens. Second, China's administrative apparatus for managing and enforcing copyright has been supine and ineffective for most of its existence because of personnel and budgetary scarcity and because of its embeddedness within another powerful bureaucracy that often pursued different priorities. Finally, in order to recast itself as a viable instrument for copyright protection, China's copyright bureaucracy has undertaken several strategies, ranging from Maoist-style campaigns to more recent alliances with certain segments in Chinese society arranging for the latter to help underwrite and otherwise reduce the enforcement costs of protecting copyright in China.

The Evolution of China's Legal Copyright Regime

Even more so than was the case with patents, establishing a copyright regime in the People's Republic of China never really enjoyed a "natural" trajectory. There are several reasons for this. China has a cultural and historical aversion to the basic philosophical underpinnings underlying copyright protection. Second, the political regime in China placed, and continues to place, an enormous emphasis on ideological control. Third, copyright-friendly norms have been slow to take root in China's consumer base. Finally, technological advancements have made it exceedingly easy to produce greater quantities of pirated merchandise of increasingly high quality. In terms of substance and timing, therefore, China's Copyright Law and the society-wide dialogue on copyright protection emerged largely from pressure brought about by the United States.[1]

The Development of the Copyright Law

On September 7, 1990, at the Fifteenth Plenum of the Standing Committee of the Seventh National People's Congress (NPC), the People's Republic of China promulgated the first copyright law in its history, with 102 votes in favor and ten opposed or abstaining. The establishment of the Copyright Law marked the end of a tortuous road that had snaked through the Mao era and spanned the entire first half of the reform era as well.[2]

1. According to the Economist Intelligence Unit, "the principle engine of IPR development in China . . . has been direct pressure brought by other countries, chiefly the USA. Since 1992, China and the USA have signed three IPR agreements that have essentially set the pace and priorities of China's drive to establish an IPR regime." Economist Intelligence Unit, *China Hand: The Complete Guide to Doing Business in China* (Hong Kong: Economist Intelligence Unit, 1996), 5. Of the three IPR subfields, copyright received the most attention during the Sino-U.S. bilateral dialogue, as argued in chapter 2.

2. Shen Rengan, "*Youguan zhuzuoquan fa zhiding de huigu*" [A Look Back at the Drafting of the Copyright Law and Related System], in *Zhongguo zhishi chanquan ershi nian* [Twenty Years of Intellectual Property in China], ed. Liu Chuntian (Beijing: *Zhuanli chubanshe,* 1998), 27.

The research into the drafting of what would eventually become the Patent Law and the Copyright Law began in 1979, as relations with the United States were being normalized.[3] At a time when Deng Xiaoping was visiting the United States, the director of the State Science and Technology Commission, Fang Yi, was holding discussions with the U.S. Energy Secretary. These talks resulted in the Sino-U.S. Agreement on High Energy Physics, in which the issue of mutual protection of copyright was addressed. In March, the United States and China began negotiations on a trade agreement, during which the United States again raised the issue of copyright protection, requesting that international copyright treaties be invoked to protect (U.S.) copyright in China prior to the promulgation of a copyright law. In Article 6 of the 1979 Agreement on Trade Relations between the United States of America and the People's Republic of China, Beijing and Washington formally attested to the following:

> Both Contracting Parties in their trade relations recognize the importance of effective protection of patents, trademarks and copyrights.

> Both Contracting Parties agree that on the basis of reciprocity legal or natural persons of either Party may apply for registration of trademarks and acquire exclusive rights thereto in the territory of the other Party in accordance with its laws and requisitions.

> Both Contacting Parties agree that each Party shall seek, under its laws and with due regard to international practice to ensure to legal or natural persons of the other Party protection of patents and trademarks equivalent to the patent and trademark protection correspondingly accorded by the other Party.

> Both Contracting Parties shall permit and facilitate enforcement of provisions concerning protection of industrial property in contracts between firms, companies and corporations, and trading organizations of their respective countries, and shall provide means, in accordance with their respective laws, to restrict unfair competition involving unauthorized use of such rights.

> Both Contracting Parties agree that each Party shall take appropriate measures, under its laws and regulations and with due regard to international practice, to ensure to legal or natural persons of the other Party protection of copyrights equivalent to the copyright protection correspondingly accorded by the other Party.

In April 1979 the State Press and Publications Administration (*Guojia chuban ju*) requested that the State Council establish an administrative

---

3. This discussion draws from conversations with a Chinese official intimately familiar with the drafting process of China's original Copyright Law. Interview 99BJ33, July 30, 1999.

organization charged with drafting what would become China's Copyright Law. CCP Secretary General Hu Yaobang, in particular, was very much behind the momentum to develop these IPR laws. Hu is reported to have said: "I concur with the report, go ahead and start as soon as possible; organize a team to draft a Copyright Law."[4] The drafting group was christened "the China publishers association copyright research" small group and began to draft a tentative copyright law. However, for several reasons, the legislative process was much faster for the Patent Law than it was for the Copyright Law.[5] First, there was a very strong emphasis on national economic development (*guomin jingji fazhan*), and patents were seen as contributing more directly to this goal than the more narrowly applied "tool" of copyright. Second, the concept of "copyright" was not well understood by many people, including those in the government. It was regarded more as a means of regulating the publishing industry than a mechanism for protecting the rights of authors.[6] Finally, there was a tremendous amount of resistance by some bureaucracies.

After more than six months, in December 1979, the group put forward a draft law that combined the publishing and copyright laws. The proponents of combining the laws argued that the term "copyright" was the result of a mistranslation from the Japanese. Moreover, they claimed that publishing rights included the rights of recording, broadcasting, and performance, which could not be separated from one another. The notion of "publishing" was already in common international usage, this line of thinking went, and "copyright" was easy to confuse with the rights of expression; in any case, publishing was enshrined in the Chinese constitution, so it was unnecessary to create a separate provision for copyright. The proponents of separating the two laws argued that the term "copyright" provided a direct connection between the author and his or her work, while simply maintaining a "right to publish" invited confusion regarding the right of the publisher.[7]

This draft law was discussed at a copyright work meeting in Changsha, the capital of Hunan province, in which the majority of the participants felt that combining the publishing and copyright laws was inappropriate, and that it would be best to separate the two. This gave rise to the debate over the sequencing of the publishing and copyright laws. Those who opposed shelving the Copyright Law until after the promulgation of the Publishing Law argued that regulations already existed that covered the latter, including the Standard for Dealing with Illegal Books and Magazines of November 18, 1955. The other side countered that in order to "manage" society, it

---

4. Shen, "*Youguan zhuzuoquan fa zhiding de huigu,*" 30.

5. This partially explains why the NCA was not established until 1985, or five years after the establishment of the Patent Bureau. Interview 99BJ33, July 30, 1999.

6. Ibid.

7. This dispute was resolved by Article 51 of the 1990 Copyright Law, which states that the term "right to publish" used in this law shall have the same meaning as the term "copyright."

was necessary to have a Publishing Law first in order to regulate what kind of books can be published; author's rights could be discussed later.[8]

In July 1980 the State Publications Bureau (SPA) prepared another draft of the Copyright Law and sent it around Beijing to solicit opinions from relevant corners of the government. Throughout the 1980s, there would be several flashpoints of debate. These included the legal rights of the individual over the individual's work unit (*danwei*); the proposed protection of computer software or folk literature under the Copyright Law; the notion of third-party or "neighbor's rights" covering the often complex legal and creative relationships among the various parties involved in producing an audio or video recording; the inheritance or transferal of copyright; and the balance between the rights and obligations of copyright holders. One other controversial issue involved the protection of foreign copyrighted works, examined in detail below. Some argued that the Copyright Law should be a domestic law and not an international one, while others were ambivalent about the distinction.[9]

Two years later, in 1982, the SPA was fused into the Ministry of Culture. In the spring of that year, the Ministry of Culture revised the working draft into what became the Temporary Statutes on the Protection of Copyright of the People's Republic of China, which were printed and distributed throughout the country for comment in July. In April 1983, the Publications Administration of the Ministry of Culture held a meeting of experts and changed the Temporary Statutes into the Experimental Statutes on the Protection of Copyright of the People's Republic of China and sent them to the State Council as a report, which was then further revised by officials from the State Council Legal Affairs Office. In October, State Council Vice Secretary Gu Mingru brought together the various State Council committees to discuss the Experimental Statutes. The consensus at the meeting was that these provided the foundation for the Copyright Law. With just a few changes, it was thought, the Experimental Statutes could be submitted to the State Council as a draft protocol. These changes proved to be somewhat more elusive than the State Council committees had anticipated. A number of organizations related to copyright management could not sign off on the draft copyright protocol, which made it impossible to adopt the draft law as it stood at that point. These actors pointed to China as being "an environment full of disorder with regard to editing, printing, and publishing, and one rife with piracy."[10]

In July 1985, the State Council established the National Copyright Administration (*Guojia banquan ju*, or NCA), which took over the main responsibility of overseeing the drafting of the Copyright Law. Between

---

8. This dispute was resolved by Article 4 of the 1990 Copyright Law: "Works that may not lawfully be published or disseminated shall not be protected under his law. The exercise by a copyright owner of his copyrights shall not violate the Constitution or the law and shall not harm the public interest."

9. Shen, "*Youguan zhuzuoquan fa zhiding de huigu*," 28–45.

10. Ibid., 31.

1985 and 1987, the NCA worked on several versions of the draft copyright law and submitted it to the various agencies for comment. One draft was sent to the State Council in May 1986. The State Council Legislative Affairs Office and the NCA solicited a number of opinions at a conference in Beijing. In the summer of 1987, at the first national copyright work conference, held in Qingdao, proponents were confronted by the challenge that there were a number of ministries and commissions that felt that the promulgation of any copyright law should be deferred. A number of officials felt that China had many other problems that were a higher priority than the enactment of a copyright law.[11]

For example, the draft Copyright Law was bitterly opposed by the science and technology units (*kexue jia*), particularly by the State Science and Technology Commission. These units argued that if China passed the Copyright Law, they would be unable to harness "the free flow of information" that China had enjoyed up to that time, as China would be forced to pay royalties it could not afford. As a result of these restrictions, China would be inhibited in fully developing its science and technology capabilities and would remain strategically vulnerable and economically noncompetitive in the international system. The top leadership found this argument particularly convincing.[12]

The NCA carefully considered this question and arrived at two possible scenarios. In the first, China could quickly accede to international copyright treaties, an outcome that was deemed to be inevitable. If this were the case, China would be bound by what its leaders saw as overly strict international standards. The other option was to develop a national copyright law that would protect Chinese copyright holders but would cover foreign works in such a vague manner, at least initially, as to render such protection largely meaningless. The logic was that a national law was "easier to manage" and that the promulgation of such a law, as well as any subsequent amendments, would be time-consuming and thus widen the window of opportunity for China to benefit from exploiting unprotected works with foreign copyrights. And it would be easier to control the situation under the framework of a national law than if China were locked into an international copyright regime.[13]

In November 1988 the NCA provided the State Council with its Report on Increasing the Speed of Work on the Draft Copyright Law. After ratification by the State Council, a copyright drafting small group (*banquan fa qicao xiaozu*) was formed under NCA Vice Director Liu Dai and Xie Huaishi, associate researcher at the Institute of Law at the Chinese Academy of Social Science (CASS).[14] The responsibility of this small group was to

---

11. Ibid.
12. Interview 99BJ33, July 30, 1999.
13. Ibid.
14. Members included officials from the CCP Propaganda Department, the State Education Commission, SSTC, the Ministry of Culture, the Ministry of Radio, Film, and Television, CASS, and the NCA—fifteen individuals in all. This group also included noted Chinese IPR expert Zheng Chengsi. Shen, "*Youguan zhuzuoquan fa zhiding de huigu*," 32.

revise the draft protocol of the NCA's Copyright Law. Progress remained slow until early 1989, when the debate was punctuated by pressure from the United States, which insisted that China establish a copyright law as a condition for renewing the U.S.-China Bilateral Trade Agreement, which was up for renewal that year. The SSTC, up to that point one of the principal opponents to the substance of the draft copyright law, feared the loss of further bilateral science and technology exchanges with the United States and did an abrupt about-face, becoming one of the strongest proponents of the Copyright Law.[15] After discussions on May 18 and 19, China and the United States signed the little-known 1989 Sino-U.S. Memorandum of Understanding on Intellectual Property Rights.

Although never ratified and very quickly overshadowed by the military crackdown in China just a few weeks later, this MOU provided the momentum to restart discussions on proposed revisions to what was now the "Draft Protocol of the Copyright Law of the People's Republic of China"; after it passed through the Standing Committee of the State Council, Premier Li Peng on December 14, 1989, called for the Standing Committee of the Seventh National People's Congress to take it up for consideration, and it was duly discussed during the eleventh through fifteenth plenums of the Standing Committee of the Seventh National People's Congress in 1989 and 1990. Members of the Legal Works Commission of the Standing Committee of the National People's Congress, the State Council Legal Affairs Office, and the NCA repeatedly went over revisions of the draft protocol of the Copyright Law; on September 7, 1990, at the Fifteenth Plenum of the NPC Standing Committee, the Copyright Law was finally passed. On the same day, President Yang Shangkun issued Order Number 31 announcing that the new law would take effect on June 1, 1991. It had taken eleven years and no fewer than six drafts, but the first copyright law of the People's Republic of China finally saw the light of day.[16]

Even though many in the government felt that China needed to have a copyright law, there remained a great deal of opposition to it, both in principle and in terms of its specific articles and clauses. Many artists, particularly composers and writers, felt that the draft law was too narrow and did not adequately protect their rights. They insisted that their concerns be addressed and included in the law. Part of Article 32, for instance, was not in the original draft and was added as a result of pressure from writers.[17] Nor were the first two paragraphs of Article 35.[18] The first paragraph

15. Interview 99BJ33, July 30, 1999.
16. Shen, "*Youguan zhuzuoquan fa zhiding de huigu*," 32.
17. "Except where the copyright owner has declared that reprinting or excerpting is not permitted, other newspaper or periodical publishers may, after the publication of the work by a newspaper or a periodical, reprint the work or print an abstract of it or print it as a reference material, but such other publishers shall pay remuneration to the copyright owner as prescribed in the regulations."
18. "(1) A performer (an individual performer or a performing group) who for a performance exploits an unpublished work created by another shall obtain permission from, and pay

of Article 37 was also not in the original draft and was added because of pressure from composers.[19]

In addition, the Copyright Law (CL) contained many provisions that diverged from the Berne Convention for the Protection of Literary and Artistic Works and the GATT IPR Regime, the Trade-Related Aspects of Intellectual Property Rights (even though TRIPS was still in draft form, it was widely circulated at the time these discussions were taking place). At issue was whether the Copyright Law should be a springboard toward harmonization or whether it should be "nationalist" in character. This would lead to perverse consequences later on.[20]

There were also ideological issues. In the post–June 4 period, many conservative elements in the government felt that the copyright debate involved issues of ideological "correctness" and that such issues should be explicitly included in the CL.[21] By contrast, copyright proponents argued that ideological issues should not clutter up the Copyright Law—that the CL should not be used as a blunt instrument for meting out punishment for ideological crimes—and that such issues should be covered by the Criminal Law. This debate was particularly protracted, and it resulted in the compromise that was enshrined in Article 4: "Works the publication or distribution of which is prohibited by law shall not be protected by this Law; Copyright owners, in exercising their copyright, shall not violate the Constitution or laws or prejudice the public interest."

Following the promulgation of the Copyright Law, the NCA, in discussions with experts from the World Intellectual Property Office (WIPO), was informed that the CL as it stood deviated too much from Berne. The Chinese took these considerations into account when drafting the Implementing Regulations of the Copyright Law of the People's Republic of China. However, because the CL had already been made public, the drafters were constrained in what they could do by the CL. For example, the "fair use" provisions of Article 22 of the Copyright Law were clarified and narrowed in scope by Article 27 of the Implementing Regulations. This was an issue that was comparatively easy to resolve. By contrast, Article 43 stated:

---

remuneration to, the copyright owner; (2) A performer who for a commercial performance exploits a published work created by another does not need permission from, but shall, as prescribed by regulations, pay remuneration to, the copyright owner; such work shall not be exploited where the copyright owner has declared that such exploitation is not permitted."

19. "A producer of sound recordings who, for the production of a sound recording, exploits an unpublished work created by another, shall obtain permission from, and pay remuneration to, the copyright owner. A producer of sound recordings who, for the production of a sound recording, exploits a published work created by another, does not need permission from, but shall, as prescribed by regulations, pay remuneration to, the copyright owner; such work shall not be exploited where the copyright owner has declared that such exploitation is not permitted."

20. Interview 99BJ33, July 30, 1999.

21. In a more recent example of this tendency, the editor of *Marxist Theory*, Duan Ruofei, attempted unsuccessfully to use the Copyright Law to silence his more free-market critics, charging that they were distorting his theories by "using excerpts instead of the whole article." "Marxist Suffers Copyright Defeat," *South China Morning Post*, April 23, 1999.

A radio station or television station that broadcasts, for non-commercial purposes, a published sound recording needs [sic] not obtain permission from, or pay remuneration to, the copyright owner, performer or producer of the sound recording.

This was more difficult to harmonize with Berne.[22] Article 43, which will be discussed in more detail below, became a politically charged issue in China. According to one well-placed source, "no movement was possible" on Article 43 at that time. Thus, the "Implementing Regulations" were a small, partial step toward harmonization with the international copyright regime, but such harmonization was constrained by the existing Copyright Law. Any ham-fisted revision of the CL, however noble its intentions, would question the very legitimacy of the legislative process and risk mass defection from all the units that were involved in—and that had made significant concessions—during the debate that led to the adoption of CL.[23]

Software and its industry-specific provisions were not included in the Copyright Law because when the debate over the content of the CL was taking place, "there really *was* no software in China," according to my source, who was only slightly exaggerating the reality at the time.[24] There were some ambiguities in the Copyright Law, as software was explicitly protected in Article 3 but not in Article 35. Because the Chinese felt that the CL "had already been perfected," it was necessary to create separate regulations. Article 21 of the Software Regulations comes straight from U.S. case law and is very different from the provisions protecting software in the CL.[25] These and other inconsistencies and loose ends became the flashpoints of what would become the Sino-U.S. IPR negotiations, which were entering full steam by 1991. This was particularly true with regard to the asymmetrical protection of Chinese and foreign works as a result of China's adoption of the Provisions on Implementing International Copyright Treaties.

External Shocks and the "Double Standard" in Chinese Copyright Protection

As argued in chapter 2, copyright issues dominated the substance of the Sino-U.S. IPR negotiations and marked the most contentious of the three IPR subfields, as well as the one in which the U.S. "footprint" on China's subsequent legislation was most clearly visible. At the same time that the Chinese were working on the Implementing Regulations and the

22. The result, ironically, was that Berne protection was ultimately extended to foreigners, while the Chinese were left with less protection afforded by their own domestic legislation. This is discussed in greater detail below.
23. Interview 99BJ33, July 30, 1999.
24. Ibid.
25. Interview 99BJ33, July 30, 1999.

software provisions, the United States had started negotiating with Beijing to avoid having to impose sanctions that were looming under Special 301. The United States was also consciously using the draft TRIPS agreement as a "carrot" (to mitigate against the "stick" of Special 301) to get China to agree to better protection of U.S. copyright in China: if China made sufficient progress, according to one U.S. negotiator, the United States would support China's bid to be a founding member of the World Trade Organization.[26] Thus TRIPS provided a convenient substantive and symbolic link between U.S. IPR concerns and China's desire to join the WTO.

The Chinese, of course, could have rejected this approach. Not only had TRIPS not yet been formally adopted—that would have to wait until 1995—but the PRC was not a member of GATT. Because the Chinese were not bound by TRIPS, it is all the more extraordinary that Beijing was willing to use TRIPS as a template for what would eventually become the 1992 Sino-U.S. Memorandum of Understanding on Intellectual Property Rights. One U.S. negotiator at the time was surprised at the degree to which China went "beyond TRIPS" in its commitments under the 1992 MOU. He attributed this to China's "GATT fever," as well as to the fact that the Chinese negotiators, especially director general of the Department of Treaties and Laws, Zhang Yuejiao, had spent time in Geneva and therefore "knew TRIPS inside and out" and were comfortable working within an established framework—however tentatively—in 1991.[27]

Nevertheless, most of the negotiations did not go this smoothly. During the 1991–92 negotiations, the then Ministry of Machinery and Electronics Industry (MMEI) and the Ministry of Chemical Industry (MOCI) were both particularly hostile to such U.S. demands. The MMEI had an important interest in lax copyright laws because of its responsibilities over the registration and distribution of computer software in China. These dissemination responsibilities—making such software available throughout China's vast State-Owned Enterprise (SOE) network—gave it great power within the Chinese system. This, in turn, was possible because the MMEI required an "excessive" amount of technical proprietary information during the registration process, information that made it quite easy for the MMEI to reverse-engineer the software, isolate the source code, and circulate it.[28] The MOCI was also one of the largest distributors of pirated industrial computer software. At one point in the negotiations, the U.S. delegation held up a pirated "process software" package that had been traced to the MOCI. The U.S. negotiator was blunt: "This is *theft!* Does the Ministry of Chemical Industry want to be known as the 'Ministry of *Theft*'?"

26. The United States had its own reasons for using TRIPS. Until the later 1980s and early 1990s, intellectual property was not generally considered a trade issue. Therefore, by invoking TRIPS, the USTR was attempting to establish a closer link between IPR and trade. Interview 98US10B, December 4, 1998.

27. Interview 98HK06, June 24, 1998.

28. Interview 98HK02, June 22, 1998.

The Chinese response was summed up by the MMEI representative's argument that such computer software was not covered by the Copyright Law, so it wasn't illegal.[29] As noted in chapter 1, the MMEI representative said, "We cannot afford to pay royalties, we don't want to, and what is more, you cannot make us," adding that it is an internal affair and thus outside the jurisdiction of the United States.[30]

Ultimately, the MMEI lost its copyright-related portfolio, partially because the United States was able to demonstrate to the Chinese that they were on the losing side of international IPR trends. For example, software had by that time largely been regarded in international circles as a "literary work" and not, as the MMEI insisted, as a "tool." Nor did it help the MMEI's case that it had succeeded in alienating its administrative counterparts almost as much as it had antagonized the U.S. negotiators.[31] Eventually, the copyright registration portfolio was handed over to the NCA, although it took some time for this to finally go through.[32] By the 1994–95 negotiations, "the MMEI was nowhere to be seen," according to one USTR official.[33]

But this jurisdictional restructuring was only the tip of the iceberg as far as U.S. influence in Chinese domestic politics was concerned. The 1995 agreement and Action Plan, in particular, were described to me as "unique" and "unprecedented" by a former USTR negotiator, as noted in chapter 3. Encroachment on China's sovereignty, however, was not limited to the 1995 agreement. Earlier agreements also encroached on what the Chinese regarded as their national sovereignty. One of the centerpieces of the 1992 MOU was China's promise to accede to international IPR treaties, specifically the Berne Convention for the Protection of Literary and Artistic Works and the (Geneva) Convention for the Protection of Producers of Phonograms Against Unauthorized Duplication of Their Phonograms. This had been a demand of the U.S. IPR industry associations for years. These demands demonstrate the degree of exogenous pressure that came to bear on China's evolving IPR regime and the degree to which this pressure shaped the latter. Article 3, paragraph 3 of the 1992 MOU stated:

Upon China's accession to the Berne Convention and the Geneva Convention, these Conventions will be international treaties within

29. Interview 98US10B, December 4, 1998.

30. Interview 98US09, November 30, 1998. The end-user problem, particularly the use of such pirated software in government offices, remained a huge problem throughout the 1990s. On February 24, 1999, the State Council finally released a "red top directive" (*hongtou wenjian*) to symbolize its opposition to the practice, but this was little more than the re-release of pre-existing regulations with a new State Council cover page. General Office of the State Council Document 19.

31. Interview 99BJ23, July 19, 1999; and Interview 99BJ33, July 30, 1999.

32. "*Guowuyuan bangong ting guanyu jianli Guowuyuan he zhishi chanquan bangong huiyi zhidu ji youguan bumen zhize fengong wenti de tongzhi*" [General Office of the State Council Notice Regarding the Establishment of the State Council and the Intellectual Property Working Conference System and the Issue of Related Units' Division of Responsibilities], no. 82, 1994.

33. Interview 98US20, December 11, 1998.

the meaning of Article 142 of the General Principles of the Civil Code of the People's Republic of China. In accordance with the provisions of that Article, where there is an inconsistency between the provisions of the Berne Convention and the Geneva Convention on the one hand, and Chinese domestic law and regulations on the other hand, the international Conventions will prevail subject to the provisions to which China has declared a reservation, which is permitted by those Conventions.[34]

This was a major victory for the United States because it bound China by both international and domestic law to protect foreign copyright holders to the same degree that other signatory countries were obliged to. Specifically, Article 19 of the Provisions on Implementing International Copyright Treaties, promulgated on September 25, 1992, stated: "Where pre-existing administrative regulations relating to copyright may conflict with these Rules, these Rules shall apply. . . . Where these Rules may conflict with international copyright treaties, the international copyright treaties shall apply." However, a particularly ironic unintended consequence was that Chinese copyright owners received *less* protection in China than their foreign counterparts because the Chinese were covered by their own domestic laws in China.[35] This not only revealed the impact of exogenous pressure on China's evolving IPR regime, it also undermined China's original strategy of using the Copyright Law to hold "foreigners at bay"—it led to precisely the opposite outcome that the SSTC and other units sought in enacting a Chinese copyright law.[36]

As a response to this reality, one that grew increasingly unacceptable politically to the State Council, by the first half of 1998 the National Copyright Administration was under pressure from the State Council to solicit input from relevant agencies about what needed to be changed in the revised Copyright Law. These "relevant units" included universities, associations, and government organs, primarily the local Copyright Bureaus. The NCA then drafted a very carefully worded document that made these suggestions explicit and submitted it to the State Council Legislative Committee. The document consists of three parts: a summary of shortcomings in the old law, a list of areas where the two differ (in the framework that the old law has to be changed), and a proposal for a revised Copyright Law.[37]

---

34. Paragraph 9 stated: "The Chinese Government will recognize this MOU as an agreement under Article 2 of the Copyright Law of the People's Republic of China which shall provide a basis for protection of works, including computer programs, and sound recordings of U.S. nationals published outside of China until such time as China accedes to the Berne Convention and the Geneva Convention. Such protection shall become effective 60 days after signature of this MOU."

35. A relatively rare, although not unprecedented, phenomenon in the intersection of domestic and international law.

36. Interview 99BJ33, July 30, 1999.

37. Interview 98BJ09A, July 10, 1998.

The State Council was reportedly not at all pleased with the NCA-proposed Copyright Law revisions. Members of the State Council believed that it remained "too foreign" and not sufficiently sensitive to "Chinese circumstances." It ignored the stages of economic development in China that make IPR a difficult concept to implement. Some in the State Council even described proponents of IPR as "people in white shirts and suits who sell things to China that cost many tons of rice, and which are too expensive."[38] The State Council made its displeasure known: "Since our country acceded to the International Copyright Convention, there arose a double standard (*shuangchong biaozhun*) in which the level of protection for foreigners' copyright is greater than the level of protection for the copyright of the Chinese people." The document then outlined the areas in which foreign copyright was accorded greater protection than those of domestic copyright holders, as summarized below. The State Council ordered the NCA to take these matters into account and to draft a revised Copyright Law by December 1998.

Indeed, it was this last article (Article 43) that would also provide a particularly contentious lightning rod for domestic political conflict and maneuvering in anticipation of the revised Copyright Law. The NCA submitted a draft Copyright Law to the Legislative Affairs Office of the State Council, where it was signed by Premier Zhu Rongji. It was then sent to the Legal Work Committee (*fazhi gongzuo weiyuanhui*) of the National People's Congress (NPC). Finally, it was sent to the NPC Standing Committee, according to the December deadline stipulated by the State Council. The NPC Standing Committee debated the issue from December 23 to 26, 1998, but the draft was sent back to committee. Another version was sent up to the NPC Standing Committee in April 1999; it was also sent back. There was an aborted attempt again in June, but too many conflicts remained, especially those pertaining to Article 43.[39]

The debate over Article 43 involved two broad groups of political actors in China. On the one hand were artists, the representatives of Chinese units and enterprises involved in recording audio materials, and published authors. This group was stronger than it might initially appear because more than 150 members of the Standing Committee of the NPC were themselves artists, authors, and educators who fell into this category and had a considerable degree of empathy for this group. Their demands included being allowed copyright protection of their work when it was broadcast on state-controlled media outlets, whether through television, radio, or some other public broadcast system. The other side was represented by the Ministry of Radio, Film, and Television and the powerful Central Committee Propaganda Department. This group was firmly opposed to such a change because it would mean having to compensate the former group from a

---

38. Ibid.
39. Interview 99BJ26, July 21, 1999; and Interview 99BJ33, July 30, 1999.

TABLE 4.1.

Summary of state council objections surrounding foreign-Chinese copyright protection

Provisions on implementing international copyright treaties	Copyright law/regulations on protecting computer software	Explanation (*shouming*)/comment by the state council
Article 6	N.A.[1]	Foreigners utility designs are protected while those of Chinese are not.
Article 7	Article 24 (Regulations) Article 15 (Regulations)	Nonregistered foreign copyright (registration optional for foreigners) are valid 50 years, Chinese (required) registered copyrights valid 25 years, with option for another 25 years.
Article 10	Article 22 (CR Law)	The strictness of use rights that protect foreigners is greater than those protecting Chinese copyright owners.
Article 11	N.A.	Copyright owners of foreign works have the exclusive right to authorize any performance, while Chinese copyright holders do not have these rights for "mechanized" performance (*jiqie biaoyan quan*).
Article 12	N.A.	Copyright owners of foreign cinematographic works, television works, and works of video recordings have greater rights to authorize public performances of their works than their Chinese counterparts.
Article 13	Article 32 (CR Law)	Prior authorization of the copyright owner shall be required for newspapers and periodicals to reprint a foreign work, except the reprinting of articles on current political, economic and social topics; for Chinese copyright owners, after their work is printed, it can be reprinted without the permission.
Article 14	N.A.	Only foreigners have lease rights over their copyrighted cinematic works; Chinese do not.
Article 15	N.A.	Copyright owners of foreign works have certain rights that prohibit the importation of their works; Chinese do not.
Article 16/18	Article 35 (CR Law)	In the case of public performances, recording and broadcasting of foreign works, and sound recordings, the provisions of the Berne Convention shall apply, but not to Chinese works.
	Article 37 (CR Law)	A producer of sound recordings who, for the production of sound recordings, exploits an unpublished work created by others shall obtain permission from,

---

1. *No specific corresponding legislation.*

(continued)

TABLE 4.1.—*cont.*

Provisions on implementing international copyright treaties	Copyright law/regulations on protecting computer software	Explanation (*shouming*)/ comment by the state council
		and pay remuneration to, the copyright owner. A producer of sound recordings who, for the production of a sound recording, exploits a published work created by others, does not need permission. This limited protection is offered to Chinese; foreigners enjoy fuller protection based on the Berne Convention.
	Article 43 (CR Law)	A radio station or a television stations may broadcast, for noncommercial purposes, a published sound recording without seeking permission from, or paying remuneration to, the copyright owner, performer, and producer of the sound recording. This limited protection is offered to Chinese; foreigners enjoy fuller protection based on the Berne Convention.

Source: Limited Circulation State Council Document, 1998

dwindling pool of budgetary outlays for operating costs.[40] Given NPC support of the first group, the two sides were more evenly matched, making the debate particularly difficult to settle.[41]

Nevertheless, most of these issues were resolved by the time the revised Copyright Law was promulgated in 2001, but they continued to defy resolution at the local level. Resistance to the Copyright Law or to the notion of copyright more generally made it very difficult to convince people in the localities, whether officials, consumers, or pirates, to take the law seriously, especially if important political actors signaled their hostility to the law by vigorously opposing measures contained in it.[42] Indeed, the domestic debate over Article 43 provides a window into the fragmentation of the

40. See Daniel C. Lynch, *After the Propaganda State: Media, Politics, and "Thought Work" in Reformed China* (Stanford: Stanford University Press, 1999).

41. Interviews 99BJ26, July 21, 1999; and Interview 99BJ33, July 30, 1999.

42. Activities that further undermined the credibility of the notion that strong laws protect copyright came from an unexpected source. After the 1996 agreement, the by now infamous Shenfei Laser Corporation in Shenzhen, previously one of the chief Chinese manufacturers of pirated CD-ROMs, became a legitimate Warner Bros. licensee. By 1998, however, Shenfei was "getting clobbered" by pirated audiovisual products produced in Hong Kong and exported to China. One industry insider, a staunch supporter of copyright but nonetheless sympathetic to Shenfei's plight, noted of the U.S. response, "We didn't realize that the problem would move to countries with good copyright laws [i.e. Hong Kong]," which did little to convince Shenfei that it had "done the right thing." Interview 98US17, December 9, 1998.

political system and the sometimes diametrically opposed interests surrounding the specific provisions of the Copyright Law among various actors that were in some cases charged with some aspects of enforcement of these very laws and regulations. Nevertheless, the issue was not purely political; it had an institutional and organizational basis as well. Indeed, the layout of the administrative infrastructure for copyright management and enforcement in China is such that the Copyright Law and related laws and regulations cannot be effectively enforced. Much of the story of China's inability to implement its own copyright law effectively has to do with the structure of the administrative apparatus for protecting copyright.

China's Copyright Administration

Even while these developments were unfolding, it was becoming increasingly clear that the principal arena for compliance was not the legal-judicial realm but rather the administrative enforcement apparatus. The laws are extremely important in that they shape and constrain the outer parameters of enforcement, but they do not guarantee actual compliance on their own. Nor, taken alone, do they anticipate actual patterns of enforcement or, for that matter, *non*-enforcement. The Chinese were able to implement the 1992 MOU, which largely called for legislative action, to the general satisfaction of most people. The problem grew to be one of enforcement, thus becoming an issue of *administration*. The next two sets of negotiations, culminating in the 1995 and 1996 bilateral agreements, focused overwhelmingly on enforcement. However, even these agreements did not fully take into account the enormous difficulties in actually implementing these copyright-related laws and regulations. To understand the degree of copyright protection that exists in China, we must shift our focus to the administrative bureaucratic apparatus charged with copyright enforcement. The following sections will show that this institutional environment is defined by the copyright bureaucracy's fragmentation, embeddedness, and dependency on its various host bureaucracies.

Organizational History

The organizational history of China's copyright bureaucracy is similar in some ways to that of the patent bureaucracy. They are both relatively young organizations, both endured their formative organizational years in the early to mid-1980s, and both were under the yoke of a superior, or host, bureaucracy, the priorities and goals of which could not be expected to be the same at all times. In other ways, however, the two bureaucracies are quite different. Patent matters revolve largely around science and technology issues, and the patent bureaucracy is firmly nestled within the science and technology *xitong* (cluster of functionally-related bureaucracies). The copyright bureaucracy, by contrast, is embedded within a *xitong* that concerns itself with cultural, ideological, and value-laden media and is therefore involved in a more politically sensitive environment, even if technical copyright issues themselves are no more or less "political" than those pertaining to patents or trademarks.

The Central People's Government Publishing General Administration (*Zhongyang renmin zhengfu chuban zongshu*) was established in November 1949 in accordance with Article 18 of the Central People's Government Organic Law. Exactly five years later, it was reorganized and subsumed under the Ministry of Culture and renamed the Ministry of Culture Publications Bureau (*wenhua bu chuban ju*). In May 1970, publications work was placed within the State Council, under the State Council Culture Organization (*Guowuyuan wenhua zu*). From September 30, 1975, to May 1982, publishing responsibilities remained directly administered by the State Council, but under the newly named National Publications Enterprises Management Bureau (*Guojia chuban shiye guanli ju*). In 1982, it was placed within the Ministry of Culture, and on July 25, 1985, it was renamed the National and Publications Administration of the Ministry of Culture. At the same time, the National Copyright Administration was established, although organizationally it was largely the same unit as the Press and Publications Administration (they enjoyed a "one organization, two signboards" relationship). In June 1986, these offices were moved out from under the Ministry of Culture and directly administered by the State Council; in January 1987, the Publications Bureau was renamed the National Press and Publications Administration (*Guojia xinwen chuban shu*).[43] Finally, in April 2001, it was made the National Press and Publications General Administration (*Guojia xinwen chuban zongshu*) and upgraded to ministry-level rank.[44]

One of the first local-level (in this case, provincial) Copyright Bureaus was that of Sichuan, which was established in 1987, and in the next two to three years, many other provinces followed suit.[45] Shanghai established the Copyright Division (*Shanghai shi banquan chu*) in 1988, while Chongqing did not establish one until 1990. Yunnan province set up its Copyright Department the same year as Sichuan, although like all of its counterparts, its beginnings were modest. Its evolution is typical: Founded on August 27, 1987, a year after the provincial Press and Publications Administration was separated from the provincial Culture Bureau, the Yunnan Copyright Department originally had a staff of two. In 1990, on the eve of the promulgation of the Copyright Law, the staff allocation (*bianzhi*) was raised and three new people were hired (one legal expert, one expert in foreign languages, and a computer specialist). Although the official staff allocation stood at four, the Yunnan

---

43. *Zhonghua renmin gongheguo zhongyang zhengfu jigou 1949–1990* [Central Government Organs of the People's Republic of China, 1949–1990] (Beijing: *Jingji kexue chubanshe*, 1993), 518–20; and *Zhonghua renmin gongheguo zhengfu jigou wushi nian* [Government Organizations of the People's Republic of China over Fifty Years] (Beijing: *Dangjian duwu chubanshe yu Guojia xingzheng chubanshe*, 2000), 149–50.

44. Interview 02BJ07, August 9, 2002.

45. Interview 99CD01, June 25, 1999.

Copyright Bureau was eventually able to hire more than that number.[46] However, it was in 1995–96, after the signing of the "Exchange of Letters" and the "Action Plan" annex between the United States and China, that the Yunnan Copyright Bureau received a major boost: its staff allocation was increased to include a ten-person "investigation team [brigade]" (*jicha dui*), which it shared with the Press and Publication Bureau (in a "one set of people, two different signboards" relationship), and it was given a one-time budgetary supplement of 400,000 yuan ($48,000) for cars, computers, and monitoring equipment.[47] The nature of the personnel allocations shifted in 2002 from a "quasi-enterprise/commercial" allocation (*shiye bianzhi*) to a purely administrative allocation (*xingzheng bianzhi*), meaning that a greater share of the operating cost is borne by the provincial government.[48] This is due in part to a desire for increased professionalism on the part of these teams and other bureaucratic actors and the granting of "civil servant" status, a trend that is occurring in all of the IPR bureaucracies and other government agencies.[49]

In the past several years, the *bianzhi* for the Yunnan Copyright Bureau went up to five and back down again to four; the Shanghai Copyright Bureau also had its personnel allocation reduced from fifteen to six.[50] This reflects the fact that even the thinly staffed copyright departments were not spared the knife during the bureaucratic downsizing of 1998–99. On the plus side, however, in 1999 all provincial-level press and publications administrations were upgraded from a second-tier bureau rank (*er ji ju*) to a first-tier bureau rank (*yi ji ju*).[51] Although the Copyright Bureaus remain subordinate to the press and publications administrations (discussed in detail in the next section), in the past few years they have been able to ride the latter's coattails up a bureaucratic half-step.

Structure: Scarcity, Embeddedness, and Dependency

The behavior of the copyright bureaucracy, particularly at the local level, often has as much to do with *where* it is as with *what* it is.[52] Although it

---

46. Interview 98CQ03, March 25, 1998; Interview 99SH13, May 20, 1999; and Interview 03KM01, July 15, 2003.

47. Interview 99KM03, June 18, 1999. The annual budget for this investigation team is 100,000 yuan.

48. Interview 03KM01, July 15, 2003. This occurred in Sichuan and other provinces throughout China at around the same time. Interview 03CD04, July 16, 2003.

49. This also requires higher standards of recruitment in order to increase the quality of personnel while the actual quantity of staff levels is being reduced or remains unchanged. Interview 03CD01, July 14, 2003 and Interview 03GY01, July 19, 2003.

50. Interview 02SH07, June 28, 2002; and Interview 03KM01, July 15, 2003.

51. Interview 02KM02, July 23, 2002.

52. This section is based on the following interviews: Interview 98CQ06B, August 10, 1998; Interview 98GY02, August 18, 1998; Interview 98GY06A, August 21, 1998; Interview 98KM02, September 1, 1998; Interview 99BJ29, Beijing, July 28, 1999; Interview 02SH07, June 28, 2002; Interview 02CD05, July 12, 2002; Interview 02KM02, July 23, 2002; and Interview 02GY01, July 24, 2002; Interview 03KM01, July 15, 2003; Interview 03CD04, July 16, 2003; and Interview 03GY02, July 19, 2003.

is physically separate from the National Press and Publications Administration, the National Copyright Administration (NCA) remains a subordinate organization. The director general (*shuzhang*) of the Press and Publications Bureau has five deputies (in charge of, respectively, books, periodicals, anti-pornography/anti-illegal [*saohuang dafei*] work, distribution, and copyright).[53] The NCA has a director (*sizhang*) and vice directors and oversees the following departments (*chu*). Traditionally, there were two "copyright departments" (numbered "1" and "2") that were merged after 1998 with a corresponding staff cut from six to three.[54] There is also a legal department (*falu chu*) and an administrative reconsideration department (*xingzheng fuyi chu*), which actually are the same office with two different formal names,[55] a comprehensive department (into which the international service department [*guoji yewu chu*] was merged in 1998), and an information and propaganda department (*xinxi xuanchuan chu*).

There have been some important changes at the legislative and policy levels in the past few years. In addition to the promulgation of the revised Copyright Law in 2001, more recent developments point to the notion that the national-level authorities are taking copyright protection increasingly seriously. For example, a recent judicial interpretation issued by the Supreme People's Court makes it a civil liability (*minshi zeren*) to use unauthorized software in a commercial environment.[56] This is the first time that the end-user is specifically mentioned in the law, which makes it very difficult for judges to sidestep the issue. Of course, there are procedural problems, as always, but this is a significant step forward in publicly committing the Chinese government to going after end-users. It is less clear how this extends to government units or to individuals. As far as individual end-users are concerned, the law remains ambiguous but the thinking seems to be: "We do not say that 'individual end user piracy is OK,' we just simply do not have the energy to regulate this huge phenomenon at the present time."[57]

In another development, in 2002 the General Office of the State Council issued Document 47, "Vigorously Promote the Strength of Software Production Activity" (*zhenxing ruanjian chanye xingdong gangyao*), which covers a range of issues, including those directly related to copyright. One of its stipulations is that if a government agency initiates an information technology project, software must account for at least 30 percent of the total project cost. The logic is that such a regulation will force the purchase of legitimate

53. Because no formal, open organizational chart is available, this reconstruction is based on interviews with NCA officials and others in 1999 and 2002.

54. Interview 99BJ11A, March 18, 1999.

55. Like the comprehensive department/international service department, these two units are formally treated separately, but are in fact the same office. Interview 02BJ07, August 9, 2002.

56. *Zuigao renmin fayuan guanyu shenli zhuzuoquan minshi jiufen anjian shiyong falu ruogan wenti de jieshi* [Interpretation by the Supreme People's Court on Some Issues Regarding the Application of the Law to Hearing Cases of Civil Copyright Disputes], October 15, 2002.

57. Interview 03BJ03, July 24, 2003.

software. Other ministries, such as the Ministry of Commerce and the Ministry of Education, have also issued similar, follow-up documents.

These developments are positive; nevertheless, the piracy rate for software remained at 92 percent in 2002, with China outpaced only by Vietnam as the greatest pirater of software.[58] The majority of problems faced by the copyright bureaucracy exist below the national level, in the context of local administrative enforcement, where the structure of the bureaucracy is breathtakingly weak. One NCA official expressed his frustration to me with the stunning statistic that "there are only 200 people in all of China engaged in full-time copyright management work." In contrast to the NCA, which endeavors to be a showcase for China's progress in copyright protection, its provincial-level counterparts are little more than lonely outposts scattered along China's copyright protection frontier.[59]

The copyright bureaucracy at the provincial level is nestled within the Provincial Press and Publications Bureau (PPPB, or *xinwen chuban ju*). The office of the "Provincial Copyright *Bureau*" (PCB, or *banquan ju*) is nothing more than a formal title to give it a nominally higher bureaucratic rank (and increased bargaining power) vis-à-vis its dealings with other provincial administrative units. The office in the PPPB charged with day-to-day copyright management work is the copyright *department* (PCD, or *banquan chu*), which is a "department" (*chu*) and thus an administrative step down in rank from the bureau (*ju*) level.[60]

This reflects a curious but deliberate organizational logic. Administrative rank is very important in the bargaining nexus of Chinese politics. The ranking system enables each unit to appraise its status with respect to all other units. At the provincial level, the top ranking is that of a "first-tier bureau" (until 1999, the Press and Publications Bureau was a second-tier bureau). A "bureau," whether first- or second-tier, outranks the copyright department (which is a "department," or *chu*), the administrative unit charged with provincial-level copyright-related work. Although two administrative units with a *ju* ranking cannot issue binding orders to one another,

58. Ibid. See also Chris Buckley, "Helped by Technology, Piracy of DVD's Runs Rampant in China," *New York Times*, August 18, 2003.

59. U.S. negotiators saw that NCA officials were "very smart" but that they had "no teeth." Interview 98HK02, June 22, 1998. A former NCA official was unsparing in his criticism of his local level counterparts: "The cadres in charge of managing the provincial-level copyright bureaus are severely lacking in ability [*banquan guanli de ren shi wuneng de*]. . . . It does not matter if you have three or three hundred or ten thousand people because the result would be exactly the same. . . . These people tend to be reactive instead of proactive. . . . Nobody will know who you are if you do not make an effort to establish a name for yourself and this is why the provincial-level copyright bureaus remain understaffed and under funded." Interview 99BJ23, July 19, 1999.

60. In practice, what this means is that the "director" (*juzhang*) of the PPPB is the *juzhang* of the PCB/PCD. One of several vice directors (*fu juzhang*) of the PPPB is assigned to be the vice director of the PCB. This latter individual is the administrative superior of the "department head" (*chuzhang*) of the copyright department (PCD), who is charged with the day-to-day responsibilities of the copyright department and all copyright-related work at the provincial level.

a *ju* is more likely to take the issues that vary with its own priorities into account if they originate from a unit with the same administrative rank than from a lower-ranking "department," or *chu*. To compensate for this, the provincial copyright department has been given the *ju* ranking (through the creation of its "shadow" organization, the PCB, or *banquan ju*) so that it can enter into interagency negotiations with other administrative units on a nominally equal footing. One provincial-level copyright official put it this way: "In public we regard [the copyright office] as a 'bureau' [*ju*], but in private we consider it a 'department' [*chu*]."[61] In practice, this has the effect not of elevating the copyright departments beyond a nominal *ju* ranking but rather of obliterating the separation between the copyright departments and the Press and Publications Bureaus in which the former units are embedded. Another official was even less charitable, calling the PCD "an empty shell" (*kongde jiazi*).[62]

The provincial Copyright Bureau, as part of a "one organization, two signboards" relationship (that is, with the PPPB), is completely subordinate to the Provincial Press and Publications Bureau. This means that the copyright department/Copyright Bureau lacks any organizational identity apart from the Press and Publications Bureau.[63] Personnel and budgetary allocations for the copyright department are decided by the Press and Publications Bureau, and any PCD requests for additional human or financial resources must be addressed to the PPPB and not to the provincial government (doing so would be a significant breach of organizational reporting relationships).[64]

The PCD is responsible for carrying out the relevant Chinese copyright laws, regulations, and policies; hearing cases of copyright disputes and providing administrative decisions and punishments according to Article 46 of the Copyright Law[65]; supervising copyright-related commercial activities in the province; providing copyright-related training to administrative officials at the provincial level and below; organizing the examination and verification of copyright contracts and participating in related arbitration proceedings; providing recommendations for the contractual registration of foreign audio and visual products and publications; and awarding practical use rights for copyright. The PCD is also charged with achieving local,

---

61. When I asked this official—the ranking official of the copyright bureau of the province—if he was the vice bureau chief of the press and publications bureau or the vice bureau chief of the copyright bureau, his response was, "Yes, of both" (*dou shi*).

62. Interview 99NJ01B, July 9, 1999; and Interview 99BJ29, July 28, 1999.

63. Interview 98GY06, August 21, 1998.

64. Interview 02SH07, June 28, 2002; Interview 02CD05, July 12, 2002; Interview 02KM02, July 23, 2002; and Interview 02GY01, July 24, 2002.

65. Article 46 of the Copyright Law stipulates that "anyone who commits . . . acts of infringement shall bear civil liability for such remedies as ceasing the infringing act, eliminating its ill effects, making a public apology or paying compensation for damages, etc., depending on the circumstances, and may, in addition, be subjected by the copyright bureau department to such administrative penalties as confiscation of unlawful income from the act, or imposition of a fine."

provincial-level compliance with national and international copyright laws, regulations, and agreements.

These subdivisions notwithstanding, there are generally no formal functional divisions (*ke*) within the PCD; these tasks are assigned to individual staff members, and the scope of the copyright department's responsibilities lies in sharp contrast to the number of people assigned to perform these tasks and to the general resources at hand.[66] In theory, the institutional framework of the Press and Publications Bureau in which the PCD is embedded mitigates these constraints—for example, additional staff may be allocated on a temporary basis from other PPPB units. In practice, this institutional framework serves to further exacerbate these constraints. In particular, the embeddedness of the copyright department within the PPPB results in a severe constriction of the available options for independent action on the part of the copyright department and a corresponding overreliance on the Press and Publications Bureau.

Although officials in these units are usually quick to assert that additional personnel can be drawn from other Press and Publications Bureau offices when needed, the associated coordination costs are often very high, and such activity only serves to underscore and to reinforce the dependency of the PCD on the PPPB.[67] Mobilizing extra personnel from the Press and Publications Bureau and from other provincial-level administrative offices requires drawing them away from their regular duties, as well as expending time and other resources in training them for the new tasks to which they have been temporarily assigned. Doing so requires a great deal of preparation and involves a significant amount of intra-agency bargaining. As one official colorfully put it, "There is only one cake, and many people are eating from it (*yige dangao xuduo ren chi*)."[68] Moreover, the frequency of this type of mobilization is determined by other PPPB priorities, not by the needs of the copyright departments.[69] As the Economist Intelligence Unit has written:

> For most copyright holders, the main impediment to copyright enforcement is the [National Copyright Agency] itself, which is horribly understaffed and lacking in a well-developed network of local

66. A selected list places these numbers, as of 1999, as follows: Anhui (3 to 4), Chongqing (3), Gansu (6), Guizhou (5), Heilongjiang (6, with an allocation for 10), Henan (6), Hubei (4), Jiangsu (3), Shaanxi (4, allocation for 10), Shanghai (11), Sichuan (5), and Yunnan (6). Moreover, in many areas since 1999, these numbers have actually gone down because of bureaucratic downsizing, although not by much.

67. Interview 98CQ06, August 10, 1998; Interview 99SH13, May 20, 1999; Interview 99CD01, June 25, 1999; Interview 02SH07, June 28, 2002; Interview 02CD05, July 12, 2002; Interview 02KM02, July 23, 2002; and Interview 02GY01, July 24, 2002.

68. Interview 98GY02, August 19, 1998.

69. The exception is when the campaign is national in scope. In such instances, money is made available through nationally mandated, top-down channels, and the local copyright departments do not have to go begging with their hats in their hands. Interview 99SH13, May 20, 1999.

agencies with strong enforcement capacity. Furthermore, the [NCA] suffers from a conflict of interest with its parent body, the [Press] and Publications Administration (PPA). The PPA is concerned mainly with censorship and has no interest in promoting the rights of authors or creating a free market in publishing. *The [NCA's] lack of funding is at least partly because of a conscious decision by the PPA to ignore copyright issues.*[70]

Because of the substantial transaction and opportunity costs involved, such mobilization tends to be irregular and short-lived and to revolve around *organizationally* mandated timing. It is not based on the fluid "piracy situation" on the ground. It is therefore not surprising that mobilization at the provincial level often takes the form of political campaigns of the pre-reform period. These "enforcement events" are sporadic, incapable of responding swiftly to specific problems, and are not sustainable over time. This stands in marked contrast to the operations of the pirates, who are often scattered throughout a given geographical area, highly mobile, and prone to exploiting flexible and sophisticated "exit strategies" to stay several steps ahead of the authorities.[71]

Nowhere does the copyright department's subordination to the Press and Publications Bureau have a more direct impact on copyright enforcement than in the restrictions on the PCD's ability to mobilize PPPB investigation teams (*jicha dui*). The Press and Publications Bureau and the copyright department share the services of these enforcement teams, but the teams report to the Press and Publications Bureau and not to the copyright department.[72] In some instances, requests for the establishment of copyright-specific investigation teams have been rebuffed with the argument that "an investigation team already exists; why do we need another one?"[73] The Provincial Press and Publications Bureau investigation teams supervise publishing houses (and to a lesser extent, retail markets) to ensure production quality, appropriateness of content, and the legitimate operation of publishing enterprises, which can include, but does not *necessarily* consist of, copyright enforcement.

70. Economist Intelligence Unit, *China Hand: The Complete Guide to Doing Business in China* (Hong Kong: Economist Intelligence Unit, 1999), 51 (italics mine). This is at least equally the case (and often more so) with regard to the culture bureaucracy at the sub-provincial level, as described in the next section.

71. Interview 98SH07, May 13, 1998; and Interview 98BJ09B, July 16, 1998. One method to decrease this enforcement shortfall has been the establishment of copyright piracy hotlines for consumers to report incidences of illegal sales of pirated products. However, because the average price of a pirated DVD is one-sixth the cost of a legitimate DVD, there is little, if any, incentive for consumers to use these hotlines.

72. Moreover, the investigation teams and the Provincial Copyright Department share the same administrative rank, so the Provincial Copyright Department cannot compel the PPPB investigation team to assist in copyright enforcement work. Interview 99KM03, June 18, 1999.

73. This is compounded by the difficulty of increasing *bianzhi* allocations for investigation teams as a result of national efforts to curtail the use of investigation teams to generate illicit revenue for local governments. Interview 99BJ35, August 3, 1999.

In some cases, as in Sichuan, the investigation teams concentrate on the campaign against pornography and illegal publications (discussed below). As a result, the Sichuan Copyright Department has been forced to recruit the support of other administrative enforcement units, such as those under the Public Security Bureau, to assist in copyright enforcement.[74] In Yunnan, by contrast, the provincial-level investigation teams are somewhat more involved in copyright enforcement. However, the current Yunnan PPPB investigation team of ten (with an estimated annual budget of 100,000 yuan, or $12,000) is hardly able to monitor the more than 2,000 stalls (*tandian*) in the capital city of Kunming alone, many of which (probably the overwhelming majority) are at least partially engaged in the sale of pirated compact disks and video compact disks (VCDs).[75] In Shanghai, the municipal copyright department's investigation team leaves "pornography investigation" to other agencies and concentrates its scarce resources on copyright enforcement.[76]

Process: "Sweeping Away Pornography, Striking Down Illegals" (Saohuang Dafei)

As a result of limited personnel and budgetary resources, the provincial copyright department, through the Provincial Press and Publications Bureau and the provincial copyright department's nominally superior alter ego, the Provincial Copyright Bureau, often ends up recruiting extra personnel from other administrative agencies to undertake coordinated action on a larger scale.[77] This activity increased after June 1996 in the wake of the Sino-U.S. IPR negotiations and is discussed later in this chapter. However, the nature of this coordinated activity only underscores many of the problems outlined above, but on a larger scale: transaction costs through larger coordination problems substantially hinder efforts at swift and sustained enforcement. Moreover, in practice, copyright issues are often subsumed to other enforcement goals of the participating government units. A good example of the convergence of all of these dimensions is the campaign against pornography and illegal publications (*saohuang dafei*).[78]

74. Interview 99CD01, June 25, 1999. Many Chinese software producers avoid the Provincial Copyright Department altogether, preferring to engage the Administration for Industry and Commerce's Economic Inspection Teams to crack down on copyright pirates by invoking China's Unfair Competition Law. Interview 99BJ24, July 20, 1999; and Interview 99BJ25, July 21, 1999. This has had the effect of arousing resentment in the copyright bureaucracy. Interview 03BJ03, July 24, 2003.
75. Interview 99KM03, June 18, 1999; and Interview 99KM05, June 22, 1999.
76. Interview 99SH13, May 20, 1999. This problem is not unique to copyright. The same scarcity of resources and bureaucratic wrangling for the services of investigation teams is faced by the Administration for Industry and Commerce (AIC). However, as we shall see in chapter 5, this resource scarcity and institutional embeddedness is mitigated by interbureaucratic competition and exogenous pressure.
77. See, for example, "Yunnan Increases IPR Protection: Yunnan Province Steps up Protection of Intellectual Property Rights," *Yunnan Daily*, January 29, 1995, 1; translated in FBIS.
78. For a brief summary of this campaign, see *Zhongguo da juece jishi, 1978–1998* [Record of Important Decisions in China, 1978–1998] (Beijing: *Guangming ribao chubanshe*, 1998), 432–52.

Established at the Fourth Plenum of the Thirteenth Central Committee in 1989, the *saohuang dafei* campaign has evolved into a semi-regular movement to "sweep away pornography" (*saohuang*) and to "strike out against illegal publications" (*dafei*).[79] "Illegal publications" include those deemed "anti-government" or "anti-Party," but they can also include illegally produced (i.e., copyright-violating) published works.[80] At the national level, this campaign brings together a host of administrative enforcement units under the guidance of a *saohuang dafei* leadership small group (*saohuang dafei lingdao xiaozu*), including representatives from the Ministry of Culture, the National Copyright Administration, the Administration for Industry and Commerce, the General Administration of Customs, the Bureau of Radio, Film, and Television, and the Ministry of Public Security.[81] In addition, the day-to-day coordinating liaison, the *saohuang dafei* working office, placed within the National Press and Publications Administration, coordinates among these other administrative units to pool human and financial resources in mobilizing these regular campaigns, which take place once or twice a year and can last for up to several months. This organizational structure, with some variation, is replicated at the provincial level.[82] As of 2002, this office holds a second-tier bureau-level (*futing ji ju*) rank at the provincial level.[83]

Although for functional reasons the *saohuang dafei* working office is placed within the national- and provincial-level Press and Publications/Copyright

79. *Zhongguo chuban nianjian 1996* [China Publications Yearbook 1996] (Beijing: *Zhongguo chuban nianjian bianji*, 1996), 33. "*Saohuang dafei*" can be translated as "sweep away pornography and strike out against illegally-published materials." For narrative smoothness, I refer to the campaign by its Chinese name.

80. As a rule, these publications list an authorized publishing house (and a corresponding SID, or source identification code) as the place where these goods were published. Very often, these publishing houses have no idea that their names and addresses are being used in these illegal publications, and the only way to confirm whether such material is illegal is to contact the publishing house listed and inquire whether it is publishing the work in question (pirated publications often list a different publishing house, which, although legitimate, is not actually authorized to produce these particular works). This, however, offers no clue as to the actual origin, which is often located in a different province than is indicated on the copyright-infringing work. Interview 99KM05, June 22, 1999.

81. Other agencies include the state security bureaucracy; the post office (pornography-related mail fraud); the railway, traffic, and airline bureaucracies. The travel-related organizations are more closely connected to piracy than one might think: as the U.S. consul in Chengdu joked to me: "The Chinese premiere of Western movies in the Southwest is often on the Chengdu-Chongqing bus!" The number of participating units in Sichuan and Guizhou is around sixteen, while in Yunnan the number is twice that. In some cases, the public security bureaucracy has its own separate *saohuang dafei* office that handles prostitution. Interview 02CD01, July 11, 2002; and Interview 02KM02, July 23, 2002.

82. Before the *saohuang dafei* office was moved into the press and publications bureaus from the Ministry of Culture's cultural market management departments in or around 1998, there was a "one organization, three different signboards" situation in the cultural market management department involving the cultural market management department, the office of commission on social culture, and the *saohuang dafei* office. Below the provincial level, *saohuang dafei* offices are in the bureaucracy headed by the Ministry of Culture. The head of the *saohuang dafei* leadership small group is the vice secretary of the provincial Party committee and the director of the provincial party propaganda department. Interview 02GY03, July 25, 2002.

83. Interview 02CD05, July 12, 2002.

Figure 4.1. *Saohuang Dafei* and related propaganda banners, Kunming (top) and Beijing (bottom), 1999. Photos by author.

Bureau apparatus, it is somewhat more powerful than such placement implies.[84] The director general of the National Press and Publications Administration is also vice director of the Chinese Communist Party Propaganda Department.[85] Moreover, as a result of several factors, including political salience, leadership support, and gradual institutionalization over time, the *saohuang dafei* campaign's transaction costs have been mitigated to some degree. The campaign itself is often highly visible; propaganda banners prohibiting the sales of such goods are prominently displayed in wholesale and

84. Below the provincial level, it is housed within the culture bureaucracy. Interview 03GY02, July 19, 2003.

85. In Guizhou province, the leader of the provincial *saohuang dafei* leadership small group is also the director of the Guizhou province propaganda department. Interview 99GY01, June 14, 1999. However, the propaganda bureaucracy appears to be playing less of a day-to-day role, although it is instrumental in establishing the broad policy goals for *saohuang dafei*. Interview 03GY02, July 19, 2003.

retail markets (albeit in close physical proximity to a brisk and voluminous trade in pirated compact disks and video compact discs [VCDs] and DVDs).

Yet this last point illustrates the tension between *saohuang dafei* and copyright enforcement. Although some officials point to the *saohuang dafei* campaign as an example of enforcement action against copyright pirates (or, at least, with positive externalities that spill over into copyright enforcement), these same officials do not regard the campaign as an explicit anti-piracy movement.[86] The logic behind such reasoning is that because the sale of pornographic and antigovernment works is illegal in China, it is by definition an infringement of copyright (or represents, in theory at least, the illegal licensing of the pornographers' copyright). However, although one can liberally interpret the sale of pornography and antigovernment works as an infringement of copyright, most copyright piracy in China (one official placed it at 80 percent) is *not* pornographic or antigovernment in nature. The majority of copyright infringement in China is politically neutral: computer application software, compact disks, VCDs, DVDs, technical books, journals, and other publications. Most copyright piracy in China falls outside the spirit and the letter, and thus the crosshairs, of the *saohuang dafei* campaign. Even when such "apolitical" and "nonpornographic" goods are seized, the violators are typically issued a fine, while those violating the *saohuang dafei* targets are jailed or even executed.[87]

The *saohuang dafei* campaigns thus reflect many of the problems associated with copyright enforcement in China. First, the principal targets are pirated publications and audiovisual goods, but they are not usually regarded as copyright-infringing products (which often involve civil penalties), but rather as "reactionary" and "socially disruptive" commodities, which carry far more severe criminal penalties. This reinforces the disinclination to use existing copyright legislation and regulations, undercutting the importance of copyright more generally.

Second, although the political salience and the gradual institutionalization of the issue can substantially reduce coordination problems, it does not eliminate them. Part of the problem is the growing complexity of the membership rolls for the *saohuang dafei* movement—at the provincial level in Yunnan, for example, there are more than *thirty* participating units.[88] Significant lead time is thus required to launch the campaign, which takes the form of waves, rather than consistent and sustained enforcement. Once the campaign is over, the status quo ante often returns until the next campaign. One retailer in Kunming told me that "there is a crackdown twice a week by the investigation teams, but everybody hides their illegal VCDs while they are here and only puts the legal ones on display."[89] On

---

86. These officials see *saohuang dafei* as a movement separate from copyright enforcement work. Interview 99CD01, June 25, 1999; Interview 99SH13, May 20, 1999; and Interview 03GY02, July 19, 2003.
87. Interview 03GY02, July 19, 2003.
88. Interview 03KM01, July 15, 2003.
89. Interview 99KM04, June 23, 1999.

many occasions, street merchants offering pirated VCDs apologetically told me to "come back again next week" because a piracy crackdown was underway. Indeed, by the summer of 2002, this response to crackdowns was so streamlined that the ubiquitous DVD street pirates on North Shaanxi Road in Shanghai would simply close their briefcases and disappear when their lookouts spotted enforcement agents, only to return in hours, if not minutes. Others worked out of legitimate clothing stores (for a fee to the owner) or from adjacent construction sites, casually handing out their cell phone numbers to "preferred customers."[90] This testifies to the inability of the *saohuang dafei* or any such campaign to provide sustained and expeditious responses to the infractions it targets.

Finally, the *saohuang dafei* mechanism simply reflects the inability of the Press and Publications/Copyright Bureau system to mobilize the resources necessary for such activity on its own and thus its dependence on other local enforcement units. Moreover, this dependency is even more pronounced below the provincial level, the focus of the next section.

The "Mother of all 'Mothers-in-Law'": The Culture Bureaucracy

In the summer of 2002, I met with three provincial-level officials in the copyright bureaucracy who regaled me about the sub-provincial level exploits of "their" (i.e., copyright) enforcement team, a team that appeared to be quite large, well-paid, and effective. I was impressed and surprised, but I remained skeptical. After they finished their account, I probed with some follow-up questions. Finally, they grudgingly acknowledged that this enforcement team did not, in fact, belong to the copyright department; it belonged to the Provincial Culture Bureau, which in effect "loaned it out" to the copyright department. *This* was not surprising, because below the provincial level the copyright bureaucracy (and the Press and Publications Bureau, its "host" unit) is subordinated to the bureaucracy headed by the Ministry of Culture,[91] which, in a policy environment described by many officials as having "too many mothers-in-law" (*popo duo*), is the most important of them while remaining one of the least understood.[92]

The National Press and Publications Administration, which is the host unit of the National Copyright Administration, was formerly housed within the Ministry of Culture (MOC). These two units were separated from one another in 1986, but this bifurcation only extended down to the provincial

90. This is somewhat in contrast to certain areas like the Zhongguancun district in Beijing, where the street touts can be found all over certain areas, but once somebody expresses an interest to buy pirated software or DVDs, they are accompanied by "middlemen" through a warren of alleys (*hutong*), courtyards, and construction sites before descending on the small room in which the actual sales take place, often in someone's home.

91. I refer to this as the "culture bureaucracy."

92. The best systematic account of this bureaucracy can be found in Lynch, *After the Propaganda State*.

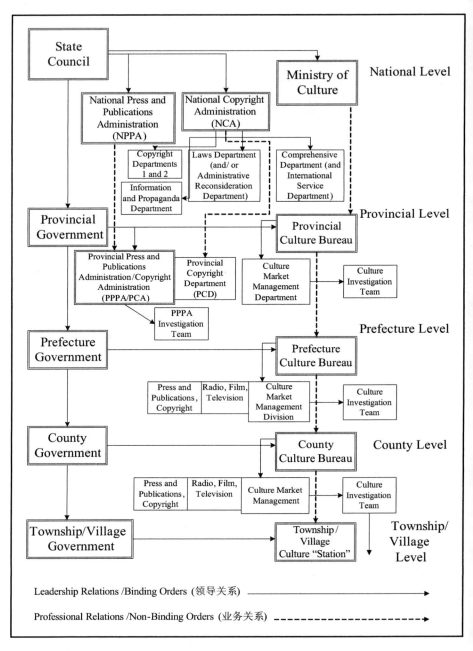

Figure 4.2. China's copyright bureaucracy

level and ground to a halt before this separation could be extended to the sub-provincial level.[93] Below the province—at the prefecture, municipality, county, township and village levels—the Press and Publications/Copyright Bureau systems are merged with, and subsumed under, the bureaucracy headed at the national level by the MOC. As a result, these sub-provincial units combine press, publication, and copyright responsibilities with the local organizational goals of the MOC system (*xitong*).[94] The division of these three sets of responsibilities has traditionally been skewed in favor of the priorities of the culture bureaucracy, particularly the local cultural market management units, and this significantly limits the degree of copyright enforcement below the provincial level. In the last few years has this begun to change, and only gradually.[95]

The culture bureaucracy, and specifically the cultural market management units within it, is charged with supervising the "cultural market" (encompassing movies, live performances, books and periodicals, audiovisual products, crafts and fine arts, gaming establishments, restaurants and karaoke parlors, and recreation centers) and with contributing to the development of related laws and regulations. Altogether, there are 11,000 people involved in full-time cultural market management work throughout China (as compared with the 200 engaged in full-time Copyright Bureau and enforcement work nationwide), with another 30,000 people from other offices who can be recruited to assist in cultural market management work as the need arises.[96] More recently, their responsibilities have evolved alongside technological changes and economic development. In Guizhou, for example, in 2003 there was a shift toward the regulation of Internet cafés for reasons ranging from cracking down on minors surfing pornographic websites (*huangse wangzhan*) to truancy and staying up after hours.[97]

The cultural market management department (*wenhua shichang guanli chu*) at the provincial level often has an administrative personnel allocation of about five people and works together with a "general investigation team" (*jicha zongdui*).[98] The next administrative levels are marked by a muddying of jurisdictional lines of authority over the cultural market between the

---

93. Interview 99BJ35, August 3, 1999.
94. There is, inevitably, some variation from one region to another.
95. Interview 02GY03, July 25, 2002.
96. Interview 99BJ28, July 27, 1999.
97. Interview 03GY02, July 19, 2003.
98. There seems to be some disagreement (or variation) on whether the culture investigation teams follow the same division of prefixes: provincial level (*zong dui*), prefecture level (*zhi dui*), and county level (*da dui*).

culture bureaucracy, the Press and Publications/Copyright Bureau system, and the units under the Bureau of Radio, Film, and Television (*guangdian ju*), although the general shift in overall authority has been in the direction of cultural market management.[99]

Directly below the provincial level (at the prefecture level) the corresponding office is the cultural market management division (*wenhua shichang guanli ke*), which has its own investigation teams (*jicha zhidui*).[100] This office is merged with the corresponding offices of the culture bureaucracy and those of the Press and Publications/Copyright Bureau system, and can invoke any of three office titles (cultural market management, press and publications, or copyright), depending on the particular tasks at hand.[101] The director of this office is always somebody from the culture bureaucracy, while the vice directors are officials from the copyright, press and publications, and other internal sub-bureaucracies.[102] Like all units within the culture bureaucracy, this office is decentralized, having principal and binding "leadership" relations with the local government and nonbinding consultative "professional" relations with its superior functional units (the Provincial Press and Publications/Copyright Bureau and the Provincial Bureau of Culture). The simplest way to navigate through this jurisdictional quagmire is to focus on one dominant set of responsibilities. As this configuration of offices is formally under the culture bureaucracy, its activities are often weighted in favor of managing the "cultural market." The personnel allocations for the investigation teams at the prefecture level are almost always larger than those at the provincial level, as cultural market management is regarded as a local matter.[103]

99. Lynch, *After the Propaganda State*, 205.

100. Although the investigation teams hold the same administrative rank as the cultural market management units with whom they work—and thus have the potential for the same coordination problems as the provincial copyright department and the PPPB investigation teams—the sheer number of personnel allocated to the culture administration investigation teams provides the cultural market management units (and others within the culture administration system) with a larger pool of enforcement resources than is available to the provincial copyright department. Interview 99GY01, June 14, 1999. At the provincial level, they are called "general enforcement teams" (*zongdui*), at the prefecture level they are "brigades" (*dadui*), and at the county level they are simply called "teams" (*dui*). Interview 02CD05, July 12, 2002; and Interview 02KM02, July 23, 2002.

101. Sichuan and Hunan provinces provide partial exceptions to this rule. Generally speaking, however, copyright bureau units (*banquan ju/chu*) do not extend below the provincial level. In other words, the lowest administrative level (with the exceptions noted) at which full-time staff are allocated to engage exclusively in copyright-related work is at the provincial level. "*Sichuan fan daoban cuoshi tixi*" [A Brief Introduction to Sichuan System to Fight against Piracy] (Sichuan: *Sichuan sheng banquan ju, MCSC Sichuan daibiao chu*). One reason for this variation is that after the Sino-U.S. negotiations were concluded in 1996, the Action Plan was presented to the provinces, and each province was given some discretion in establishing its own framework for implementing the Action Plan. Interview 02KM02, July 23, 2002. Since 1999, thirteen out of Sichuan's twenty-one prefecture-level offices have contained a formal copyright "signboard." Interview 03CD04, July 16, 2003.

102. Interview 02CD04, July 12, 2002.

103. Interview 98GY02, August 19, 1998.

At the county level, the cultural market management office is combined with the offices of the radio, film, and television subsystem as well as those of the press and publications and copyright subsystems into the Culture Broadcasting Bureau (*wenhua guangbo ju*). Under the director (*juzhang*), there are three vice directors (*fu juzhang*). The first holds a culture portfolio and heads the cultural division (*wenhua ke/gu*); the second has a broadcasting portfolio and is in charge of the broadcasting division (*guangdian ke/gu*); the third has a press and publications (and copyright) portfolio and is responsible for the publications and copyright division (*chuban [banquan] ke/gu*).[104] Further complicating matters is the considerable variation along this dimension. For example, some counties combine sports and athletics management (instead of broadcasting) into this bureaucracy (the office is known as the *wen-ti ju*, or the "Culture-Athletics Bureau").[105] These functional divisions notwithstanding, the vice directors are directly subordinate and report directly to the *juzhang*, whose primary professional association is with the culture bureaucracy. The priorities at this level are also often shaped to reflect those of the culture bureaucracy: one official, echoing the general consensus, said that investigation teams below the provincial level have a relatively large scope of responsibilities (*fanwei bijiao da*) and therefore focus less on copyright (*guji banquan bijiao shao*).[106]

The lowest administrative level is that of the township and village. The culture bureaucratic unit at this level is the "culture station" (*wenhua zhan*), and it is firmly nestled within the township and village government. These "stations" are staffed with generalist cadres, although the staff levels range from two or so in the northeast to a dozen or more in such provinces as Guangdong.[107]

There are two explanations for the differences in the development of the enforcement capacities between the culture bureaucracy and the press and publications/copyright system. The first is historical: a result of the incomplete separation of the press and publications/copyright system from the culture bureaucracy. The principal result is that copyright enforcement per se does not extend locally below the provincial level and must rely on officials within the cultural market management system to undertake such enforcement. Where priorities and scarce resources earmarked for the supervision of the "cultural market" conflict with or supersede those of local copyright enforcement, the latter is often sacrificed to the former.

Thus, the targets of cultural market management enforcement are often the same as those of the *saohuang dafei* campaigns, of which the cultural market management is an active participant. Materials that are produced

104. Such offices are a "*kĕ*" at the prefecture level and a "*gu*" at the county level.

105. Interview 03XJ01/6, July 17, 2003; and Interview 03GY02, July 19, 2003.

106. Interview 03KM01, July 15, 2003. The subdivisions of this bureaucracy at the prefecture level and below contain a fairly large degree of variation, so this paragraph describes a composite of the general layout of these offices.

107. Interview 99BJ08, July 27, 1999; and Interview 03GY02, July 19, 2003.

or imported illegally and which are antigovernment or pornographic are by definition "pirated" works in China, and it is in this way that the *sao-huang dafei* campaign extends into copyright enforcement. However, copyrighted products that do not have a pornographic or antigovernment or anti-Party orientation, such as computer software, many movies, and most books, are not included under the broad heading of the "cultural market" and are generally accorded a lower priority.[108] Thus, although the cultural market management bureaucracy has an extensive enforcement apparatus, its activities have only recently started to overlap in a significant way with the scope of responsibilities of the Copyright Bureau system.[109]

There is a second, functional explanation: the different administrative and enforcement jurisdictions between the two systems. The responsibilities of the Press and Publications/Copyright Bureau system emphasize the production and manufacture of publications, while the cultural market management system is responsible for investigating and enforcing its legal/administrative mandate vis-à-vis wholesale and retail *sales*.[110] As a result of the momentum generated by the Sino-U.S. IPR dialogue, there was a successful crackdown in 1996 and 1997 on the illegal manufacture of audiovisual publication products.[111] Many of the targeted manufacturers were either closed down or retooled for "legitimate" manufacturing, while the majority of the illegal manufacturing moved into Hong Kong, Macau, and Southeast Asia.[112]

Thus, in the late 1990s there was a dramatic shift in China from the *production* of pirated audiovisual materials to the *sale and distribution* of these products (fueled by the ever-increasing consumer demand for VCDs and DVDs), the enforcement—as distinct from the registration or mediation—of which lies largely outside the jurisdiction of the Provincial Press and Publications/Copyright Bureau.[113] This mandate belongs to the cultural market management enforcement apparatus, which has seen its enforcement responsibilities and resources increase alongside the heightened consumer demand for pirated movies and other audiovisual products. The strength and corresponding effectiveness of the cultural market management system is partly due to the Chinese government's

108. Interview 03GY02, July 19, 2003.
109. Interview 99BJ26, July 21, 1999; Interview 02CD04, July 12, 2002; and Interview 02GY03, July 25, 2002. More recently, Shanghai has experimented with the creation of an independent general culture inspection team (*wenhua jicha zongdui*) with personnel culled from various relevant agencies; it now boasts around sixty people. This team is administered directly by the Shanghai municipal government and is responsible for carrying out *saohuang dafei* and other "culture-related" campaigns. Interview 02SH07, June 28, 2002.
110. Interview 99KM03, June 18, 1999; Interview 99GY01, June 14, 1999; and Interview 99BJ28, July 27, 1999.
111. Seth Faison, "China Jails Audio and Movie Disk Pirates," *New York Times*, April 17, 1997, section D, 18.
112. Seth Faison, "China Turns Blind Eye to Pirated Disks," *New York Times*, March 28, 1998; and Interview 98HK03, June 25, 1998.
113. This trend appears to be reversing itself as production lines are starting up again in China.

emphasis on maintaining vigilance against "spiritual pollution" and "unhealthy tendencies" while simultaneously building "socialist civilization" within a value-based commercial medium, the cultural market.[114]

This raises the issue of the value-based concerns of the culture bureaucracy and its relationship with copyright protection in China. It is difficult to generalize about the character of this bureaucracy and the other important actors that make up the "gatekeeping" functions for such cultural products. This is because it is difficult to generalize about a bureaucratic cluster as large as this one. But it also stems from the fact that this bureaucracy is extremely difficult to penetrate. On the one hand, there is a close relationship with the CCP Propaganda *xitong*, which sets the general "line" and which does infuse an ideological and, more recently, a nationalistic character, into the mix. For example, there is a strict quota of how many foreign films can be shown in Chinese movie theaters (in an exception to the "one country, two systems" formula, Hong Kong motion pictures are considered "foreign"). The decisions on which films can be shown, according to one insider, are often based on such value-laden criteria. *Independence Day* was reportedly rejected because it is the United States, and not China, that saves the world from destruction.[115] This also extends beyond motion pictures:

> In the [mid-1990s] campaign to promote "Socialist Spiritual Civilisation," foreign movies, television programmes and music are looked at suspiciously by the authorities. President Jiang Zemin has staked his claim to leadership on tightening Chinese Communist Party control over culture. In the second half of 1996, the Ministry of Radio, Television and Film shelved a plan to broadcast ten major foreign films a year. It also ordered television stations to keep foreign programmes to no more than 15% of total programming time. Separately Chinese record companies have been told that they must distribute three domestic tracks for every foreign track.[116]

This describes one dimension of the culture bureaucracy. On the other hand, many culture officials are quite market-savvy and surprisingly open-minded. The representatives of the Ministry of Culture during the Sino-U.S. negotiations did not appear to the U.S. negotiators to be "sinister keepers of the ideological flame." Rather, they were quite receptive to the

114. This effectiveness should not be overstated. As Lynch documents, there are considerable pockets of resistance in which local retailers are able to flourish despite the presence of the CMM enforcement apparatus. Lynch, *After the Propaganda State.*
115. Alternatively, *Titanic* was allowed to be shown, racy sex scenes and all, because it was about universal theme of "love and loyalty." It also helped that President Jiang Zemin, a well-known movie buff, reportedly loved the film, thus clearing away any ideologically based resistance to showing it nationwide. Interview 98BJ09A, July 10, 1998.
116. Economist Intelligence Unit, China Hand: The Complete Guide to Doing Business in China (Hong Kong: Economist Intelligence Unit, 1997), 45.

economic arguments of market access.[117] The cultural market sub-bureaucracy is by definition charged with market regulation, and the officials I interviewed who work there were a far cry from the Cultural Revolution–esque caricatures that many have of them. That said, one Ministry of Culture official did confirm that China's opposition to U.S. market access demands for audiovisual products had to do with maintaining social order more than (but not entirely independent of) economic calculations, and this makes it especially difficult for foreign actors to apply pressure in this area of intellectual property enforcement.[118]

This remains a particularly difficult cleavage to resolve because the USTR and the copyright lobby regard China's market access restrictions as a principal factor leading to the environment of piracy in China. Such restrictions severely curtail the legal importation of foreign audiovisual products, and the gaps in supply are filled by the pirates who satisfy the dramatically increasing consumer demand for such products by making a wide array of foreign (and domestic) titles available at very low prices (music CDs, VCDs, and DVDs often cost less than two dollars apiece). In this sense, the culture bureaucracy's successful execution of its duties actually *contributes* to the piracy situation on the ground in China.[119]

Future Enforcement Scenarios

Faced with such severe budgetary and personnel constraints and by its dependence on other agencies for the critical mass necessary to wage an effective campaign against piracy, China's copyright bureaucracy has responded by passively accepting assistance from on high for substantive enforcement campaigns and, more recently, by forging relationships with nongovernmental agencies and actors that assist with information-gathering, which helps spread the costs of enforcement. The next three sections explore these alternative strategies.

The 1996–97 "Winter Action"

The 1996–97 "winter action" against copyright piracy is an example of a full-scale campaign instituted from the Center. It was a "one-shot" campaign that identified a finite and manageable set of targets, mobilized a considerable array of enforcement actors *outside* the Copyright Administration apparatus, and provided a scheme of powerful (and unsustainable) financial incentives for informants.[120]

117. Interview 98US15, December 8, 1998.
118. Interview 99BJ28, July 27, 1999.
119. Florence Lu, "State's Heavy Hand Gives VCD Pirates Edge Over Cinemas," *South China Morning Post,* February 22, 1999.
120. Michel C. Oksenberg, "The Chinese Policy Process and the Public Health Issue: An Arena Approach," *Studies in Comparative Communism* 7 no. 4 (Winter 1974): 401.

What made such a campaign possible? First of all, there was a significant degree of political momentum created by the Chinese leadership as a result of exogenous pressure from the United States in order to prevent a recurrence of IPR negotiations with the USTR. The Chinese leadership feared that the Sino-U.S. dialogue over intellectual property was evolving into a semi-institutionalized annual process, drawing unwanted attention to China's shortcomings, as was the case with the yearly debate in Congress over renewing China's Most-Favored Nation trade status. Therefore, the IPR issue was included in the measures for "cleaning up" the cultural market, a principal theme of the Sixth Plenum of the Fourteenth Central Committee meeting in October 1996.[121] The *People's Daily* underscored this shift in emphasis:

> The Resolution of the Sixth Plenary Session pointed out that "we will by no means allow the cultural market, an important front for promoting spiritual civilization, to become an area where decayed ideology and culture breed and spread," and stressed that "we must make unremitting efforts to wipe out pornographic publications and crack down on illegal publishing practices." *The party Central Committee has all along taken seriously the campaign against "pornography" and "illegal publications," but this is the first time it has, to add emphasis, written the campaign into its resolutions.*[122]

Such indications of the importance the top leadership attached to local compliance with the 1996 agreement contributed to the political momentum necessary to free up resources not usually earmarked for the more standard "recurring" political campaigns.[123]

The second factor is the increasing narrowness of the U.S. negotiators' minimum acceptability set, in other words the bare minimum of Chinese actions that would be sufficient for the USTR to remove China from the Special 301 Priority Foreign Country list. This focused on the closing down of some thirty-odd manufacturing plants inside China that were producing illegal compact disks, CD-ROMs, and laser disks, and any remaining plants engaged in such activity. As long as China closed down these factories, any agreement that included these closures would be supported by the U.S. IPR lobby and provide informal "ratification" of the agreement sought by the USTR. According to a knowledgeable official at the USTR, the set of

121. Although Lynch notes that this meeting "appears to have created an atmosphere reminiscent of 1958" in that an unmanageable number of targets and strategies were affirmed in the fight to establish "socialist spiritual civilization," the timing was perfect for the "winter action," which kicked off barely two months later. The goals of the "winter action" thus became a focus of the political momentum that emerged from the Sixth Plenum, even as the government backtracked on a number of other goals initially settled upon at the meeting. Lynch, *After the Propaganda State*, 201–2.

122. "Make Persistent Efforts to 'Eliminate Pornography' and 'Illegal Publications,'" *People's Daily*, December 11, 1996, 1; translated in FBIS (italics mine).

123. Oksenberg, "The Chinese Policy Process and the Public Health Issue," 401.

U.S. demands to shut down the pirate compact disk manufacturing operations was by far the most high-profile—and the most important—component of the 1996 agreement. It seems that Beijing picked up on this as
well.[124] The Chinese appeared to have calculated that closing down the factories in question would satisfy the minimum U.S. demands and make it far
more difficult for the United States to level further IPR-related demands at
China in the near future.[125]

Targeting these factories was an inspired political strategy for both sides.
First, it offered a tangible way to measure China's progress in IPR enforcement and offered the Clinton administration a quantifiable means to demonstrate China's compliance with the agreement (which, in turn, was a
necessary tactic to demonstrate the results of the U.S. "get tough with China"
strategy in order to secure the votes necessary for the passage of Most-
Favored Nation trade status renewal for Beijing).[126] Second, and related to
the first, it gave China a manageable and solvable set of tasks, which gave
Beijing the incentive to muster the considerable short-term resources and
formidable political capital necessary to meet these goals. Third, it got at
the heart of the concerns on the part of the International Intellectual Property Alliance and the Motion Picture Association of America over China's
export of illegal audiovisual products abroad; it did not address the issue
of domestic consumption, which, because of market access restrictions, was
not as great a concern for the copyright lobby at the time.[127] Finally, the closure of these factories did, in fact, provide a lethal blow to the *manufacture*
of copyright-infringing products *inside* China, at least for a while (although
it did nothing to reduce demand for such products).

The third factor that explains the success of the "winter action" was the
mobilization of public security and military units to lead the crackdown on

---

124. "On the eve of the present talks, *the issue of concern to the United States has actually been
basically solved.* The Chinese side recently redoubled its efforts to crack down on illegal duplication of compact discs . . . by the dispatch of supervisors to 30-plus CDs and software manufacturing plants to ensure that these plants strictly observe discipline and law in the future. . . .
[C]ustoms in Guangdong Province and the coastal areas recently have tightened inspection of
CDs and software taken out of the country and arrested a number of businessmen engaged in
smuggling activities and even plant directors involved in the production of pirated products."
"Sino-U.S. Trade War Can Hopefully Be Checked—Written on the Eve of the Reopening of
the Sino-U.S. IPR Protection Talks," *Wen Wei Po*, June 11, 1996, A2; translated in FBIS (italics
mine).

125. In addition to sustained U.S. pressure, this enhanced political emphasis on the part
of the top leadership in China was also a result of domestic factors. In the four months following the negotiations, the Chinese government planted officials in the compact disc, CD-ROM,
and laser disc manufacturing plants to monitor production. During this time, Chinese and foreign JV manufacturers of these goods complained to the government that pirate factories were
severely compromising their bottom lines, appeals that became increasingly difficult for the government to ignore. Interview 99HK04, June 3, 1999; and New China News Agency, "Pirated CD
Operations Shut Down in Guangdong," October 24, 1996.

126. Interview 98SH02, March 19, 1998.

127. Interview 98US17, December 9, 1998; Interview 98US18, December 10, 1998. In any
event, a focus on curbing retail sales and domestic consumption would be—and remains—a
singularly impossible task.

these manufacturing operations. The copyright administrative system was effectively bypassed or, more accurately, co-opted into this temporary alliance of policing and combat units.[128] The most prominent of these were units within the local Public Security apparatus.

The goals of the "winter action"—particularly the closure of underground factories—made it clear that the police (and, in some cases, the military) would be required to take on a leading role in order for the campaign to be successful. The vice director of the National Press and Publications Administration and the National *Saohuang Dafei* Working Office, Gui Xiaofeng, and the director of the Propaganda Department Publication Bureau, Gao Mingguang, outlined the strategy of the 1996–97 *saohuang dafei* campaign as a "five grouping" (*wuge yipi*) approach:

> This refers to efforts to wipe out one group of major criminal rings involved in illegal publications; wreck one group of dens for both copyright piracy and the printing of pirated publications; crack one group of "black production lines" of laser discs; rectify one group of wholesale markets for books and publications, as well as distribution markets for audio-video products; and deal with one group of publishing units which sell for profit book numbers, publication numbers, and order numbers of an edition, with a view to further standardizing the order of publishing, printing, wholesale, marketing, and import of publications.

Significantly, they went on to state that "of all these, thoroughly cracking underground production lines is a job to which we have devoted greater efforts during the present period."[129] Doing so, however, required an extensive enforcement network capable of withstanding the often considerable political and physical risks inherent in such activity.

Part of the reason is that a number of these factories were operating under the auspices of the local governmental units themselves, particularly the Ministry of Electronics Industry and the People's Liberation Army (PLA), and although press accounts may have overstated the role of the military in the operations of these underground production lines, many individual PLA units were "indirectly, indirectly involved."[130] An operation with PLA involvement is widely regarded as being "untouchable," and the

128. One case of military involvement included sealing off a street in Guangdong so that 200 soldiers could raid six separate compact disc factories. Many people at this time were also given lengthy prison sentences, a fact that put the United States in the uncomfortable position of being partially responsible for these incarcerations, while at the same time pressuring Beijing to improve China's human rights record. Interview 99HK04, June 3, 1999.

129. "We Must Be Thorough in Eliminating Pornography and Illegal Publications," *People's Daily*, January 4, 1997, 2.

130. Lynch, *After the Propaganda State*, 154. Other factories were operated by secret societies, or "triads," which also enjoyed a considerable degree of insulation from government enforcement agencies. Information about the military role comes from Interview 98US15, December 8, 1998.

copyright administration system—and even the Administration for Industry and Commerce (AIC) and the Quality Technical Supervision bureaus (QTSB), and the cultural market management investigation teams—were no match for the "protection" offered by the factory's military connections.[131] Nevertheless, according to one knowledgeable source, the military is not "invincible." The key to understanding how a military-run operation can be closed down involves a basic understanding of the power balance in a given relationship: if a more powerful unit can be identified and mobilized for the task at hand, even a military target can be brought down.[132]

In one case, a pirate compact disk factory housed inside an air force base was closed down after central government intervention, and its owner was sent to prison for three years. In another incident, another compact disk plant in southern China had been targeted for a raid by the AIC, but because the owner had a relationship with a local military commander, the latter sent troops into the warehouses where the merchandise had been bonded by the AIC and simply took the CD-producing machinery away in the presence of open-mouthed AIC officials. Reportedly, after intervention from the top, the military commander was ultimately court-martialed.[133] In such cases, enforcement units included those within the Public Security or National Security *xitong*, which are far more powerful than the traditional administrative agencies devoted to local copyright or trademark enforcement.

A final critical factor in the success of the "winter action" was the reward scheme for information leading to the location of the illegal manufacturing plants. To operate, pirates must be creative in establishing—and in concealing—their operations.[134] It is only through local residents-cum-informants that such operations can be uncovered, as in the case in Henggang, where two illegal compact disk production lines secretly located inside a rural duckling hatchery were identified by local peasants.[135] Therefore, it was necessary to create an incentive structure to motivate these individuals to risk physical injury or possibly even death by informing the government about the whereabouts of such factories; in other words, the rewards had to be

131. These two bureaucracies, the AIC and the QTSB, are discussed at length in Chapter 5.
132. Interview 99HK04, June 3, 1999.
133. Ibid.
134. In the words of one official: "The underground production line . . . in Haipang Village, Shiji Town, Panyu Municipality, Guangdong Province is a typical case. Collaborating with confederates both inside and outside the country, law-breakers shipped in the equipment through illegal channels, and installed the production line in a relatively quiet and concealed village. . . . They introduced a totally enclosed management, under which production staff were not allowed to leave the factory without permission, and all their day-to-day activities and recreation were conducted inside the factory. Moreover, [only] a single line of contact was established between each link of the provision of master discs and of the shipment and sales of manufactured goods, which could be cut off immediately should anything go wrong. . . . Some lawbreakers spared no pains to [bribe] local cadres and functionaries of management bodies with a considerable amount of money." "We Must Be Thorough in Eliminating Pornography and Illegal Publications," People's Daily, January 4, 1997, 2.
135. Seth Faison, "China Appears To Crack Down On CD Pirating," *New York Times*, April 7, 1997, section A, 1.

substantial. In Beijing, these rewards ranged from 10,000 to 100,000 yuan ($120 to $12,000).[136] Not to be outdone, on December 11, 1996, the provincial government of Guangdong announced a reward scheme of 300,000 yuan ($36,000) for each illegal production line found.[137] This is an astronomical sum, for some workers nearly the equivalent of a fifty-year salary.[138]

The deep financial pockets necessary for such reward schemes are obviously outside the scope of the press and publications/copyright system (each individual reward, for example, equals a nine-year operating budget for the Guizhou Provincial Copyright Bureau) and, in any case, are unsustainable over the long run unless special, extra funds are earmarked for the purpose.[139] Nevertheless, they were a critical factor in the success of the 1996–97 "winter action," as evidenced by the discoveries and closures of a string of hitherto "invisible" underground manufacturing operations. By late October of 1996, China had shut down ten such operations.[140] By contrast, in the first ten days after announcing the 300,000 yuan award, nine more underground compact disk production lines were closed down.[141] Three more were shut down within the next ten days, and five more within the month.[142] All together, by early January 1997, twenty-five illegal production lines had been closed down in Guangdong province alone.[143]

"Small Government, Big Society"

The nonsustainability of campaigns like the 1996–97 "Winter Action" had Chinese copyright officials scrambling to find alternative means by which to effectively counter widespread copyright piracy. However, the organizational structure described in the previous sections has remained largely intact. Therefore, the copyright departments have turned to "outsourcing" in order to achieve more effective enforcement, particularly through the growing network of anti-piracy alliances. This falls under the rubric of what has been termed "small government, big society" (*xiao zhengfu da shehui*).[144]

136. New China News Agency, "Report on Beijing Municipality's Crackdown on Pornography," January 7, 1997.

137. New China News Agency, "Nine Illegal CD Production Lines Demolished in Guangdong," December 21, 1996; and Interview 99BJ39, August 14, 1999.

138. This calculation is based on an average worker salary of 500 yuan a month. In some areas, basic worker wages were higher, ranging between 800 and 1,000 yuan a month. Most workers in China, particularly in underdeveloped areas, had salaries closer to the lower wage of 500 yuan in 1996.

139. The annual operating budget for the Guizhou Province Copyright Bureau is a paltry 36,000 yuan, although additional monies may be made available on an ad hoc—and tightly controlled—basis. Interview 98GY02, August 19, 1998.

140. New China News Agency, "Illegal CD-ROM Disk Plants Closed," October 22, 1996.

141. "Nine Illegal CD Production Lines Demolished in Guangdong."

142. "We Must Be Thorough in Eliminating Pornography and Illegal Publications."

143. "Guangdong Rewards Units Excelling in Underground CD-ROM Production Line Crackdown," *People's Daily*, January 22, 1997, 5; translated in FBIS.

144. See *"Xiao zhengfu da shehui" de lilun yu shijian: Hainan zhengzhi tizhi yu shehui tizhi gaige yanjiu* [Theory and Practice of "Small Government, Big Society": The Study of the Reform of Hainan's Government and Social Systems] (Beijing: *Shehui kexue wenxuan chubanshe*, 1998).

An interesting indigenous development is the creation of a number of local ad hoc groups that focus on enhancing and deepening the ability of the NCA to enforce copyright. At this relatively early stage of development, there is considerable variation as to the structure, responsibilities, and makeup of these groups, but most fall under the broad heading of the Anti-Piracy Alliance (*fan daoban lianmeng*). Essentially, these groups are associations that include domestic software producers, retailers, and publishing houses that donate money, information (in the form of market inspections, for instance), and other resources to help the local copyright departments locate piracy within their jurisdictions and go after such violators.[145] Although the *2001 Press and Publications Yearbook* states that the anti-piracy alliances were initially floated in three experimental provinces (Sichuan, Jiangsu, and Guangdong), as early as 1999, Shanghai and Chongqing municipalities had also drawn up blueprints for and actually established their own anti-piracy alliances.[146] By 2000, eleven such alliances had been formed.[147] Sichuan province and Chongqing municipality both have anti-piracy alliances, which join together with the local police and other administrative units to undertake anti-piracy actions.[148] Liaoning province has its own copyright association (*Liaoning sheng banquan xuehui*), which carries out similar functions.[149] Sichuan province has also started to extend its anti-piracy alliance network of representative organizations (*peichu jigou*) down to the prefecture and municipal levels.[150]

The Shanghai Anti-Piracy Alliance, formed in 1999, includes among its membership Shanghai's local print publishing houses, audio-video publishing houses, and software companies—more than sixty companies in all. Significantly, the anti-piracy alliance—and not the Shanghai Copyright Department—actually pays the annual 120,000 yuan ($15,000) salary itself (and underwrites some additional operating expenses) for a ten-person press and publications/copyright enforcement team (*jicha dui*).[151] Anecdotal evidence supports the notion that, combined with consumer "hotlines" (*rexian* or *jubao*), these alliances seem to be making a positive, albeit limited, dent in the piracy situation on the ground in

145. The member list in Sichuan rose to sixty-eight by 2002. Interview 02CD05, July 12, 2002.

146. *Zhongguo chuban nianjian 2001* [China Publications Yearbook 2001] (Beijing: *Zhongguo chuban nianjian bianji*, 2001), 92.

147. Ibid., 94. As of 2002, Yunnan Province has yet to establish its own formal alliance, but the Yunnan Copyright Department is already managing informally many of what is de facto an APA. Interview 03KM01, July 15, 2003.

148. *Zhongguo chuban nianjian 2000* [China Publications Yearbook 2000] (Beijing: *Zhongguo chuban nianjian bianji*, 2000), 128, 337.

149. Ibid., 326–27.

150. Interview 02CD05, July 12, 2002.

151. Interview 02SH07, June 28, 2002. Some areas have been more successful in securing such funding. Guangdong and Jiangsu provinces reportedly were able to raise 1,000,000 yuan apiece, while other areas, like Yunnan, are scrounging for even a fraction of such operating funds. Interview 99KM03, June 18, 1999.

China.[152] Some observers remain skeptical: as one industry representative put it, the anti-piracy alliance is "a loose organization with no objective to speak of" aside from a general desire to wipe out piracy.[153]

In addition, even before the creation of the anti-piracy alliances, foreign associations had established a presence in China to work together with the NCA and its local counterparts to improve the copyright enforcement situation in China.[154] The International Federation of the Phonographic Industry is a nongovernmental trade association that established a presence in China in order to monitor the evolution of China's copyright regime and to protect the interests of its member companies operating in China. Indeed, the IFPI has been so successful that it appears *by name* in some Chinese copyright-related regulations, particularly those pertaining to copyright registration.[155] The United States Information Technology Office (USITO) was a quasi-governmental unit that moved out of the government and became a private association representing the interests of U.S. and other information technology–related industries with operations in China. The Business Software Alliance (BSA), well-known on Capitol Hill, has established operations in China, as has the Motion Picture Association of America (MPAA). All of these agencies work together with the copyright and other bureaucracies in order to educate local officials and the public through workshops and publications, among other means, about the importance of protecting copyright in China.

One big step forward in allowing foreign actors to work more closely with local copyright administration offices is the recent set of changes enshrined in the revised Copyright Law and its related Implementing Regulations. Article 37 of the Implementing Regulations of the Revised Copyright Law, by not distinguishing between foreign and Chinese actors, makes it legally possible for foreign entities to work together with *local* Copyright Bureaus without prior NCA approval.[156] This is different from the original Copyright Law, which stipulated that foreign actors must appeal to the National Copyright Administration if they wished to take action against the

152. Although most consumers appear to "vote with their pocketbooks" over the issue of pirated consumer goods, making such "hotlines" appear somewhat anachronistic, one way of obtaining mass support is over the issue of viruses that can be found in much pirated computer software. On April 26, 1999, about 100,000 computers in China were "paralyzed" by the Chernobyl computer virus. Experts noted that one of the reasons this virus was so effective was the widespread use of pirated software in China. "Rampant Computer Virus Hits 100,000," *South China Morning Post,* April 28, 1999.

153. Interview 03BJ03, July 24, 2003.

154. This trend has also been occurring on the anticounterfeiting front, with arguably more success. I discuss this in chapter 5.

155. See, for example, "*Guojia banquan ju guanyu tongyi guoji changpianye xiehui zuowei qihuiyuan luyin zhipin quanli renzheng jigou de tongzhi*" [National Copyright Agency Circular Concerning the Agreement with the International Federation of the Phonographic Industry Regarding the Organization for the Authentication of its Members' Rights over Audio Products].

156. Article 37 of the Implementing Regulations, referring to Article 47 of the revised Copyright Law, lifts the restrictions that foreign actors must pursue their claims via the NCA, thereby clearing the way for them to engage provincial-level copyright departments directly.

violations of their copyright in China. However, one source intimately associated with copyright administration said that it will take some time for
local Copyright Bureaus to achieve the requisite "comfort level" to work
effectively with foreign actors.[157]

Moreover, there are limits to what foreign and Chinese NGOs can do in
the often "rough-and-tumble" environment of local Chinese politics. The
IFPI, for example, has enjoyed a formal presence in China since 1994 largely
due to its adroitness in cultivating national and local political support.[158] By
late 1995, however, the IFPI found itself in an uncomfortable position. As a
direct result of the momentum and the political pressure arising from the
formal Sino-U.S. IPR negotiations, local Chinese enforcement units began
to crack down in earnest against illegal compact disk manufacturing operations. One such manufacturer, located in the Shenzhen Special Economic
Zone in southern China, enjoyed the protection of an extremely powerful
local government office.[159] Because of this political patronage, the factory
was considered immune from governmental "interference," a euphemism
for "the effective enforcement of copyright," and its leaders were outraged
when the factory was finally investigated at the end of 1995.

Rumors quickly began to circulate that the IFPI was providing the USTR
with information to support the latter's investigation into China's IPR
enforcement, including one that specifically targeted this factory. Amid
these rumors, representatives from the factory paid a visit to the IFPI office
in the provincial capital of Guangzhou, demanding that the IFPI call for
an end to the investigation and withdraw its "allegations." One evening not
long thereafter, the entire Guangzhou IFPI staff of twelve was taken away
and detained for several days, while the IFPI office was closed down for a
week. When it reopened, some key staff reappeared but had been "reas-
signed" to work on behalf of the local government to investigate "IFPI's
leaking of state secrets." Because of the conflicting reports from the IFPI
and the infringing factory in question, the local Guangzhou municipal government found itself in the difficult and politically charged position of trying to arrive at an accurate assessment of what had transpired; until then,
all actors in this drama were suspect.

---

157. Interview 03BJ03, July 24, 2003.

158. The IFPI began negotiations to establish an office in China in 1993, but it almost immediately became entangled in both ideological and bureaucratic politics. At the time, foreign
record companies were banned from operating (or even establishing a representative office)
in China because audiovisual products were deemed to possess potentially harmful ideological
effects. Moreover, there was no precedent for an IFPI-type quasi-commercial NGO in China,
and it was difficult to find a host with the "correct" organizational "fit." MOFTEC, the Ministry of Civil Affairs, and the Administration for Industry and Commerce were all considered
but deemed inappropriate. Eventually, the IFPI cultivated a relationship with the National Press
and Publications Administration (NPPA), which took the lead in obtaining consent from other
government organs. Rather than "gaining approval," this arrangement received "no objection"
from MOFTEC, the AIC, the Ministry of Public Security, the Ministry of Culture, as well as tacit
consent from the Propaganda Department. Interview 99HK04, June 3, 1999.

159. Ibid.

Ultimately, the factory's efforts backfired: the general manager was put on trial and received a relatively severe sentence of twelve years in jail. Nevertheless, this was also a significant setback for the IFPI. Local government officials, with whom contact was absolutely essential for the IFPI to maintain its operations, studiously avoided the IFPI because of the increased scrutiny that emerged from this investigation, and it was only after eighteen months of intensive confidence-(re)building efforts by the IFPI that its relations with local officials began to return to some semblance of normalcy.[160]

"Laid-Off" (Xiagang'd) Officials and "Undertaking Units"

Finally, many government bureaucracies, including the copyright bureaucracy, have been forced to cut their staff levels by as much as 50 percent or more. In order to provide a "soft landing," these workers are herded into both existing and new "undertaking units." "Undertaking units" (*shiye danwei* or *shiye jigou*) are extensions of administrative bureaucracies that offer some sort of service paid for by the consumer. Examples include hospitals, specialized training schools, hotels, and many other types of undertakings, including investigation teams. It has traditionally been easier to receive personnel allocations from the Commission for the Composition of Government Offices (*bianwei*) for undertaking units because these units underwrite a portion of the budget with the profits they earn and are thus not a net drain on budgetary outlays. In the new climate of bureaucratic downsizing, however, "undertaking units" provide a sort of "halfway house" between a hitherto insular bureaucratic career and one that is governed by the uncertainties of the market.[161]

The China Copyright Protection Center (*Zhongguo banquan baohu zhongxin*) is an offshoot of the Press and Publications Administration/National Copyright Administration as a result of the administrative restructuring that came out of the Ninth National People's Congress of March 1998 and was founded in September of that year. The CCPC has been housed together with several other copyright-related undertaking units, such as the China Copyright Agency, the Software Registration Center of China, the Remuneration Collection and Distribution Center of China, and the

---

160. Ibid. See also "Piracy Fighters in China Fear Killings; IFPI Withdraws Staff in Wake of Violent Rumor," *Billboard*, 107, 51 (December 23, 1995): 9. In some rare perverse circumstances, however, organized crime has actually *assisted* with copyright protection. Hong Kong and Macau mobster "Broken Tooth" Wan Kuok-koi was reportedly approached by a Hong Kong movie company that wanted to do a movie about him. He was very pleased and offered all sorts of help to the people involved with making the movie. However, when "Broken Tooth" heard that pirated versions of the movie were being produced, he found out where they were being sold and warned the people selling them that if they did not "trash" the pirated versions of the movie, then they themselves would subsequently be "trashed." Interview 98US19, December 11, 1998.

161. Interview 03BJ03, March 9, 2003.

Editorial Office of *Copyright* magazine, the official Press and Publications Administration/National Copyright Administration trade publication.[162]

The China Copyright Protection Center (CCPC) is charged with the registration and informational responsibilities of the NCA:

> Several functions formerly assigned to the NCA have been transferred to the CCPC, including registration of computer software copyrights; registration of copyrights of works by foreign authors; verification of international copyrights; and registration of contracts for publishing international audio-visual and electronic publications. It also offers legal services ranging from copyright consultation to mediation and advocacy for copyright disputes and lawsuits. . . . The CCPC has also assumed responsibility from the NCA for administrating several existing collection societies, including the Copyright Agency of China (CAC), the Computer Software Registration Centre and the National Centre for the Collection and Distribution of Authors' Remuneration. In addition, the CCPC has taken over as editor and publisher of the *Copyright Bulletin,* the NCA's official publication for copyright-related announcements and registration information.[163]

The CCPC is a revenue-generating unit, a subordinate unit to the Press and Publications Administration from which it takes its marching orders. Most of the lower-ranking personnel can be recruited at the discretion of the CCPC. The more than fifty people at the China Copyright Protection Center are divided into eight departments, including the general office, copyright agencies "1" and "2," the legal office, the collective management office, the product registration office, and the *Copyright* magazine publishing office. The leadership of the China Copyright Protection Center and its other units, however, were recruited directly from the ranks of the Press and Publications Administration/National Copyright Administration, in part to avoid laying them off.

Initially, the Press and Publications Administration provided start-up funds for the CCPC to begin its operations. These funds were released by the Planning and Finance Section (*jihua caiwu si*) of the Press and Publications Administration. However, it was a one-time payout: thereafter the CPCC and other "undertaking units" were responsible for financing their own budgets through the revenues they received through the services they provided.[164]

Of course, this works marvelously when the market can bear the legitimate operations of the unit in question: if it provides a service that is in sufficient demand. But this is not the case. As part of this shift toward better

162. The secretariat of the Anti-Piracy Alliance was slated to be placed within the China Copyright Protection Center.

163. Economist Intelligence Unit, China Hand: The Complete Guide to Doing Business in China (Hong Kong: Economist Intelligence Unit, 1999), 48.

164. *Zhongguo zhishi chanquan nianjian 2000* [China Intellectual Property Yearbook 2000] (Beijing: *Zhishi chanquan chubanshe,* 2001), 59–60; and Interview 99BJ12, March 19, 1999.

accountability, in 1999 a classified document was distributed announcing that all undertaking units were planned to be "weaned" (*sannian yihou duannai*) away from the administrative apparatus by 2002 in order to be financially self-sufficient.[165] However, as recently as 2002, during informal conversations one Chinese official echoed a widespread sentiment when he volunteered that "maybe we were a bit optimistic" about the three-year timetable.[166] Moreover, some activities, like enforcement, do not easily lend themselves to legitimate money-generating activities. As a result, it is easy to cross over into activities that deemphasize piracy enforcement in favor of income generation—taking a cut of legitimately imposed fines or even to outright extortion.[167]

Until some significant, sustained changes take place, the most likely "enforcement scenario" will continue to be when consumers voluntarily vote with their pocketbooks whether to purchase a legitimate or a copyright-violating product. What is particularly interesting is that, of all these enforcement scenarios, none embrace a convergence with the State Intellectual Property Office. This is not accidental. When discussing such a merger with copyright officials in 1999, the national officials were somewhat agnostic, but the local officials were downright hostile to it. By 2002, these same officials were even more dismissive about the possibility of such a merger. In April 2001, one of the principal inducements to the move disappeared when the Press and Publications Administration and, by extension, the National Copyright Administration became a ministry-level bureau (*zheng bu ji ju*). Because these two interwoven bodies now formally outrank SIPO, the merger would mean a loss of rank for the NCA, further scuttling any movement toward the merger. One NCA source mused that combining "three independent bureaucratic clusters. . . . That is a pretty difficult thing to accomplish" (*sange duli de xitong. . . . kunnan bijiao da*).[168] The opposition of the copyright bureaucracy and other relevant units pales in comparison, however, to that of the trademark/anticounterfeiting bureaucracies discussed in the next chapter.

165. Interview 99NJ01C; see also "*Guowuyuan guanyu bianzhi 1999 nian zhongyang yusuan he difang yusuan de tongzhi*" [State Council Notice Regarding Personnel/Budgetary Allocations for 1999, Central Budgets, and Local Budgets], which states: "Accelerating the reforms in undertaking units, we will cut the financial subsidies to undertaking units, except for a small number of educational and other undertaking units, in principle we will reduce the subsidies by one-third each year so that in three years they will each be responsible for their own profit and loss."

166. Interview 02KM01, July 23, 2002. An additional problem is that personnel allocations for "undertaking units" (*shiye bianzhi*) were traditionally easier to secure because the enterprise was self-funding to some degree. Hence there would be less budgetary allocation than would be the case with a purely administrative personnel/budgetary allocation (*xingzheng bianzhi*). As a result, many "undertaking units" retain an inordinately large number of employees, a situation that is inconsistent with the process of becoming completely self-funding.

167. Interview 99BJ32, July 29, 1999. The Yunnan Provincial investigation team, which used to receive a personnel and budgetary allocation as an "undertaking unit," has now been changed to an administrative unit with an administrative personnel allocation (*xingzheng bianzhi*) in order to nip this problem in the bud. Interview 02KM02, July 23, 2002.

168. Interview 02BJ07, August 9, 2002.

CHAPTER 5

Trademarks and Anticounterfeiting

The holy grail for any researcher of IPR in China is to be allowed to directly observe an anticounterfeiting raid. In mid-1999, during the course of my fieldwork, I was invited to do just that. I made my arrangements directly with a private investigation firm working on behalf of a U.S. company operating in China. I was instructed to phone the investigation company's Hong Kong office every day to inquire whether I would be able to take part in the next day's raid. One morning in early June, I was told to meet my interlocutors in the bar of a Guangdong hotel the following day. Upon my arrival at the hotel the next afternoon, they introduced themselves as the representatives of the investigation firm. The five men were led by a gentleman in his late forties I will call Liu. Like many private investigators, Mr. Liu was formerly with the Hong Kong police force but had moved into the private sector in anticipation of the changes following Hong Kong's reversion to Chinese sovereignty in 1997. It did not matter much that he was not a mainlander; what was important was that he was ethnically Chinese, that he "blend in." Liu briefed me on the day's activities, and we went to the local Administration for Industry and Commerce (AIC) office, the official Chinese agency undertaking the raid.

Half an hour later, we boarded two taxis to the AIC building, where I was introduced to the division chief of the economic crimes unit. While I waited, Liu and the AIC agents pored over two sets of handwritten maps that marked the location of the targeted market stalls. Only now did Liu inform the AIC of the identity of the targets, a measure necessary to prevent leaks. Before we left, I noticed that an AIC agent "deputized" Liu by giving him an AIC ID card to wear (backward so that nobody could tell that it had somebody else's picture on it) during the raid. This further blurred the boundaries between the government agency (the AIC) and the private investigation firm working on behalf of the foreign client. Once the group of seventeen assembled, we all went downstairs and got into three unmarked black minivans.

When we reached our target, the enforcement team of private investigators and AIC agents walked into the arcade and stopped at the first targeted stall, just inside the entrance. This stall was situated next to a security guard (*bao'an*), who did not take part in the raid. As soon as the enforcers descended on the stall, a man ran to a second one and started to pack away the goods being sold there. A moment after that, the enforcers came over to his stall and began the long process of questioning him and cataloguing the offending merchandise.

An hour after the raid began, the boxes of confiscated goods were put onto a truck and taken away. We returned to the minivans and proceeded back to the AIC office, where the staff made photocopies of the confiscated sales receipts in order to calculate the punishments and to use them to try to locate the middlemen (warehouses, wholesalers, and producers) involved in the production and distribution chain. Liu said that it was the policy of his client (the foreign company) to destroy all confiscated goods, which is no small issue. Destruction is expensive, and the local enforcement offices are loath to expend scarce resources to destroy merchandise if a cheaper solution is available; one possibility is to take off the violating trademark and sell the goods as generic. These costs are often borne by the trademark holder, not by the enforcement agency.

After this stage, as it neared 6:00 P.M., we all got into the minivans and went to dinner. Only the male AIC members who participated in the raid attended; the two women went home. We were later joined by the municipal AIC bureau chief and his assistant, neither of whom personally participated in the raid. The dinner was a typical Chinese banquet, but what was remarkable was Liu's ability to ingratiate himself with the AIC people. He had been doing this all day long, telling jokes, trading war stories, and, often fawningly, reminding the AIC how important their work is. For his part, the bureau chief did a masterful job at making himself appear not too eager to be enjoying himself. He seemed far less interested in trademark protection than in the fact that his counterparts in other regions of China had comparatively more power, that they could carry firearms, and other similar complaints.

There was some discussion among the higher-ranking cadres as to how to get rid of the lower-status officials, and they eventually settled on the line that the rest of us were "going to play mah-jongg." This was code for "karaoke," and we all got into taxis and went to a somewhat rough-looking karaoke parlor, where there was plenty of alcohol, food, and hostesses. Indeed, when I finally turned to leave at 1:30 in the morning and sought out the bureau chief to thank him, I was told, after several requests to meet with him, that he was upstairs "getting a massage" and could not be disturbed. The raid, the banquet, the karaoke, and the massage were all paid for by the foreign company on whose behalf the private investigation firm had coordinated this series of raids with the AIC.

This extended anecdote is important for several reasons. First, although no two enforcement actions are ever exactly alike, it confirms a general pattern in the relationship between private investigators and Chinese administrative agencies in terms of functional divisions of labor: the former lay the groundwork and absorb the costs, the latter provide the official authority (i.e., legitimacy and legality) and take the credit. Second, it underscores another crucial pattern in such cooperation between external actors and Chinese administrative agencies: this enforcement action and others like it would not have taken place were it not for the expectation of some sort of side payment, either in the form of direct monetary transfers (which I did not observe directly in this case), payments in kind (dinner, karaoke, and massages), or some sort of other, more symbolic direct benefit (the giving of "face" to the AIC by the investigation agency representatives, especially Mr. Liu). It should finally be noted that this investigation firm, like many others, undertakes several enforcement actions like this on a typical day.

What is the impact of such activity on anticounterfeiting enforcement efforts in China? How is it possible for such unlikely alliances to take shape and to flourish? What can this tell us about the effects of foreign pressure on policy enforcement in China? As was shown in chapters 2 and 4, exogenous pressure from Washington was concentrated mostly around copyright issues. Chapter 2 demonstrated that because the trademark lobby was unwilling or unable to pursue its goals under Special 301, it was largely left out of the trade policy formulation and negotiation process. It is all the more remarkable, therefore, that it is in the IPR subfield of trademarks that exogenous pressure has been the most successful. Why is this?

There are several interrelated dimensions, which, taken together, provide an explanation for this increase in the effectiveness of anticounterfeiting enforcement in China over the past several years. First of all, anticounterfeiting enforcement falls into the domain of not just one but two bureaucracies, the Administration for Industry and Commerce and the Quality Technical Supervision Bureau. Second, and related to the first, each of these bureaucracies extends all the way down to the county level; in the case of the AIC, all the way to the township level. Thus, these two bureaucratic structures are not merely independent from one another, they also enjoy an expansive "reach" into the local nexus where most anticounterfeiting activity occurs. However, the foregoing notwithstanding, the actual anticounterfeiting offices in each of these bureaucracies are embedded within the larger organization in a way that is not unlike their counterparts in the copyright bureaucracy.

In fact, it is the third element of this equation that changes the incentive structure of these institutions and thus overcomes the embeddedness problem, thus moving this from a situation of potentially improved anticounterfeiting enforcement to an environment where it has actually flourished. This dimension is the entry of foreign actors into the process of anticounterfeiting enforcement. These include not only the trademark owners who have set up their manufacturing and sales operations in China; it also includes the growing number of private and quasi-private investigation agencies that have moved into the murky, gray area of administrative law enforcement. Why this focus on *foreign* agents? Because even though it is almost universally agreed that Chinese trademark owners suffer more from counterfeiting than do foreign companies in China, it is only the latter that have traditionally been willing and able to bring their deep financial pockets to bear on the situation, financially underwriting costly investigations and enforcement actions undertaken by the two Chinese anticounterfeiting enforcement agencies discussed in this chapter. However, these relationships between foreign actors and Chinese enforcement agencies are not simply based on bribes and side payments. These foreign actors apply a considerable amount of subtle but unrelenting pressure onto these enforcement agencies to alter the latter's preferences so that they dovetail more closely with those held by these foreign actors (as well as Chinese trademark holders): that is, more effective anticounterfeiting enforcement.

The Trademark Situation in China

Annual losses due to counterfeiting in China are estimated to be in the billions of dollars. China has acquired an international reputation as a global manufacturing base and clearinghouse for counterfeit products. Chinese counterfeiting networks have become increasingly sophisticated and decentralized over the past decade, and in most cases it is virtually impossible for Chinese and foreign consumers to distinguish genuine from fake goods at the retail level. The Nike Corporation estimates that for every legitimate Nike product made in China, one counterfeit is produced.[1] In certain retail markets, close to 90 percent of some standard household products are counterfeit, while the Chinese government has gone on record to say that the aggregate ratio of counterfeit goods to legitimate products is two to one.[2] Moreover, as a member of the World Trade Organization, there are concerns that China will be unable to enforce its newly revised, TRIPS-compliant IPR laws; fears that China's increased access to export markets will flood the world with Chinese-made counterfeit goods are also starting to be borne out.[3]

There are two general types of trademark violation: counterfeiting and infringement. Although this chapter tilts toward counterfeiting as the focus

---

1. *South China Morning Post,* March 4, 2000, quoted in Quality Brands Protection Committee (QBPC) Pamphlet.
2. QBPC Position Paper, quoted in QBPC Pamphlet.
3. Interview 02SH05, June 27, 2002; Interview 02SH10, July 2, 2002.

of analysis, infringement also remains a serious problem. The rule of thumb in distinguishing the two is that a counterfeit is indistinguishable from its legitimate counterpart, at least as far as the outside packaging is concerned. A trademark-infringing good has outside packaging that is intended to confuse the consumer into thinking that it is a legitimate product; it is similar, but not identical, to the latter. Two examples of a trademark-infringing good are the "W&W's" chocolate candies mentioned in chapter 1 and the "Kongalu Corn Strips" discussed below.

A trademark can include the name of the product. Hershey first started selling its chocolates to the Chinese market in 1995 under the Chinese mark *Hao xinshi* ("good thoughts"). However, after spending millions to establish a brand name in China under this mark (and uncovering massive counterfeiting of its products in the meantime), Hershey was informed that another Chinese confectioner had already registered the *Hao xinshi* name, so Hershey was forced to find another. This "re-branding process, which involved written communication with the company's distributors in China, as well as advertising campaigns and consumer promotions, took about a year."[4] Hershey ultimately benefited: after months of hard work, it was able to retain its consumer base with the even better *Hao shi* ("good times") brand name.[5]

Images are a more ambiguous area of trademark protection. But some cases are more cut-and-dry than others. An example is the dispute between the *Sonsy* and *Biaomei* soap manufacturers in Chongqing. The disagreement revolved around the face that graces the cover of *Sonsy* soaps, that of Laura Saxe, a former visiting student in China who agreed to be photographed for the *Sonsy* soap package and whose visage has since come to symbolize "class and foreign allure." Since she left China in 1993, "'Miss Laura' fever" has gripped Chongqing: "for months around Chongqing, her mug shot dominated—on buses, billboards, shopping bags, but mostly on the bar soap." This led Zeng Minhui, who started the *Biaomei* beauty products company with her husband, to "borrow" Saxe's face in order to increase sales. This "theft" was only discovered after a driver accidentally transported *Biaomei* products to a *Sonsy* factory. *Sonsy* sued *Biaomei* for $50,000, but local judges ordered *Biaomei* to pay only $1,125 in damages, the same amount paid to Saxe for the use of her image.[6]

Most counterfeiting and trademark infringement revolves around the actual packaging of the good. A case of this is that of Kongalu Corn Strips, which liberally—and quite impressively—borrowed from the packaging of Kellogg's Corn Flakes and Rice Krispies. By the mid-1990s, the Kellogg Company had invested nearly $40 million on building a manufacturing base in

    4. Economist Intelligence Unit, *China Hand: The Complete Guide to Doing Business in China* (Hong Kong: Economist Intelligence Unit, 1999), 39.
    5. Ibid.
    6. John Pomfret, "Chinese Soap Opera Has an American Star: Company That Used U.S. Woman's Image Sues Rival That Stole It," *Washington Post* News Service, May 19, 1999, A01.

Figure 5.1. Counterfeit vs. trademark-infringing breakfast cereal. Written testimony from the Kellogg Company presented at USTR hearing, January 25, 1995, on file at the USTR reading room.

China. (Corn Flakes had been sold in China since 1992.) Around August 1993, the Meizhou Kongalu Nutritious Food Company based in Guangdong province began copying the trade dress (that is, the distinctive and nonfunctional features that distinguish a product), the distinctive logo, and "the entire look of [Kellogg's] packaging," all the way down to the Corn Flakes rooster. Moreover, even though Kongalu's Corn Strips boasted nine essential vitamins and minerals (to Kellogg's seven), the product inside appeared to be "filled with significant amounts of impurities, such as insect parts." Not only was Kongalu unfairly taking market share away from Kellogg's by passing off its product as Kellogg's, it was also doing considerable damage to Kellogg's own reputation.[7] Such "appropriations" of outer packaging are not at all uncommon, ranging from *Feichang* ("Forever") Cola, which mimics the bottle shape, red and white label, and "dynamic ribbon device" of Coca-Cola, to the uncanny resemblance of the new "Red Flag" limousines to previous models of Audis sold in China.[8]

Slogans can also be afforded trademark protection. The importance of trademarking a slogan is illustrated by the case of High Status Number One (*Angli yihao*), a popular health tonic produced by the Shanghai Jiaotong

7. Written testimony of George A. Franklin presented at USTR Hearings on January 24–25, 1995 (on file at the Office of the United States Trade Representative Reading Room).

8. Red Flag's web site puts it somewhat differently: the Red Flag design is based on "*importing, digesting and absorbing* German Audi car technique." http://wwwchina.net/faw/e2/3_hongqi.htm, accessed August 9, 2003 (italics mine).

University High Status Limited Company. Its slogan, which sounds (slightly) better in Chinese, is "Eliminate the Body's Internal Waste" (*qingchu tinei laji*), and it is closely associated with the product, much as "Just Do It" recalls Nike and "I'm Lovin' It," McDonald's. However, this slogan has been picked up by other companies, such as Lebang Brand Hemp Seed Capsules (*Lebang pai maren jiaonang*) and Three Flavors Brand Sweet and Luxurious Oral Liquid (*Sanwei pai tangtai koufu ye*), with the likely intention of unfairly capturing some of High Status Number One's market share. Indeed, as one commentator points out, the slogan is even being used for products that do not perform the same function as High Status Number One.[9] The idea is simply to raise the cachet of the product in question by associating it with the popular product High Status Number One through the latter's slogan. The result is that it dilutes the value of High Status Number One, especially if the other products are of poor quality.[10]

Of course, there has been some exogenous pressure from the USTR and the IPR lobby to change China's trademark legislation, particularly with regard to the scope of infringements, the scope of registration of marks, the scope of eligible rights holders, and territorial extension. Much of this external pressure, however, focuses on the issue of well-known trademarks.[11] The Provisional Regulations on Identification and Administration of Well-Known Trademarks promulgated by the State Administration for Industry and Commerce (SAIC) in 1996 provide such protection in China and are compliant with the Trade-Related Aspects of Intellectual Property (TRIPS), the World Trade Organization's IPR regime. The problem has been that the SAIC Trademark Office has refused to extend this protection to foreign marks. A common argument invoked in support of this position is that such marks may be "well-known" outside of China, but not among the Chinese population.[12] This issue has been at the forefront of the trademark lobby's demands for China to revise its trademark regime.

However, as argued in chapter 2, the trademark lobby has largely been a passive actor in the Special 301 process. Apart from the well-known marks

9. See http://www.cnad.com/news2001/20010303/2001033002.htm, accessed July 2, 2003.

10. In a twist to the expectation that counterfeits are of poor quality, Anheuser-Busch markets Budweiser (*Baiwei*) as a "premium" beer in China. As a result, Chinese counterfeiters of Budweiser use a higher-quality beer than the lower-quality beer they use for fake Carlsberg or San Miguel beers. Interview 99SH01, April 5, 1999.

11. "Well-known" trademarks, as the title implies, refers to those marks that are easily recognizable by, and which have a relatively high reputation for, the average consumer. Because the mark is well known, its owners can expect it to be afforded protection by countries in which such a mark is not registered—in part because of prior registration by pirates. Protection for well-known trademarks includes unauthorized use on dissimilar items. For example, when registering a trademark, the owner registers it in accordance with the types of merchandise upon which it expects to affix the mark. Well-known trademark protection makes it impossible for such a mark to be used on merchandise for which it has not been registered, such as the *Pabst Blue Ribbon* mineral water available in China. "The Risks are Rising in China," *Fortune*, March 6, 1995.

12. Economist Intelligence Unit, *China Hand: The Complete Guide to Doing Business in China* (Hong Kong: Economist Intelligence Unit, 1999), 30–31.

issue, the principal complaint of trademark holders has been enforcement, and although there has been some coordination with the USTR at the association level, much of the most interesting (and least known) work in this regard has been occurring at the local level, where the lion's share of counterfeit manufacturing, distribution, and sales takes place.

Manufacture

Manufacturing of trademark-infringing and counterfeit products is spread all over China. Sometimes the production of trademark-violating merchandise takes place in factories that also produce legitimate merchandise (this is also the case with copyright). Either these factories sell production overruns illegally or they maximize profits by simply manufacturing the same merchandise for the legal trademark owners and, after hours, for the counterfeiters in "fly-by-night" operations.

In most instances, the factories make perfectly legal "generic" merchandise that violates trademarks only when the offending mark is affixed. Taking the case of the ubiquitous counterfeit Dunhill shirts that line the stalls of local markets as an example, the counterfeiters purchase legitimate generic shirts in Chaoyang, Guangdong province, and contract them to peasants and migrant workers in Shantou (also in Guangdong) who then sew the counterfeit Dunhill logos. There is often a tremendous incentive for these migrant laborers to engage in this type of work: this type of moonlighting often brings a sorely needed extra 400 yuan or so a month. These laborers also add counterfeit Dunhill buttons made in Shenzhen. The labels and boxes are manufactured and assembled in southern Zhejiang province. Finally, delivery to markets such as the infamous Huating market in Shanghai (since relocated and renamed the Xiangyang market) is incremental and on a "need to sell" basis: retailers do not want to be saddled with too much merchandise because the more counterfeit product there is, the greater the likelihood of a raid—and the larger the financial loss and administrative penalty. Often, customers are told to come back the next day to purchase a specialty item that may not be immediately available on the shelves.[13] Because of the diffuse nature of the production chain, it is very difficult to disrupt it.

However, even when large numbers of counterfeit goods are concentrated in a single area, enforcement can also be difficult. This is the case with the "distribution centers" that are scattered throughout China.

Distribution

"Distribution centers" can range from small nondescript warehouses to operations that encompass entire towns and local economies. These

13. Interview 98SH03C, May 29, 1998.

distribution centers are often managed by local government agencies
(such as the AIC), or they have quasi-private ownership but include officials such as former vice mayors or former AIC directors on their boards
of directors. An estimated 30 percent of these distribution centers are
in eastern China, and there is an extensive network in the northeast as
well. A well-informed source estimates that anywhere between one-fifth to
one-third of merchandise passing through any of these clearinghouses is
counterfeit, violating both domestic and foreign marks. The largest and
most notorious of these distribution centers is located in Yiwu municipality, Zhejiang province, which enjoys a staggering annual turnover of
around two billion dollars a year.[14] Exacerbating the enormous scope of
the problem is the skillful and deliberate diffusion of the actual counterfeiting networks described above, a development made even worse by the
growing army of laid-off (*xiagang*) workers, many of whom have become
"counterfeit entrepreneurs."[15]

In 1999, the only way to get to the backwater of Yiwu directly from Shanghai was five hours by train or an even longer bus ride (although there were
direct flights to and from Beijing and Guangzhou). One of the most striking observations one has walking out of the Yiwu train station is the relative
absence of sedans. Most of the vehicles in Yiwu are trucks, loading and
unloading merchandise from surrounding areas. One is also struck by the
immense warehouses that make up the downtown area. It is a city that owes
its success to its role as a distribution center. The local economy is therefore dependent on the influx and outflow of manufactured goods, many
of which are trademark-infringing or counterfeit. And such operations are
protected by the local authorities. Indeed, among the private investigators
I interviewed (and their clients), the name "Yiwu" has become synonymous
with a "local government-protected counterfeiting center gone amuck."

Retail Sales

The "Silk Alley Market" (*xiushui jie shichang*) on Jianguomenwai in Beijing has operated for years and openly sells an array of counterfeit goods,
particularly North Face, Timberland, and Lowe. One private investigator
recalled a visit to a retailer during an investigation during which the retailer
showed off his tiny apartment where he kept his counterfeit merchandise.
Located behind his retail booth, it was little more than a tiny single room for
which he paid a monthly rent of 40,000 yuan ($4,800).[16] Nor was this retail-
er's booth in a particularly desirable location in the market, where rental

14. Interview 99SH06B, May 18, 1999.
15. On the consumer end, the growing number of unemployed workers has led to an
increase in the demand for counterfeit (read: cheaper) products. Interview 99GZ01A, April 26,
1999.
16. This room held, at most, two dozen pieces of merchandise, in part to discourage raids:
there is less chance of a raid if the stocks are kept low because the expected payoff for the
enforcement agencies is low.

fees are much higher. Rent was paid directly or indirectly to the Chaoyang district AIC. Given that there are more than a hundred of these booths, the amount of income that ends up in the Chaoyang AIC's coffers is enormous.[17] This reportedly goes to the Chaoyang government as locally remitted taxes (*dishui*), not as remittances to the central government (*guoshui*). Moreover, it is often difficult for foreign companies or the U.S. government to make a moral case against IPR infringement in "Silk Alley," as the overwhelming majority of its customers are non-Chinese.[18]

However, most counterfeit and trademark-infringing merchandise ends up in legitimate retail outlets; often the retailers themselves are unaware that the product is illegitimate. Although the foregoing paints a rather bleak picture, trademark enforcement has met with much more success than has been the case with patents or copyright. To begin to understand why, it is necessary to look at the bureaucracies charged with trademark protection and anticounterfeiting.

The Organizational History of China's Anticounterfeiting Bureaucracies

Perhaps the most important difference between trademark and copyright enforcement in China is the degree to which their respective administrative structures penetrate into the localities. Unlike the copyright enforcement apparatus, which below the provincial level is co-opted into the cultural market management subsystem described in chapter 4, the trademark management subsystem and the fair trade/economic inspection subsystem are both part of the AIC system, which extends all the way down to the township and village level. In short, any discussion of policy compliance and enforcement must begin with the physical presence of a viable enforcement apparatus within the nexus in which IPR-violating behavior takes place. In chapter 4, it was shown that no such independent apparatus exists for copyright enforcement. In the following sections, I argue that as far as trademark (or, more accurately, anticounterfeiting) enforcement is concerned, China benefits from not one but *two* such administrative systems, those of the AIC and the QTSB.

Organizational History of the Administration for Industry and Commerce (AIC)

The State Administration for Industry and Commerce (SAIC; *Guojia gongshang xingzheng guanli ju*) is distinguished from many of its contemporary bureaucratic counterparts by its long and relatively uninterrupted

17. Interview 99BJ01, March 4, 1999.
18. Interview 99BJ21, April 1, 1999.

institutional history. Although it has experienced some administrative shuf-
fling and was not immune to the political convulsions of Maoist China, its
institutional culture was allowed to evolve largely intact. And although its
functional responsibilities have shifted somewhat to converge with the growing marketization of China's economy, the residual artifacts of its core functional responsibilities throughout the pre-reform era continue to inform
some of its behavior. The contradictory responsibilities that the SAIC has
acquired throughout its history have served to create an ambiguous organizational mission that can be easily manipulated from within to serve parochial interests at the expense of its current, official responsibilities.

After the establishment of the People's Republic of China in October
1949, the Political Council's Finance and Economic Commission established the State Administration for Private Enterprises, which was responsible for registering private enterprises and joint venture enterprises and
for supervising related laws and regulations. In 1952, after the creation
of the State Planning Commission, organizations in the Finance and Economic Commission underwent a restructuring, and the State Administration for Private Enterprises was abolished and the State Administration of
Industry and Commerce (SAIC) was established in its stead. After the creation of the State Council in 1954, the Finance and Economic Commission
itself was abolished. On November 25, 1954, the SAIC was enshrined as
an administrative office directly administered by the State Council. The
State Council placed the SAIC in charge of managing the transformation
of capitalist commercial and industrial activity into socialism. As early as
1954, the SAIC had established its Trademark Office, although there was
quite a bit of reshuffling throughout the 1950s within the SAIC, especially
from 1957 to 1959.

In 1959, as the Great Leap Forward (1958–61) and its radical approach
to economic development was reaching its peak, central planning and management of the economy was coming under increasing fire by Mao Zedong.
Reflecting the political trends that were transforming the country at the
time, it was decided that socialist transformation had been completed. The
SAIC was then placed under the leadership of the State Council's Office
on Finance and Trade.[19]

In 1960, perhaps as a reflection of the liberal trends toward quasi-private
markets that were seen by some of the top leadership as a way out of the
devastation of the Great Leap Forward, a market department was added to
the SAIC and some of the other departments were reconsolidated. In 1963,
the passage of the revised Statutes on Trademark Management (*shangbiao
guanli tiaolie*) and the Detailed Rules on Trademark Management Statutes
(*shangbiao guanli tiaolie shixing xize*) indicated a setback for general trademark-related concerns and reflected the growing radicalism that would

19. *Zhonghua renmin gongheguo zhongyang zhengfu jigou 1949–1990* [Central Government
Organs of the People's Republic of China, 1949–1990] (Beijing: *Jingji kexue chubanshe*, 1993),
400–401.

soon erupt into the Cultural Revolution (1966–77).[20] During this time the SAIC was largely in charge of managing simple commercial activity for foodstuffs and other basic goods. Although it managed to avoid decimation by the Red Guards during the Cultural Revolution, the AIC system was reduced to a skeleton staff.[21] In June 1970, the SAIC was placed within the Ministry of Commerce (*shangye bu*), where it remained until after the death of Mao in September 1976.

Two years later, on September 25, 1978, the State Council issued a circular, Regarding the Establishment of the General State Administration for Industry and Commerce. It ruled that the SAIC (in this incarnation, *Guojia gongshang xingzheng guanli zongju*) would be reinstated as a directly administered office under the State Council and that it would be represented at the elite level by the State Council's leadership small group on finance and trade. The responsibilities of the SAIC at this time are noteworthy, particularly in light of the discussion of institutional character in the sections to follow. These broad responsibilities included protecting the socialist system of public ownership, maintaining the state plan, safeguarding the honest operations of economic enterprises, "*striking down capitalism, and guarding against development in the direction of capitalism.*"[22]

Institutional Structure of the AIC

The SAIC in its current incarnation was established on August 23, 1982. The broad responsibilities of the SAIC include implementing policies, laws, and Party and government directives; drawing up laws and regulations relevant to the administration of industry and commerce; supervising the economic activities of industrial and commercial enterprises; protecting legitimate enterprises and clamping down on illegal enterprises; safeguarding the "socialist economic path"; and increasing production, mobilizing labor, and ensuring the implementation of the national economic plans. Specifically, the SAIC's responsibilities include supervising the growing local market economies and ensuring that pricing and other related behaviors remain legal and above board; managing all administrative aspects of enterprise and business registration; supervising contracts and mediating contract disputes; registering and protecting trademarks; managing advertising; supervising individual/self-employed economic undertakings (*getihu*); striking out against speculation; and inspecting groups, units,

20. *Zhonghua renmin gongheguo fagui huibian* [Compilation of Laws and Regulations for the People's Republic of China] (Beijing: *Falu chubanshe*, 1982), 162–70.

21. Interview 99SH08, April 29, 1999.

22. "*Daji zibenzhuyi shili, fangzhi zibenzhuyi qingxiang de fazhan*" (italics mine). Other responsibilities included striking out against speculation and black markets, enforcing contracts, mediating economic disputes, managing markets, supervising the registration of enterprises, and registering and managing trademarks in accordance with the law. In 1981, the SAIC also took on the responsibility of managing commercial advertising by establishing an advertising department. See *Zhonghua renmin gongheguo zhongyang zhengfu jigou 1949–1990*, 401–2.

enterprises, undertaking units (*shiye danwei*) to ensure production by legitimate means.[23]

These responsibilities were reflected in the expansion of the departments within the SAIC, as well as their upgrading in rank.[24] By 1991, the policy research department was changed to the laws and regulations department, but perhaps most important for the subsequent discussion on local enforcement, the economic inspection department had also been established by this time.[25] During the 1993 bureaucratic restructuring of government units, the new departments within the SAIC similarly reflected the growing SAIC responsibilities as China's market economy grew in sophistication and complexity.[26]

The institutional structure of the national SAIC office is more or less replicated throughout the AIC administrative system, or *xitong*. At the level of province, provincial-level municipality, and in the more important municipalities (such as Dalian and Ningbo, for example), the Administration for Industry and Commerce is divided, with some variation, into a general office, personnel department, policy and regulations department, fair trade department, enterprise registration and management department, foreign-invested commercial enterprise registration and management department, trademarks and advertisement department, market supervision and management department, self-employed and private enterprise economic supervision department, economic contracts department, and a property auditing department.[27] The number of staff in any particular locale depends largely on what is often referred to as "the level of economic development." In all of greater Chongqing municipality, there are 8,000 AIC personnel, with about one-third in Chongqing city.[28] In 1998, the municipality of Shanghai had a total of 5,700 AIC personnel.[29]

What is critically important in comparing trademark enforcement with the dynamics surrounding copyright enforcement described in chapter 4 is the fact that the AIC system does not stop at the provincial level: the AIC extends through the prefecture (*di zhou shi*), municipal (*shi*), county (*xian*), and urban district (*shiqu*) levels. These offices tend to be quite large, and their responsibilities often mirror their vertically superior counterparts. In fact, it is only at the township (*zhen*) and village (*xiang*) levels that the AIC offices (*gongshang suo*) become significantly

23. Ibid., 402–3.

24. Before 1982 these departments were at the *chu* level; after 1982 they were at the higher *si* level.

25. *Zhongguo zhengfu jigou 1991* [China Government Organizations 1991] (Beijing: *Zhongguo renshi chubanshe*, 1991), 367.

26. *Zhongyang zhengfu zuzhi jigou* [Central Government Organizations] (Beijing: *Zhongguo fazhan chubanshe*, 1995), 341–43.

27. *Zhongguo zhengfu jigou minglu 1996* [Directory of Chinese Government Offices 1996] (Beijing: *Xinhua chubanshe*, 1996).

28. Interview 98CQ26, September 14, 1998.

29. Interview 99SH08, April 29, 1999.

smaller and take on almost completely generalized functions.[30] Even before the AIC restructuring that began in 1998–99, county- and urban district–level AICs had binding leadership relations with their counterparts at the township and village level. However, this did not preclude a substantial amount of collusion between township and village AICs and their corresponding local governments. Since 1999, there has been an attempt to centralize the AIC system all the way to the provincial level.[31]

Two of the most relevant internal departments within the AIC system are the trademark and advertising department and the fair trade department (also known as the economic inspection department). At the provincial level, trademark-related work is handled by the trademark and advertising department (*shangbiao guanggao chu*).[32] Its responsibilities include supervising and investigating the use of trademarks, assisting the process of registering trademarks, and providing an administrative forum to settle trademark-related disputes (80 percent of disputes are below the provincial level, and these may even be mediated at the township or village levels). In Guizhou, this office contains five to six people, two handle trademarks, two deal with advertising, and the rest manage departmental finances. In Shanghai, the office has a staff of around ten, but it no longer handles registration work because of the growth in the complexity of coordination problems; these responsibilities are handled by the growing number of trademark agencies in Shanghai.[33]

At the prefecture level, the trademark and advertising office (*shangbiao guanggao ke*) can have as few as one or two or as many as six people on its staff, although in larger cities (i.e., provincial capitals) the number may equal or even exceed their counterpart offices at the provincial level. At the county and urban district level, it is within the contract advertising and trademark section (*guanggao shangbiao gu*), which also has a staff anywhere between one and four people. The more comprehensive "AIC post" (*gongshang suo*) at the village and township levels is actually a division of the county-level AIC, as noted above, and handles trademark issues as well as many other AIC responsibilities.[34] These offices employ as few as five to as many as thirty people.[35]

30. Interview 98GY04, August 19, 1998.

31. Andrew C. Mertha, "China's 'Soft' Centralization: Shifting *Tiao/Kuai* Authority Relations since 1998," forthcoming in *China Quarterly*.

32. In some localities, such as Inner Mongolia, these two responsibilities are handled by two separate offices (*Zhongguo zhengfu jigou minglu*).

33. Interview 98GY04, August 19, 1998; Interview 99SH08, April 29, 1999.

34. The AIC is not alone at penetrating this sub-county level of government; the Township Industries Bureau, the Finance Bureau, the Land Bureau, the Justice Bureau, the Civil Affairs Bureau, the Public Security Bureau, the Statistics Bureau, and others have offices at the township level. Marc J. Blecher and Vivienne Shue, *Tethered Deer: Government and Economy in a Chinese County* (Stanford: Stanford University Press, 1996), 39–40. See also Vivienne Shue, *The Reach of the State: Sketches of the Chinese Body Politic* (Stanford: Stanford University Press, 1988, 57).

35. Interview 98GY04, August 19, 1998; Interview 99CD04, June 28, 1999.

AIC Enforcement Units

At all levels below the province, the trademark offices of the AIC are involved in investigation and enforcement, not registration. Local AIC units do not have the right to register trademarks; they pass trademark registration up to the national-level SAIC. But local AICs do have the responsibility of enforcing trademarks, and therein lies an important source of tension. The local AICs are charged with protecting trademarks but do not derive any income from doing so because trademark registration income is collected and largely retained by the national-level SAIC. Therefore, all things being equal, if there are other sources of income at the local level that conflict with trademark enforcement, there is little incentive for local AICs to enforce trademarks.[36]

The Fair Trade/Economic Inspection (*gongping jiaoyi/jingji jiancha*) Bureaus are offices within the AIC that handle the investigation and enforcement of commercial laws and regulations (although it can also call upon other parts of the AIC to assist with enforcement, when necessary), including trademark enforcement. Its staffing levels underscore its importance to the AIC: at the urban district and county level throughout Shanghai municipality, for example, the AIC staff numbers around a thousand people. Up to one quarter (between 230 and 250) of these people engage in economic inspection and enforcement. By contrast, only about seventy individuals handle trademark management work (and this is usually in addition to other responsibilities).[37] The fair trade/economic inspection department has the authority to investigate factories and retail outlets, confiscate illegal merchandise, and fine individuals and businesses violating China's commercial laws and regulations. Beyond this general outline, there is a considerable degree of confusion regarding this office.

In some areas, there is a clear distinction between two discrete sets of offices with their own functional responsibilities. In Chongqing, for example, the AIC houses both a fair trade department (*gongping jiaoyi chu*) and an economic enforcement team (*jingji jiancha dadui*). These used to be combined in the same office but were separated sometime around 1998. Although there is some overlap, and in some cases there is ambiguity surrounding the proper jurisdictional parameters, the fair trade office focuses on the "higher ground" of enforcement, including directing and supervising the laws of consumers and industry, and supervising the work "at the county [and urban district] levels." By contrast, the economic enforcement team is involved in "street level" enforcement. In some cases, the fair trade and the economic inspection departments are divided into two offices, in others they are merged into one. At the village and township levels, the *gongshang suo* has no enforcement

36. Interview 98GY04, August 19, 1998.
37. Interview 99SH08, April 29, 1999.

power of its own; it requires assistance from the county or urban district AIC and its enforcement teams.[38]

In other cases, the AIC fair trade departments are actually the same units as the AIC economic investigation units, with the same offices and the same personnel.[39] Whether they carry the formal title of "fair trade department" or "economic investigation department" is often decided by the provincial leadership. In other words, some areas in China use the "fair trade" appellation, while others use the "economic investigation" title. In some cases, there is variation between these two titles *within* a province. One reason for this confusion is that in the mid-1990s, as a result of the 1993 Unfair Competition Law of China, the enforcement arm of the AIC was to be renamed in order to coincide with its responsibilities in enforcing the new law. However, some areas in China have not gotten around to changing their names. In the past, other locales, such as Shanghai, had deliberately refrained from taking on the "fair trade" moniker because the Shanghai AIC regards doing so as unnecessarily narrowing the scope of AIC responsibilities to issues of unfair competition.[40]

Another source of confusion is the opaque—and often seemingly peculiar—nature of the AIC bureaucracy itself. An extreme form of this is found in Guizhou province. Even before the economic inspection units were changed to fair trade offices, there had been a parallel set of offices: at the provincial level, the fair trade department (*gongping jiaoyi chu*) and the fair trade post (*gongping jiaoyi suo*); at the sub-provincial level, the fair trade section (*gongping jiaoyi ke*) and the fair trade team (*gongping jiaoyi dui*).[41] The division of labor between these two sets of parallel offices has to do with the first of these offices (department/section) having the explicit power to enforce, unlike the second of these offices (post/team). However, what is intriguing is that at each of these administrative levels, these two offices are staffed by the *same exact people*. In effect, at any given time, one of these subsystems is a shadow organization of the other, and the personnel simply don the particular "hat" that is appropriate for a given undertaking.[42]

In some other cases the division of labor for enforcement is even more complicated. In Guangzhou, for example, the municipal AIC economic inspection department does not usually "dirty its hands with lower-order" issues such as typical counterfeit crackdowns; it prefers to crack down

38. Interview 98CQ26, September 14, 1998.
39. Interview 99HK01, June 1, 1999.
40. Interview 99SH08, April 29, 1999.
41. Interview 98GY04, August 19, 1998 and Interview 99GY03, June 14, 1999.
42. Much like the more institutionalized upgrading of the provincial copyright departments (*banquan chu*) to Provincial Copyright *Bureaus* (*banquan ju*) described in chapter 4, the creation of this "phantom army" of enforcers is to demonstrate strength and to create leverage in the inevitable interbureaucratic negotiations that characterize Chinese politics. Indeed, by maintaining this fiction, the AIC may be strategically creating the momentum to eventually obtain personnel allocations that are commensurate with its formal offices, which would effectively double the ranks of its AIC enforcement system personnel and, equally important, its corresponding budgetary outlays. Ibid.

on counterfeit manufacturers or focus on altogether different economic crimes, such as those involved in "gray market" exports. It hands over such enforcement to a specialized team (*lianhe zhiqin dadui*).[43]

Nevertheless, the above irregularities of the AIC enforcement system should not obscure the most important fact here: the AIC system is characterized by its comparatively large pool of commercial enforcement units, regardless of formal title. The problem, as will be discussed below, is that there have traditionally been many competing interests within the AIC for these enforcement-based resources. How these limited resources have been channeled into anticounterfeiting enforcement through bureaucratic competition will be analyzed later. It is thus necessary to introduce the competing bureaucracy, the QTSB.

Organizational History of the Quality Technical Supervision Bureau (QTSB)

Unlike the SAIC, the State Quality Technical Supervision Bureau (SQTSB; *Guojia zhiliang jishu jiandu ju*) in its present form (since 1998, it has been renamed the State Quality Examination Supervision and Quarantine General Bureau, *Guojia zhiliang jiandu jianyan jianyi zongju*) has a short institutional history.[44] Much of the analysis in this chapter draws from the fact that over the past several years, units in the QTSB system have actively and effectively used their narrow, streamlined institutional configuration to their advantage in broadening their political jurisdictions, in this case in the direction of anticounterfeiting (de facto trademark) enforcement. However, it is first necessary to lay out the institutional history of the SQTSB to suggest why the proactive organizational behavior of QTSB units, in this case with regard to aggressive anticounterfeiting/trademark enforcement, is considered by many observers to be as good if not better than that of the AIC. Such behavior is especially surprising because, the SQTSB does not hold an official trademark enforcement mandate.

Today's SQTSB is primarily responsible for maintaining product quality and overall standardization in China. Its institutional forerunners, therefore, are to be found in these functional areas. Specifically, these antecedent units include the State Bureau of Measurements, the State Bureau of Standards and Measurements, and the State Standards Bureau. What is striking is that, unlike the SAIC, which remained largely intact throughout the past half-century, even as it moved from one superior unit to another, the history of the antecedent units that make up the SQTSB is one of organizational reconstruction and administrative reconstitution. Therefore, the SQTSB can trace its uninterrupted history only as far back as 1988, more than three decades after the establishment of the SAIC.

---

43. Interview 99GD01, June 9, 1999.
44. I use the comparatively more manageable acronyms "SQTSB" for the national level and "QTSB" for the local levels.

The State Technical Supervision Bureau (*Guojia jishu jiandu ju*) was formally established in December 1988 in the context of China's desire to further develop its market economy. Its predecessor bureaucracies, the State Bureau of Measurements and the State Bureau of Standards, were abolished, and the product quality responsibilities of the State Economics Commission were transferred to the STSB. The broad responsibilities of the STSB were in effect a combination of the responsibilities of its two former antecedent units, albeit with more emphasis on the growing marketization of the Chinese economy.

At the time, the STSB was responsible for regulating the formulation, revision, examination, approval, and promulgation of national standards, as well as the subsequent supervision of their implementation. It was also responsible for establishing basic measurement standards and regulating systematic national recording of measurement-related appliances, managing the registration process for national product quality and issuing relevant production licenses, examining and commenting on enterprise compliance with quality regulations, coordinating all work specific to technical supervision, organizing propaganda, and establishing research and publication institutions. It was also charged with leading and managing enterprises, work units, and special learning institutes directly administered within the QTSB system, as well as leading relevant professional and academic associations and representing China in related international events and exchanges. The responsibilities for supervision and enforcement of the QTSB's product quality mandate were housed within the quality supervision department (*zhiliang jiandu si*), specifically within the supervision and inspection section (*jiandu jiancha chu*).[45]

In 1993, the STSB was placed under the direct leadership of the State Economics and Trade Commission (the successor of the SEC) and upgraded to vice-ministerial rank (*fu bu ji*). Its responsibilities remained largely the same, although there was a subtle shift in the direction of increased penetration into local markets, particularly with regard to investigation and inspection. Since 1998, the STSB has again been in the process of reorganization. Renamed the Quality Examination Supervision and Quarantine General Bureau at the national level, and the Quality Technical Supervision Bureau at the provincial level and below, its responsibilities were left largely unchanged, although they did reflect greater emphasis on industries in which worker safety was dependent on the technical supervision of production facilities and other capital-intensive goods.[46]

Institutional Structure of the QTSB

The QTSB likewise boasts an impressive local network of offices, although unlike the AIC, the QTSB does not formally extend below the

45. *Zhongguo zhengfu jigou 1991* [China Government Organizations 1991], 365.
46. *Zhongyang zhengfu zuzhi jigou* [Central Government Organizations], 420–26.

county level (work at the township and village levels is undertaken by the county-level QTSB). At the provincial level, the QTSB often has a staff of around four dozen people. In Yunnan province alone, the QTSB network employs around two thousand people, or ten times the entire *nationwide* staff dedicated to full-time copyright enforcement. Although the functional jurisdictions of the QTSB will be discussed in more detail in the next section, it is helpful to lay out the internal organization of the QTSB here.

With some variation, provincial and municipal QTSBs mirror the national SQTSB, containing a general office, scientific education and laws and regulations departments, a quality department, a measurement department, and a standards department. In some locales, there are two other offices that fall under the heading of enforcement (investigation, levying fines, and confiscating merchandise), each with a staff of about a dozen: they are the provincial "strike down fakes" law enforcement team (*sheng dajidaoban zhifa dui*) representing the provincial government, and the Provincial Technical Supervision Bureau investigation team (*sheng ji jishu jiandu ju jicha dui*)[47]

Official investigation teams did not exist much before 1994, but at that time there were people who were informally involved in such work. After 1994, this type of work was institutionalized into the investigation team system in which QTSBs at the provincial, municipal, and county levels all have their own investigation teams. The number of personnel in a given investigation team varies from around a half-dozen to thirty people. For example, Liaoning province has more than twenty people in its provincial-level QTSB investigation team. The number of personnel depends on the size of the market, the "behavior" (*xingwei*) of the individual QTSB unit, and the preferences of the local government.[48] In an attempt to increase enforcement, the QTSB investigation teams (like those of the culture market management bureaucracies) have seen their personnel allocations (*bianzhi*) shift from a purely administrative (*xinzheng*) *bianzhi* to an "enterprise/undertaking" (*shiye*) *bianzhi*. The reason for this, as noted in previous chapters, is that the latter type of personnel allocations are easier to come by as they are not as tightly regulated by the government; this is because

47. Interview 98KM04, September 1, 1998. The provincial-level investigation teams are "general" teams (*jicha zongdui*), the prefecture-level investigation teams are referred to as "detachments" (*jicha zhidui*), and the county-level investigation teams are known as "brigades" (*jicha dadui*). I use the generic term *team*, whenever possible to avoid confusion. In an interesting twist that harkens back to the discussion of the Copyright Bureau/department in chapter 4, the twenty-man Sichuan QTSB *jicha zong dui* is also the *jicha fen ju* ("Investigation Branch Bureau"). This is an example of "one group of people, two different signboards" (*yitao ren liangkuai paizi*). Why this redundancy? The "*fen ju*" title is a higher administrative rank, which gives this office some more power vis-à-vis other offices with which it needs to coordinate its activities, while it uses the general investigation team title ("*zong dui*") during anticounterfeiting activities. Interview 03CD01, July 14, 2003. In Guizhou, they are dispensing with the Branch Bureau (*fen ju*) altogether and simply calling them "Investigation Bureaus" (*jicha ju*) to give them added gravitas. Moreover, as of 2003, this appellation did not extend down below the prefecture level. Interview 03GY01, July 19, 2003.

48. Interview 99BJ32A, July 29, 1999.

shiye bianzhi have a lower budgetary allocation than the *xingzheng bianzhi* to match the personnel allocation and are thus cheaper for the government to provide.[49]

At the prefecture level, the QTSB units have the same functions as the provincial-level QTSB, but with fewer staff. Some of the offices are merged for the sake of convenience, although this varies by location. At this level, the QTSB office has a staff of around twenty-five people (with ten others assigned to the investigation detachments, or *jicha zhidui*). At the county and urban district levels, the QTSB's functional divisions are usually collapsed into a comprehensive office (*zonghe bangong shi*). At this level, the QTSB office has a staff of between four and eight people, with two other people allocated full-time to the investigation brigades (*jicha dadui*). The principal task of the QTSB at the county and urban district level is administrative enforcement. As mentioned above, at the township and village levels, technical supervision work is carried out by the county-level QTSB.[50] These local QTSB enforcement teams, like their AIC counterparts, have the right to enter suspected factories, to confiscate merchandise, and to levy fines. When goods are determined to have little or no value, they are confiscated. If they are determined to have some value, they can be auctioned off at prices determined by the local Pricing Bureaus (*wujia ju*).[51]

The important thing to note here is that, like its AIC counterpart, the QTSB system extends to the county level, where much of the actual enforcement activity takes place. Moreover, each of these levels boasts its own special investigation and enforcement team. This is in marked contrast to the copyright enforcement system, which only extends to the provincial level and which must rely upon the press and publication investigation teams and the cultural market management office's investigation teams below the provincial level.

However, there is also a crucial difference between the AIC and the QTSB on this score: the QTSB enforcement teams have a very narrow mandate and therefore are not faced with many enforcement trade-offs. Their goals are both more consistent and manageable than those of the AIC. The AIC, by contrast, suffers from an organizational top-heaviness in

49. Interview 03CD01, July 14, 2003; Interview 03GY01, July 19, 2003; and Interview 03GY02, July 19, 2003.

50. Interview 99CD03, June 28, 1999; and Interview 03CD01, July 14, 2003.

51. QTSB enforcement teams have specialized training and receive certification (provincial-level officials are certified by the SQTSB, while sub-provincial enforcement officials are certified at the provincial level) after passing an examination covering relevant laws, procedures, and regulations, as well as meeting specific technical requirements. Only after they pass the examination and receive their certificate (*sifa zhengjian*) do these individuals have the right to participate in enforcement actions. In some areas, enforcement agents have imposing navy blue uniforms (similar to those worn by customs officers or by the Shanghai AIC), which in some cases actually enhance their authority or at least their ability to intimidate their targets. The official symbol of this office, a chevron-like design, also contributes to the image of the QTSB as a professional institution with its own distinct identity. Interview 98GY04, August 19, 1998; and Interview 98KM04, September 1, 1998.

which many competing offices, jurisdictions, and incentives compete for
the same finite enforcement resources. The impact of these jurisdictional
dynamics on enforcement patterns is the subject of the next section.

Jurisdictional Intersection and AIC-QTSB Competition

In general, the Chinese government discourages two or more administrative agencies from sharing the same functional responsibilities. On
paper, a division of labor separates the AIC and the QTSB as far as trademarks are concerned: the AIC has sole responsibility for trademark enforcement. In reality, between 1994 and continuing up to the present, the QTSB
had carved out a substantial niche for itself within the ongoing crackdown
against counterfeit products in China. This environment of organizational
competition is partly a result of shifting interpretations of the QTSB regarding its own administrative role in Chinese society and in the marketplace.
However, such an interpretation is unlikely to have translated into action
if the AIC, left to its own devices, had not demonstrated a chronic unwill-
ingness to pursue trademark enforcement. This increase in the quantity
and the quality of anticounterfeiting enforcement in China is based on the
organizational competition to capture (or, for the AIC, *recapture*) the trademark enforcement "market." This section traces the changing jurisdictional
factors that have contributed to allowing such a "market" to arise.[52]

All commercial activity in China is regulated by the Administration of
Industry and Commerce. The responsibilities of this administrative system
are far-reaching and broad in scope. As noted in chapter 4, the only commercial activity in China in which the AIC is *not* a principal actor is the
market for "cultural products," which falls under the Ministry of Culture's
cultural market management subsystem. However, it would be wrong to
assume that the AIC has an institutionalized free market bias. As described
above, the AIC spent its formative years as a key player in China's planned
economy, and although it has changed somewhat to mirror China's evolution into a more market-based economic system, it retains some of its
pre-reform institutional character because of its relatively long and uninterrupted bureaucratic history. Therefore, any new responsibilities or free-
market orientation must be understood as having been superimposed upon
the original institutional framework of the AIC as a regulatory mechanism
within a state socialist economy.[53]

The AIC derives its power from its ability to control commercial activity
in a particular geographic area, both as an agent of the local government
(with which individual AIC units have until recently enjoyed leadership relations) and under its own organizational mandate. Moreover, in
the climate of increased economic decentralization under reform, AIC

52. Interview 99BJ32, July 29, 1999.
53. On the regulatory aspect of state socialism, see Janos Kornai, *The Socialist System: The
Political Economy of Communism* (Princeton: Princeton University Press, 1992), esp. chs. 6 and 7.

authority has increased, making the local AICs powerful and financially well-off while at the same time undermining their ability (and often their willingness) to carry out the increasingly contradictory responsibilities, both official and unofficial, they face.

For example, an important source of tension in AIC responsibilities is between enterprise registration and market management, on the one hand, and the enforcement of China's commercial laws and regulations on the other. In theory, the AIC is charged with ensuring that the economic activities within its jurisdiction are legal, and therefore these two responsibilities should not conflict. In practice, however, a combination of personnel and budgetary resource scarcity and administrative inertia results in some tasks being pursued and others abandoned. Not surprisingly, those actions that provide greater rewards to the local AIC are those that are given top priority. Many responsibilities that do not provide a net gain for the AIC in terms of money, power, or prestige end up falling through the cracks.

Simply put, enterprise registration and market management directly or indirectly provide local AICs with a substantial amount of legal or quasi-legal income. Enforcement of economic laws and regulations provides a net loss—that is, in the absence of bribery and other types of corruption. Moreover, enterprise registration and market management are relatively straightforward tasks and rarely involve any real risk. Enforcement of commercial laws and regulations necessitates locating the violating factory, warehouse, or retail outlet and confiscating the offending merchandise, time-consuming actions that often carry the threat of physical violence from the counterfeiters.

When these two sets of responsibilities clash, the outcome is not surprising: if an IPR-infringing enterprise provides the local government and/or the AIC with a somewhat steady flow of income, it is very likely that the AIC will not only refrain from closing down the factory, it may also actively "protect its investment," particularly since there is a ceiling in the neighborhood of 50,000 yuan for counterfeit-related fines.[54] By contrast, there is no such corresponding ceiling on the profit and, by extension, the local government revenues generated by the factory in question.[55] At worst, what may happen is that the AIC can close it down and then simply re-register the enterprise under a different name or person and then look the other way while the enterprise continues to pursue its infringing activities.[56]

In the southwestern province of Yunnan, the Kunming Xichang electronics and audiovisuals market was comprised of more than two hundred stalls that sold audio compact disks, video CDs, DVDs, electronics equipment, and related accessories. However, the overwhelming percentage of merchandise was in the form of illegal VCDs. It was a regional clearinghouse for merchandise from Hunan and Guangdong provinces and from locales

54. The approximate rate of exchange at this time was 8.26 yuan to one U.S. dollar.
55. Interview 99SH02, April 27, 1999.
56. Interview 99BJ06, March 15, 1999.

as far away as Indonesia. What is striking about this operation is that unlike most retail outlets that can close down and move at almost a moment's notice, this market was a large and immobile target for IPR enforcement. Yet on several weekday visits, I observed that business was brisk and concern about government enforcement almost entirely absent.[57]

When asked why such a market openly selling illegal VCDs was allowed to function, one provincial official said that the unit charged with assisting the Wuhua district cultural market management office with enforcement was the same unit that collected the rents from the various retailers—the Wuhua district AIC.[58] Passing through the district Culture Bureau's market management department and ultimately to the Finance Bureau of the Wuhua district government, the aggregation of management fees (*guanli fei*) is almost Kafkaesque in its complexity. There was, first of all, rent for the physical space (*changdi fei*), based on the location of the site within the market and on the square footage of the stall itself. There was also a tripartite breakdown of prices based on location (and considerably simplified here): one retailer toward the back end of the market paid fifty yuan per month per square meter, while other sellers toward the front paid twice or even three times this amount (i.e., for a space of twenty square meters, this price ranged from one to three thousand yuan, depending on the location).

In addition, there was an industry and commerce fee (*gongshang fei*), paid out to the AIC every two to three months, which amounted to another hundred yuan a month. There were also various local and national taxes, which came to about two to three hundred yuan a month. On top of this, there were the ubiquitous water and electricity fees (*shuidian fei*) and health fees (*weisheng fei*). One retailer in a middle-level booth estimated the whole monthly package at about four to five thousand yuan.[59]

A conservative estimate would place the average monthly fee of each stall at three thousand yuan. Multiplied by twelve months and two hundred stalls, the figure comes to about 7,200,000 yuan (about $871,700), a substantial sum for a single market to pay out to an urban district government in the interior of China. To put this into perspective, this amount is more than *seventy times* the annual budget for the Provincial Press and Publications/Copyright Bureau investigation team.[60] Moreover, as long as there were no sales of pornographic, antigovernment, or anti-Party audiovisual products, there was little reason for the cultural market management office

57. One retailer said that crackdowns occur regularly twice a week, at which time all the retailers simply hide their illegal products until the enforcement agencies leave. Interview 99KM04A, Kunming, June 21, 1999. Moreover, one provincial official cautioned that because of the increasingly good quality of packaging for pirated audiovisual goods and the shoddy quality of much legitimate product, it is often difficult to distinguish one from the other. Interview 99KM05, June 22, 1999.

58. Interview 99KM05, June 22, 1999.

59. Interview 99KM04B, June 23, 1999.

60. Interview 99KM03, June 18, 1999.

to intervene.[61] In this situation, one that is replicated throughout China, everybody is satisfied except the owners of the intellectual property being violated.

Making anticounterfeit enforcement even more daunting and less attractive is the fact that the counterfeiting problem in China is both enormous in scope and fragmented in nature, providing the worst of both worlds to a unit charged with anticounterfeit enforcement. The scope of counterfeiting is impossible to quantify in any sort of systematic fashion, although the China Anti-Counterfeiting Coalition puts estimates of annual losses in China for only seven of its members at $300 million and puts the overall figure for foreign companies in China at around 15 to 20 percent of total sales.[62]

Moreover, the counterfeiters have grown increasingly sophisticated in their operations. First of all, the technology for packaging is often of very high quality—even if the product itself is not—including special dyes, foils, and even holograms that appear on the market before their legitimate counterparts do. Second, as counterfeiting becomes more profitable, the counterfeiters themselves are able to reinvest their profits and benefit from economies of scale, producing more and cheaper counterfeit products. They have also become more creative in camouflaging the offending operations, diversifying the merchandise produced by a given factory, and establishing sophisticated distribution networks.[63]

Added to this is the low priority of trademark counterfeiting in the pecking order of enforceable economic and commercial crimes. Apart from the difficulty and the potential physical danger of challenging government- or military-sponsored "local protectionism" and the near impossibility of cauterizing a distribution network for counterfeit goods for any reasonable period of time, the attractiveness of trademark enforcement and the laurels bestowed upon successful enforcers traditionally tended to be less prized than those associated with cracking down on "gray market" goods or ambitious enforcement actions that could become a "big and important case" (*zhongda anjian*). Anticounterfeiting enforcement tended to be piecemeal and labor-intensive—requiring almost constant follow-up, which as one veteran investigator noted is particularly neglected in China[64]—and often does not carry the cachet of enforcement actions directed at other economic or commercial criminal activities.[65] Indeed, this does not appear to be significantly different than the challenges facing the copyright enforcement bureaucracy in China.

61. Interview 99KM04A/B, June 21, 1999, and June 23, 1999, respectively. In fact, there were a number of VCDs that contained patriotic documentaries of various parts of post-1949 Chinese history, including several on the bombing of the Chinese Embassy in Belgrade, a popular item at the time.

62. The China Anti-Counterfeiting Coalition (CACC), "Barriers to Effective Legal Enforcement against Counterfeiting in the People's Republic of China," November 25, 1998, 5.

63. Interview 99SH03, April 27, 1999.

64. Interview 99BJ06, March 15, 1999.

65. Interview 98SH16, May 27, 1998; Interview 99GD01, June 9, 1999.

Figure 5.2. The Kunming Xichang audiovisual market: Changing incentives and enforcement outcomes. Top: In 1999, a seemingly unenforceable situation. Bottom: By 2002, no longer open for business. Photos by author.

Given the foregoing, then, why has trademark enforcement *improved* in the past decade or so? The answer lies in the intrusion into this AIC jurisdiction by the Quality Technical Supervision Bureau, a bureaucracy that saw anticounterfeiting enforcement as a means to expand its own organizational reach. Sensing a "chance opportunity" arising from AIC sluggishness, the QTSB at both the national and local levels was able to exploit this AIC slack and recast itself as a de facto parallel anticounterfeiting enforcement bureaucracy. This understated but deliberate expansion by the QTSB of its own jurisdictional mandate into the arena of anticounterfeit enforcement has dramatically changed the situation, bringing a new bureaucratic competitor into the fray and forcing the AIC into action.

As previously noted, the most relevant QTSB responsibilities have to do with product quality and consumer protection from shoddy or dangerous goods. Insofar as counterfeit merchandise is of inferior quality relative to its legal counterparts, and insofar as the unknowing purchase of such counterfeits harms the consumer, the QTSB can legitimately target the manufacture and sales of such offending merchandise. Beginning in earnest around 1994, the QTSB has liberally interpreted its role to include directly and aggressively combating the production and sales of counterfeit goods, intruding on what had formerly been anticounterfeiting responsibilities of the AIC. This has led to a sometimes intense, albeit understated (and, officially speaking, *verboten*), interbureaucratic competition between the two agencies:

> Rivalries have developed among the various government entities charged with the public enforcement against counterfeiting. . . . A number of these entities continue to upgrade their enforcement tools against counterfeiting in an effort to increase their capabilities vis-à-vis their bureaucratic competitors in order to corner the market on intellectual property enforcement. For example, in Guangdong Province the QTSB recently had its power increased by local legislation leading to increased tensions with the AIC, which has primary authority over trademarks and believes that the QTSB is encroaching upon its authority.[66]

How has the QTSB been able to capture this enforcement jurisdiction so swiftly? First, as noted earlier, unlike the AIC, which has grown by accumulating additional administrative responsibilities over the past fifty years, the QTSB's organizational history began in 1988, a full thirty-five years after the establishment of the AIC, squarely within the reform era. The QTSB may lack the AIC's authority and power, but it is unencumbered by the institutional drag and internally contradictory responsibilities that characterize the AIC. Moreover, the QTSB has much less red tape through which it must go in order to initiate an enforcement action; it is, in the words of one official, "more 'technical' and less 'administrative'" than the AIC.[67] The QTSB has drawn upon its agility of movement and maneuvered itself into settings in which it can increase its functional responsibilities, enhance its authority, and demonstrate its overall significance to superior government organs.

Second, unlike the AIC, the QTSB has a very clear and narrow set of manageable objectives: standardization and measurement insofar as they relate to product quality, and consumer (and producer) safety. Unlike the case of the AIC, the QTSB's organizational responsibilities are limited in number, consistent in operation, largely technical, and less vulnerable to political interpretation and other organizational and geographical biases.

What, then, are the QTSB's incentives for taking on these additional responsibilities? One experienced observer summed it up this way: "To be very clear, the competition [is] over money."[68] Issuing fines, collecting fees,

---

66. China Anti-Counterfeiting Coalition, "Report on Counterfeiting in the People's Republic of China" (draft), February 25, 1999, 20–21. Document in author's possession.

67. Interview 03CD01, July 14, 2003.

68. Interview 02GZ01, July 25, 2002.

and obtaining side payments from trademark rightholding "clients" provide these enforcement agencies with extrabudgetary revenue impossible to secure through normal budgetary allocation processes. Very often, foreign firms and the private investigators acting on their behalf are required to pay "case fees" (*ban'an fei*), which are often little more than bribes. Other forms of side payment provided by these foreign companies and the investigative firms acting on their behalf may be in the form of underwriting legitimate expenses associated with enforcement, including costs associated with overtime pay, renting extra vehicles, and destroying and disposing of confiscated merchandise.[69] Investigators often provide banquets and other entertainment for cadres, and some foreign companies have taken it upon themselves to build recreation facilities for individual enforcement agencies as gestures of "goodwill."[70] This dynamic is captured in the anecdote at the outset of this chapter.

In addition to such remunerative rewards, "having authority to combat counterfeiting results in larger budgets, more staffing, power and prestige."[71] This has been in part an attempt to prevent future personnel and budgetary cuts stemming from the dramatic bureaucratic downsizing begun in 1998. More recently, the QTSB has been consolidating its gains and has moved from a somewhat narrowly technical, third-tier bureaucracy to an important player in China's recent attempts to establish a more effective regulatory environment for its commercial sector and to professionalize the ranks of its new civil service class.[72] These recent developments are due in part to the successes borne by the QTSB's aggressive approach to anticounterfeiting enforcement since the mid- to late 1990s. That said, nonmonetary incentives are generally of secondary importance, especially at local levels.[73]

The foregoing dynamics, in turn, have prompted the AIC to pursue its anticounterfeiting responsibilities more vigorously. For the AIC units, QTSB competition provides a not-so-subtle reminder that they are not operating as effectively as they could. On the one hand, this introduces pressures for the AIC to demonstrate that it can effectively undertake the duties for which it is responsible. This is akin to the bureaucratic competition dynamics in

69. In December 1998, during a meeting of what became known as the Guangdong Action Committee (GAC), AIC officials floated the idea of establishing a pricing list for AIC services in order to lower the transaction costs of AIC cooperation with foreign companies. To the surprise of many, the representatives of the participating foreign companies agreed to the suggestion. Interview 99BJ36, August 3, 1999; and Interview 99BJ39, August 8, 1999.

70. Case fees for enforcement actions have dropped in the past several years. In the past, trademark holders might have to pay up to 10,000 yuan ($1,200) on dinners and other payoffs for a single AIC enforcement action to proceed. Now, such amounts tend to be the exception. This is not because AIC officials have necessarily become more honest but is rather due to increased bureaucratic competition with the QTSB resulting in the reduction of the going price for payoffs. Interview 99BJ06, March 15, 1999.

71. China Anti-Counterfeiting Coalition, "Report on Counterfeiting in the People's Republic of China" (draft), February 25, 1999, 20. Document in author's possession.

72. Interview 03CD01, July 14, 2003; Interview 03XJ01/2, July 17, 2003; and Interview 03GY01, July 19, 2003.

73. Interview 02SH02, June 21, 2002; and Interview 02GZ01, July 25, 2002.

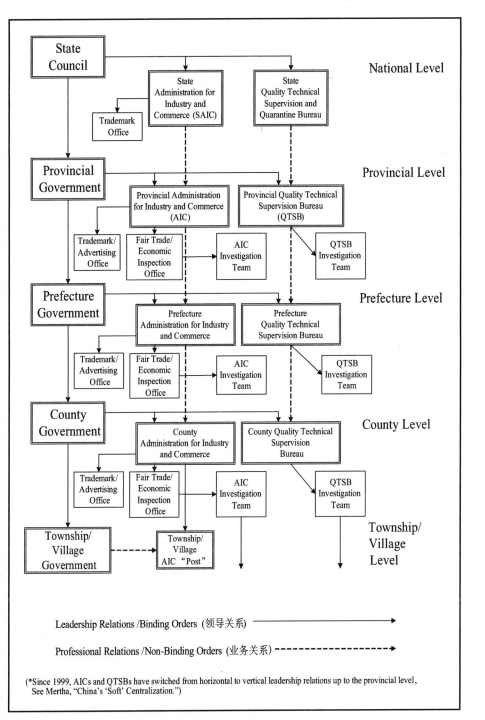

Figure 5.3. China's anticounterfeiting bureaucracies*

Japan noted by Chalmers Johnson: "This kind of conflict . . . invigorates the bureaucracy . . . and provid[es] competitive checks to complacency, bureaucratic rigidity, and arrogance."[74] On the other hand, the growing amount of money to be made provides a positive incentive to engage in effective enforcement. QTSB competition thus alters AIC incentives toward more effective trademark enforcement while raising the stakes for neglecting to do so. This initial response, in turn, has led to a recognition by AIC units that the collection of rents through undertaking effective enforcement provides a source of extrabudgetary income that is not only large but also difficult for supervisory agencies to monitor.[75]

More recently, both the AIC and the QTSB have realized that there is more money to be made not in collecting case fees or charging for their "enforcement services" but in retaining a portion of the fines they collect and subsequently redistributing it within the overall AIC or QTSB budget, a practice local officials refer to as *zishou zizhi*.[76] This has not only led to greater financial rewards for AIC and QTSB anticounterfeiting enforcement, it has also increased the stakes over which the two agencies compete. Moreover, it has led to a dovetailing of incentives between the enforcement agencies and the rightholders: levying case fees provided a *dis*incentive to retain the services of these agencies, while a shift in the focus to *zishou zizhi* created a situation whereby the enforcement agencies were very favorably disposed toward working with these (mostly foreign) actors to meet the latter's goals.

The question remains, why not simply institutionalize AIC-QTSB[77] competition and give it an official endorsement from the State Council? This is exactly what the Chinese government tried to do in the mid-1990s in the context of the emerging "strike down fakes" (*daji jiamao,* or *dajia*) campaign targeting counterfeiting in China. A national "strike down fakes" leadership small group and an attached "strike down fakes" (*dajia*) office were established in 1994. This office included representatives from the QTSB, the AIC, and several other agencies and emerged from two years of concentrated, but informal and non-institutionalized *dajia*-related work, following a set of 1992 State Council pronouncements on the importance of cracking down on counterfeits.[78] The process of establishing the "strike

74. Chalmers Johnson, *MITI and the Japanese Miracle: The Growth of Industrial Policy, 1925–1975* (Stanford: Stanford University Press, 1982), 321.

75. It is much more difficult for the finance (*caizheng*) bureaucracy to monitor the levying and collection of fines and other monies. A more recent policy of monitoring, *shouzhi liangtiao xian,* whereby fines have to be paid into a special bank account from which the AIC (or QTSB) can withdraw funds only after securing permission from the Finance Bureaus, has been established to counter this problem, but it is likely to be ineffective. Interviews 02SH13, July 5, 2002; 02GY02, July 24, 2002; and 02GY03, July 25, 2002.

76. Interviews 02SH13, July 5, 2002; 02GY02, July 24, 2002; and 02GY03, July 25, 2002.

77. At that time, the QTSB was called the Technical Supervision Bureau (TSB). I maintain the QTSB acronym to minimize confusion.

78. "*Guowuyuan guanyu yanli daji shengchan he jingxiao jiamao weilie shangpin feifa xingwei de tongzhi*" [State Council Circular regarding Striking Down Hard on the Manufacture and Sales of Counterfeit and Inferior Quality Goods and Other Illegal Behavior], no. 38, July 2, 1992; and "*Guowuyuan pizhuan weisheng bu deng bumen guanyu yanli daji zhishou jiawei yiyao shangpin*

down fakes" leadership small group began with jockeying by the QTSB (and to a lesser extent, the AIC) to institutionalize the "*dajia*" system.

Sensing an opportunity to enhance its own power, the QTSB put considerable effort into establishing its position as the lead agency for *dajia* work. Although the QTSB pushed hard for this, Zhu Rongji, a vice premier at the time, initially opposed the move, arguing that it would create a deadlock between the QTSB and the AIC. After even more QTSB lobbying, in which the QTSB argued somewhat disingenuously that such an organ was necessary for harmonizing the work of the AIC and the QTSB, Zhu relented and grudgingly gave his assent.[79]

The "strike down fakes" leadership small group was placed within the State Economics and Trade Commission (SETC). This apparently Solomonic decision placed SETC deputy director Xu Penghang at the helm of the "strike down fakes" leadership small group, an apparently nonaligned and unbiased outcome in that neither the AIC nor the QTSB would formally take the helm of this body. Xu's officially disinterested status was undermined, however, by the fact that he also happened to be the director general of the QTSB, as a consequence of which the office handling day-to-day *dajia*-related matters was ultimately placed in the QTSB. Not surprisingly, Zhu Rongji's initial concerns were borne out. Because of the AIC-QTSB deadlock in Beijing, the national *dajia* system fell apart and in 1998 was ordered to be dismantled.[80] Since then, former premier Zhu Rongji, current premier Wen Jiabao, and Vice Premier Wu Yi have all attempted, with varying degrees of success, to clarify and strengthen the division of labor between the AIC and the QTSB. By 2003, several local officials repeated to me the mantra that "the AIC investigates markets, while the QTSB investigates factories and warehouses"—but, it must be said, without much conviction.[81]

But institutions are often slow to die. As of 2003, the *dajia* offices still existed at the national level all the way down to many counties in China; however, at the national level, for all intents and purposes, it was no longer functioning. Rather, *dajia*-related responsibilities were transferred to the more comprehensive "standardize the market economy" leadership small groups (*guifan shichang jingji lingdao xiaozu*) and their attached working offices. The larger mandate of these leadership small groups makes it easier for the various units, particularly the AIC and the QTSB, to get along because there is not as much jockeying for the position of "lead agency" as was the case in a leadership small group and office with a narrower and more contestable mandate. The thinking appears to be that eventually

feifa huodong baogao de tongzhi" [State Council, Ministry of Health, and Other Offices' Circular regarding Striking Down Hard on the Making and Selling of Counterfeit and Inferior Quality Medical Products and Other Illegal Activities Bulletin], no. 57, October 5, 1992.

79. Interview 99HK01, June 1, 1999.
80. Interview 99BJ32B, August 3, 1999.
81. Interview 03CD01, July 14, 2003; Interview 03XJ01/2, July 17, 2003; and Interview 03GY01, July 19, 2003.

the *dajia* offices would be dismantled and the *guifan shichang jingji* offices would take their place, but at the national level and at local levels, the two offices currently exist side by side and, in some cases, are made up of the same individuals representing the same bureaucratic agencies.[82]

The Role of Foreign Actors

One of the most dramatic developments in the past two decades of reform in China has been the enormous rise in the levels of foreign direct investment. Accompanying these increasing levels of FDI was the parallel rise of foreign commercial actors living and working in China. When combined with the growing competition between the AIC and the QTSB, this trend has had a tremendous impact on patterns of trademark enforcement in China.

This development was not immediate; the initial learning curve was steep. The Chinese often claim that foreigners cannot ever really understand "the way things work" in China. Often, this expectation is borne out. However, many foreign actors, in part by developing a keen sensitivity to the Chinese context and by strategically employing Chinese *compradors* in key positions, have discovered that it is indeed possible to gain some degree of understanding. In engaging local AICs and QTSBs to step up their enforcement efforts, the more successful foreign companies have been increasingly able to behave more like their Chinese counterparts, with one important difference: money. Unlike their Chinese counterparts, foreign actors have traditionally brought a lot of money to the table, a critical component in their ability to assist in the transformation of the incentive structures of local government enforcement agencies with regard to anticounterfeiting.

The success of these foreign companies in establishing trademark enforcement–based alliances with local government agencies is due in no small part to the ability of these actors to mimic and expand upon previous and concurrent efforts by some of their Chinese counterparts. It is generally accepted in China that violations of Chinese intellectual property far outstrip instances involving foreign intellectual property. However, in the analysis to follow, foreign actors loom much larger than Chinese IPR holders. As noted above, this is largely due to their ability and willingness to exploit large financial resources in the hopes of changing local incentive structures for anticounterfeiting enforcement.[83] Indeed, their smaller

---

82. Interview 03XJ01/2, July 17, 2003; and Interview 03GY01, July 19, 2003.

83. One might ask why these actors, ostensibly representing mobile capital, do not exercise their "voice" option instead of their "exit" option. Part of the answer is that capital in China is not quite as mobile as one might assume, so sunk costs tend to be quite high. In addition, this raises the question of where one would move this capital. If the answer is "somewhere else in China," there is little to prevent the same thing happening in the new location. Finally, the lure of the "China market" is so seductive to many foreign firms that it undermines what might otherwise be a decision to exercise their "exit" option. See Albert O. Hirschman, *Exit, Voice, and Loyalty: Responses to Decline in Firms, Organizations, and States* (Cambridge: Harvard University Press, 1970).

number relative to Chinese firms is more than made up by the money they bring to the table.

However, simply throwing money at the problem is not sufficient. The more successful of these foreign firms have paid close and careful attention to the behavior of some of their more aggressive Chinese counterparts. Some Chinese actors have been able to establish limited defenses against counterfeiters. The example of Southwest Ink is particularly illuminating.[84] Established in 1957, its products are sold throughout China and the company is particularly renowned in the Southwest for its red ink, the trademarked *Zhu Mo*.

My source said that the counterfeiting issue became much more complicated once China began moving toward a market economy. Seeking to expand its operations, the factory in 1985 licensed its *Zhu Mo* product to five manufacturers in Sichuan and one each in Guizhou and Yunnan provinces. The agreements stipulated that the Chongqing factory would supply the materials to the "branch factories" while the latter were required to use these materials in procedures that were set by the Chongqing factory.

It quickly came to light that the licensees were quite literally "watering down" the finished product in violation of the licensing agreement—with the blessing of their local governments. Not surprisingly, the resultant ink was of inferior quality, yet legally it retained the *Zhu Mo* trademark. The "branch factories" thus increased their own short-term revenue while lowering the value of the *Zhu Mo* trademark in the long run. Moreover, former workers from these factories opened their own ink manufacturing operations and brought the *Zhu Mo* trade secrets (and sometimes even the *Zhu Mo* mark) with them, while unscrupulous private operations have illegally used the *Zhu Mo* mark (or trademark-infringing variations of it) for ink they produce without any kind of contractual relationship with the Southwest Ink Factory.

The first step taken by Southwest Ink was to sever its relationships with its licensees. In addition, the Chongqing factory started an investigation, engaged in market research, and even set up a special office at the factory to deal solely with trademark issues. It has enlisted the help of the AIC, but this has not been enough to stem the flow of counterfeit *Zhu Mo* products into the marketplace. In a strategy that is representative of many Chinese firms, Southwest Ink uses its sales staff as the front line in the fight against trademark violations. In addition to their sales responsibilities, these people are charged with investigating the marketplace and identifying counterfeit *Zhu Mo* products. These salespeople are often young and energetic, and they have far better knowledge of the product in question and can distinguish fakes from legitimate *Zhu Mo* products. As salespeople, they can "blend into" the market, are far less obtrusive than enforcement officials, and are thus able to get a far more accurate reading of the marketplace.

---

84. Southwest Ink is a pseudonym.

Finally, these salespeople also encourage consumers to contact them when they unwittingly buy a counterfeit *Zhu Mo* product and to identify the location of the sale. The salesperson will then follow up with an investigation, sending the counterfeit product to the Southwest Ink Factory's technical department for testing, if necessary.

My source also reflected the Chinese preference for handling such matters through administrative channels as opposed to legal ones. Going through administrative management authorities (i.e., the AIC or the QTSB) results in a simpler process, a lower standard of evidence necessary for an investigation, and a speedier conclusion.[85]

What is noteworthy about the experience of Southwest Ink is that it can easily serve as a playbook for the strategies foreign companies can use to manage trademark enforcement in China. Companies like Southwest Ink have served as models for how to engage this enforcement process, and foreign companies have aggressively moved up the learning curve over the past decade. The greater monetary resources available to foreign companies have allowed them to surpass their Chinese counterparts in harnessing and exploiting another critical development in the evolution of "street level" trademark enforcement in China: the rapid growth in the number of investigation agencies on Chinese soil.

Government Enforcement Agencies and Private Investigation Firms

One particularly interesting and unexpected development in China over the past several years has been the ability of private and quasi-private foreign and Chinese investigation agencies to take root and flourish. It is remarkable because it puts foreign actors and Chinese enforcement agencies in sustained, intimate contact with one another in what continues to be regarded as a sensitive issue: law (including IPR) enforcement in China. These agencies numbered around fifteen at the end of 1999 and have mushroomed since then.[86] Traditionally, these firms' client bases have been overwhelmingly foreign, not Chinese, companies.

It should be underscored that establishing these types of transnational networks has been far more difficult in sub-provincial copyright enforcement. As noted in chapter 4, below the level of the province, copyright enforcement falls under the jurisdiction of the cultural market management system. The actors in this system carry an institutionalized suspicion of, and are often sealed off from, foreign influence, which this bureaucracy sees as the principal cause of the "spiritual pollution" it is charged with combating. There has been little opportunity for foreign actors to establish relationships with this bureaucracy, as a result of which copyright enforcement is denied the potential benefits of a transnational network

---

85. Interview 98CQ07, April 8, 1998.
86. Interview 99BJ36, August 3, 1999; Interview 02SH02, June 21, 2002; Interview 02SH07, June 28, 2002; and Interview 02GZ01, July 25, 2002.

between local enforcers and the agents of foreign IPR holders. Therefore, many copyright owners utilize the AIC when the issue at hand straddles copyright and trademark violations, such as the sales in China of the "Windows 96" operating system.[87]

Trademarks, in contrast to copyright, are regarded in China as apolitical and utilitarian. Trademarks have traditionally been used to indicate the origin of manufacture for a given product. The emphasis on the actual value added offered by a trademark is a somewhat more recent phenomenon. Even regions under the control of Chinese Communist guerillas in the 1940s, such as the Su-Wan, Pu-Ji-Lu-Yu, Hua-bei, and the Shaan-Gan-Ning base areas, had established their own local trademark laws and regulations.[88] Unlike patents and copyright, trademarks existed throughout the PRC, even during the Cultural Revolution, although, as Mark Sidel points out, the constriction in the universe of "politically correct" brand names—such as Red Flag, East Wind, and Worker Soldier Peasant—often obscured the identity of the actual manufacturer—and in the process made trademarks largely meaningless.[89] Unless the trademark itself uses politically charged items—as was the case with Yves Saint Laurent, which is forbidden to sell its Opium line of perfume in China because of the country's unfortunate history with that fragrance's namesake—trademarks tend to be politically neutral.[90]

The backgrounds of these investigative agencies are far from uniform and remain shrouded in some secrecy.[91] Nevertheless, a few patterns of evolution have emerged. The first type are law firms like Rouse and Co., which take on a substantial amount of work outside of the courtroom, rolling up their sleeves and working in the trenches, much like the "consulting companies"/investigation agencies described below.

The second type of agencies are Chinese-owned (often ambiguously so) IPR investigation firms.[92] One such company, Eastern Consultants Limited (ECL), while ostensibly a joint venture with a Hong Kong consortium of lawyers, is essentially a state-owned investigation company. ECL staff includes former members of the Public Security Bureau (PSB), the AIC, and the China Patent Bureau, among others. These people are not retirees, but rather younger employees let go in the administrative downsizing

87. "War on Piracy Continues in China," *Billboard*, vol. 108, no. 29 July 20, 1996.

88. Liu Yunhan, Gao Li, and Zhao Lisheng, *Zhishi chanquan guanli* [The Management of Intellectual Property Rights] (Kunming: *Yunnan daxue chubanshe*, 1997), 104; and Tu Jialun, *Shangbiao xue* [The Study of Trademarks] (Kunming: *Yunnan minzu chubanshe*, 1990), 663–70.

89. Mark Sidel, "Copyright, Trademark, and Patent Laws in the People's Republic of China," *Texas International Law Journal* 21, no. 2 (1986): 259–89.

90. "China Bans *Opium*-Brand Perfume, Citing 'Bad Social Influence,'" *China Business Information Network*, September 7, 2000.

91. In order to protect the anonymity of my sources, some of the company names have been changed.

92. In some cases, U.S. and Hong Kong firms act as "front companies" for these investigation agencies to solicit business, preferring to keep the actual nature of the agency secret from the general public.

of the mid- to late 1990s, although their personal dossiers (*dang'an*) still reside within their former government units. ECL claims that it has around twenty licenses that empower it to undertake actions that foreign law firms in China cannot touch, such as the power to issue "seize and desist" orders and to collect debt, a highly controversial issue in China.

Formed in and around 1994 by Vice Premier Li Lanqing and the minister of justice to demonstrate China's "get tough" policies on IPR to the USTR, ECL remained a showpiece for several years. However, with the major government staff and budget cutbacks following the Ninth National People's Congress in March 1998, ECL began to take on a more concrete role in law enforcement. The advantage of ECL is that it can cut through a great deal of red tape as a result of its political connections, particularly through its network of informal relationships with the SAIC.[93]

A far better-known agency is the China United Intellectual Property Protection Center (CUIPPC), a Beijing-based investigative firm that is very well managed and aggressive and demonstrates creativity in educating its agents in the specifics surrounding a particular case. Some have suggested that this firm was established as a result of the 1995 IPR negotiations as a company formed by the Legislative Affairs Office of the State Council to demonstrate China's commitment to IPR protection, and although it is no longer "owned" by the State Council, it maintains a close relationship with its former host unit. With a half-dozen offices throughout China, in each region it has a lead investigator who reports directly to Beijing. The staff members that are recruited for a particular case are chosen for their specific expertise regarding a given investigation or enforcement action.[94]

The third type of investigative firm is the foreign-owned "consulting" firm specializing in IPR enforcement, such as Factfinders; Kroll Associates; Pinkerton; Hill and Associates; and Markvess, as well as a rapidly growing number of lesser-known firms.[95] These consulting agencies have been infused with veterans of the Hong Kong police force, who were given the "golden handshake" when Hong Kong reverted to Chinese sovereignty in 1997.[96] Although these firms do not necessarily limit their operations to intellectual property issues, 80 to 90 percent of their work is taken up with IPR enforcement. Within this area, nine-tenths of their business deals with trademark and counterfeit issues.[97] These firms have no legal authority but rather assist (and aggressively recruit) clients by identifying counterfeits in the marketplace, gathering evidence, and working together with the relevant enforcement agencies to undertake enforcement actions on behalf of their clients.

---

93. Interview 99BJ21, April 1, 1999.
94. Interview 98SH14, May 26, 1998; Interview 99HK02, June 2, 1999.
95. Anne Stevenson-Yang, "Gumshoes," Beijing *City Edition*, May 14–27, 1999, 6.
96. Interview 02SH05, June 27, 2002.
97. Interview 98SH03D, July 7, 1998; Interview 99BJ38, August 5, 1999.

The individuals on the front lines are arguably the most important people on the payrolls of these firms. These people are almost exclusively Chinese, as foreigners are generally not allowed to participate in the actual enforcement actions themselves, even as observers—although, as the anecdote at the beginning of this chapter establishes, this is not a hard and fast rule. This is due, in part, to the inclination of the AIC and the QTSB to work only with Chinese because of the sensitive nature of their work. While most of the coordination is undertaken by the investigation firms, the actual enforcement actions can only be undertaken by the actual AIC or QTSB units.

As noted above, one of the main reasons why foreign trademark interests are overrepresented by these investigative agencies is that foreign companies tend to have more money at their disposal for such activities; many Chinese companies are disinclined to use their income in this way.[98] This type of enforcement can be expensive, although in recent years, competition has driven the price down dramatically.[99] The price for a raid or enforcement action is often determined on a case-by-case basis. Investigators also incur travel and lodging expenses, sometimes for weeks at a time. They also often pose as customers and maintain their cover by purchasing a large number of samples; one investigator told me that "you cannot simply buy one [item]" in such an instance.[100] Moreover, thoroughness dictates that it is necessary to go after other actors along the supply chain, many of whom are often, and not by accident, hundreds of miles away from production and retail sites.[101]

Another substantial cost has traditionally been the trademark agent (*shangbiao daili*), a factor that foreign companies take into account when comparing the AIC and the QTSB as enforcement agents. In the early 1990s, the China Council for the Promotion of International Trade (CCPIT) had a monopoly over trademark agency; as of 1999 there were about three dozen trademark agents authorized to handle foreign requests for action; however, reportedly all but a handful of them received this authority as a political favor and were not particularly qualified, at least professionally, for such work.[102] Moreover, some trademark agents are more powerful than others vis-à-vis local enforcement units, and it is necessary to distinguish the former from the latter.[103]

These agents are usually Chinese lawyers, and are often "recommended" by the AIC unit working on a particular investigation, which can obtain

98. In the past, enforcement could cost $8,000 or more per raid. It is also the case that many Chinese companies either do not see the value in spending money on such enforcement activity or see the foreign companies taking on the full burden of providing a "public good." Interview 02GZ01, July 25, 2002 and Interview 02SH02, June 21, 2002.

99. Interview 02GZ01, July 25, 2002.

100. One African-American investigator found himself in particularly high demand for this type of work, as he often posed as a buyer from any number of poor sub-Saharan African countries.

101. Interview 98SH03D, July 7, 1998.

102. Interview 99BJ36, August 8, 1999.

103. Interview 99BJ06, March 15, 1999.

an informal "finder's fee." The agent helps draft the necessary "complaint letter," which is similar to a search warrant in the United States in that merchandise not included in the complaint letter cannot be confiscated during that raid.[104] Apart from the cost of the trademark agent, which can range between $200 and $7,000 per complaint, or as high as $150 per hour of service, going through a trademark agent represents another step in the process, a step that often allows an extra opportunity for the counterfeiters to be tipped off that a raid is imminent and a chance to close down temporarily or move their operations.[105] On the positive side, a formal complaint letter adds extra authority to the enforcement action, which helps counter the power of local protectionist tendencies.[106]

Foreign commercial actors in China have shaped enforcement patterns in at least three important ways. First, they play a vital role in raising the stakes and thereby shaping the incentive structure so that these two bureaucracies find it in their interests to become active in anticounterfeiting enforcement.[107] It is worth quoting at length from a draft report of the China Anti-Counterfeiting Coalition, as it provides a particularly good summary of this exchange. Anticounterfeiting enforcement provides

> many perks that authorities get from companies in the form of trips to conferences in the PRC and abroad, expensive post-raid dinners, lunches and other entertainment. Raids are also revenue-generating activities because authorities confiscate cash, goods, machinery and equipment, including cars and will then sell confiscated goods at public auctions. Fines imposed upon counterfeiters enrich government coffers and some administrative agencies give cash bonuses to personnel who participate in successful raids. Government authorities also routinely ask companies to reimburse the cost of lodging where travel is required, the cost of hiring trucks to load and move confiscated goods, and the cost of storing the goods if a private warehouse needs to be rented. Some government authorities will also ask companies to pay case handling fees. One local AIC has even established a special association, with a membership fee, for companies interested in around the clock twenty four [sic] enforcement services. Budget limitations are the reasons most commonly given for these fees and the reimbursement of costs, but increases in budgets and resources do not appear to change these practices. After years of these practices, a culture seems to have developed that companies should subsidize enforcement activities.[108]

104. Interview 99SH03C/D, May 29, 1998 and July 7, 1998, respectively.

105. This provides an area where the QTSB can compete favorably with the AIC because the QTSB does not require this step. Interview 03CD01, July 14, 2003.

106. Interview 98SH23, June 15, 1998; Interview 99SH06B, May 18, 1999; and Interview 99HK05, June 4, 1999.

107. Interview 99BJ06, March 15, 1999; and Interview 99BJ36, August 3, 1999.

108. China Anti-Counterfeiting Coalition, "Report on Counterfeiting in the People's Republic of China" (draft), February 25, 1999, 20–21. Document in author's possession.

As noted previously, side payments are not always remunerative. From an organizational standpoint, one such side payment is to provide "face" to the enforcement agency through expressions of gratitude in newspapers and trade journal advertisements. Although this payment of "political capital" should not be overstated, neither should it be completely overlooked: in a country that puts a premium on political symbolism, it is an effective way of providing positive exposure to a given bureaucracy, whether the QTSB or the AIC. Such nonremunerative side payments can be as mundane as helping enforcement agencies fulfill their monthly quotas of raids. The AIC often "lobbies" the investigation companies to provide such work, particularly during "lean" spells of enforcement activity.[109]

Second, while it would be an overstatement to say that these foreign actors play the AIC and the QTSB off of one another, they have adeptly fanned the flames of this interbureaucratic competition to their own advantage. Individual company representatives and even investigation firms, whether Chinese or foreign, cannot undertake enforcement actions by themselves. They must secure the cooperation of local enforcement authorities, most often the AIC or the QTSB. This involves considerable sunk costs. After identifying the least corrupt and most helpful and effective of these agencies, it can take up to eighteen months before the relationship becomes "productive."[110]

Finally, foreign companies and the investigation agencies in their employ have found that if they are willing to undertake the groundwork, and if they are able to help disentangle the potential jurisdictional disputes that may arise, Chinese enforcement agencies are far more likely to work on their behalf. That is to say, the foreign actors undertake the "wet work" and the Chinese administrative enforcement agencies act as the "white knights."

In recent years, these investigation firms have sprung up all over China. There has been fierce competition between them, making a dirty business arguably even dirtier. In some cases, competition is so intense that some less scrupulous agencies come up with "fake fakes"—that is, they invent stories about sales of counterfeit where no such sales exist in order to secure the legitimate trademark holder as a client. Nevertheless, in many cases, the degree of personal empathy and professional confidence between these agency representatives and Chinese enforcement agents is striking. Although these relationships are absolutely crucial to understanding anticounterfeiting enforcement patterns in China, they have been joined by networking at the national level as well. And although some investigators argue that these formal national-level networks are little more than window-dressing, in reality these national-level associations and networks appear to be a complement to local enforcement and an important source of pressure toward shaping the nature of anticounterfeiting efforts in China.[111]

109. Interview 02GZ01, July 25, 2002.
110. Ibid.
111. Ibid.

This is particularly true with regard to more recent moves toward making criminal prosecution the default response to counterfeiting.

The Criminalization of Counterfeiting

Perhaps the most important and glaring shortcoming in anticounterfeiting enforcement to date has been the inability to deter future counterfeiters. One investigator put it this way: "Even if a company underwrites one hundred enforcement actions a year, counterfeiting activity will continue largely unabated."[112] Because of the diffusion in the manufacturing and distribution stages described in previous sections, the merchandise on hand is always kept in small quantities in order to ensure that fines stay low, and thus can be treated as overhead. Out of the twenty-three raids from March to September 1995 in Beijing and Guangzhou targeting counterfeit Nintendo products, in only ten instances were fines levied. In these ten cases, the average fine was 8,230 yuan ($990).[113] In just two cases were business licenses invalidated; when this happens, the business is often simply re-registered under the name of another family member or business associate. In other instances, the entire economic well-being of a locality may depend on counterfeiting. Insofar as counterfeiting provides employment and therefore economic and social stability, such local protectionism is especially difficult to resolve because it nestles such economic calculations in a political context. Many foreign (and Chinese) commercial actors have concluded that it is impossible to address this problem effectively by simply increasing the number of enforcement actions and that something far more powerful is needed.

For policy to be implemented successfully and systematically, a growing number of trademark holders and investigation agencies argue that what is needed is some form of "ideology" to lower these enforcement costs to a manageable level—an ideology of deterrence.[114] Without this "fear factor," the positive economic incentive to continue is simply too great.[115] As this view has become increasingly widespread, there has been a steady effort by foreign companies and the investigation firms in their employ to revisit what has been a seemingly distant but sought-after goal for the past half-decade: to place anticounterfeiting enforcement squarely in the arena of criminal prosecution.

The 1997 revised Criminal Law contains specific provisions for intellectual property offenses. Section 7 of the Criminal Law provides for sentences

112. Ibid.
113. Nintendo Special 301 Submission, February 20, 1996, USTR Archives.
114. Douglass C. North, *Structure and Change in Economic History* (New York: Norton, 1981). North discusses such an ideology in terms of providing a positive incentive to change behavior, but he does not necessarily preclude a negative, deterrent-based "ideology" as an effective incentive structure.
115. Interview 02GZ01, July 25, 2002.

of up to three years in prison or hard labor and a fine for IPR-related crimes. If the value or the quantities involved are deemed particularly "huge" (*judade*), the sentence is between three and seven years and a fine. The baseline appears to be if the product on the market is valued at 50,000 yuan ($6,000) or more, although this appears in the "Economic Crimes" section of the Criminal Law and not the "Intellectual Property" section. Sentences of more than seven years—and even the death penalty—can be invoked if the economic crimes (i.e., counterfeit production and sales) in question result in serious injury or death of a consumer; the stipulations regarding pharmaceuticals and foodstuffs are particularly severe. According to one source, "three-time losers," that is, recidivists found guilty of three counterfeiting offenses can be automatically turned over to the Public Security Bureau (PSB).[116]

The potential deterrent effect is significant. Although the number of cases that end in criminal prosecutions is still too low to create this effect, the cases that do result in prosecution often result in sentences that are considered severe. One foreign company report stated that it was able to secure thirty-four criminal prosecutions, with an average jail sentence of three years. Even though such a sentence might appear somewhat modest, three years in prison or in a labor camp can still act as a considerable deterrent. It is not simply that prison conditions can be terrible, but there is a tremendous social stigma associated with a stint in prison. A prison sentence often means losing one's livelihood, one's family, and prospects for a decent job in the future. This is true all over Asia, but it is particularly true in China. And in China it is not possible to "trade in" one's jail time for monetary compensation, as was the case in Taiwan.[117]

The initial number of cases looks promising, but it is still extremely low. After experiencing considerable reluctance from the PSB and the People's Procuracy to intervene, the numbers have begun to increase, slowly but steadily. One investigator said that in his four years in Shanghai, he has participated in three thousand enforcement actions. In the thirteen years he lived in Taiwan, he participated in just over half that number. The difference is that in Taiwan, almost all of them were prosecuted as criminal offenses. In 1996, one quarter of one percent of all trademark-violating cases were prosecuted under China's revised Criminal Law. By 2002, the number was between 2 and 2.5 percent. Although this number is still small, it does represent nearly a tenfold increase over five years.[118] One U.S. company was able to secure only one criminal prosecution in 1999. The following year, the number went up to three. In 2001, the number jumped to twelve and then doubled in 2002. At the same time, this same company undertook almost six hundred enforcement actions in 2001 alone. Half of them were prosecutable under the Criminal Law, but only twelve of them

116. Interview 02SH02, June 21, 2002.
117. Ibid.
118. Ibid.

were actually prosecuted.[119] Another knowledgeable source indicated that nine-tenths of cases with which he was familiar that could have been handled in the criminal court were instead handled administratively.[120]

This falls short of providing an adequate deterrent. However, even this modest increase would probably not have been possible if not for the continued pressure brought by foreign companies. The investigation companies acknowledge a rising trend in which their clients are pressuring them to conduct raids so that the 50,000-yuan threshold is met and the case can be brought to criminal court. After years of undertaking hundreds, even thousands, of raids, representatives of these foreign companies realize that even though administrative enforcement is better than civil litigation, administrative enforcement cannot provide the deterrent that is necessary to get the counterfeiters to cease and desist. A group of foreign companies realized this back in 1998 and formed the China Anti-Counterfeiting Coalition (CACC).

By mid-1998, the last officials at the United States Embassy in Beijing directly involved in the Sino-U.S. IPR negotiations were being rotated to posts outside of China. One such official articulated his admiration for the International Intellectual Property Alliance (IIPA) which had, in his view, done a "great job" in using Special 301 to bring copyright concerns to the top of the U.S.-China bilateral trade agenda. At the same time, he lamented the fact that, despite being in his opinion more important, trademark issues were all but ignored in the official dialogue. He noted that economic losses from counterfeiting far exceed those of copyright piracy. As a result, U.S. Embassy officials put together a coalition of businesses to bring attention to trademark counterfeiting in China. This group, the China Anti-Counterfeiting Coalition, was formed on May 14, 1998.[121] Because U.S. officials were anxious to move this group out of the embassy to pre-empt the charge that the U.S. government was "conspiring" with American businesses against China, as well as to ensure that the CACC could be legitimately seen as espousing business interests and not government policy, CACC leadership was assumed by representatives from Proctor and Gamble and S. C. Johnson, who immediately began to recruit interested companies into the CACC ranks.

Although the CACC began as a somewhat confrontational and aggressive organization in the mold of the IIPA, these initial impulses were tempered over the course of the next two years, partially in recognition that, for pressure to be successful in China, it has to be a combination of positive and negative inducements. As a result, the approach of the CACC changed, even as its ultimate goal—the default criminalization of counterfeiting—did not. First, the CACC jettisoned its initial United States Trade Representative–style confrontational approach for one of cooperation with

119. Interview 02GZ01, July 25, 2002.
120. Interview 02SH10, July 2, 2002.
121. Interview 98BJ01, June 13, 1998.

the Chinese authorities. Second, on the "advice" of the Ministry of Foreign Trade and Economic Cooperation (MOFTEC, since renamed the Ministry of Commerce, or MOFCOM), which quickly became a sponsor, it changed its name to the more benign-sounding Quality Brands Protection Committee (QBPC) in March 2000.[122] It was also placed under the China Association of Enterprises with Foreign Investment (CAEFI, or *Zhongguo waishang touzi qiye xiehui*).[123] Although traditionally a few foreign companies have joined CAEFI, according to Pearson, "the vast majority of members have been Chinese, and the association is geared heavily toward their participation."[124] This is significant because it makes the QBPC a sub-association of foreign companies within what is largely a *Chinese* governmental association, CAEFI. It is also noteworthy that in July 2001, MOFTEC Minister Shi Guangsheng became the Chair of CAEFI, which, according to one source, is the first time that an incumbent ministry-level official has simultaneously served as the chair of an association.[125]

In 2000, the QBPC first got its foot in the door when it issued a study on the economic impact of counterfeiting that reported that the annual value of counterfeit goods in the Chinese market represented a 132 billion yuan loss (including, pointedly, 25 billion yuan in taxes) to the Chinese economy. This report made it to the desk of Liu Huaqiu, head of the Foreign Affairs Office of the Chinese Communist Party Central Committee, who then passed it on to Premier Zhu Rongji himself.[126] Zhu was supposedly so outraged at the laxity of the middle-level officials that during a meeting with QBPC representatives, he turned to them and said, "Look at how much you have shamed me."[127]

One QBPC representative struck up a friendship, quite by accident, with the same Liu Huaqiu, unaware of Liu's important gatekeeping function vis-à-vis the top leadership. Initially professing no knowledge about the scope of the counterfeiting problem, Liu reportedly became increasingly incensed as he learned more about it (the QBPC was naturally more

122. According to one QBPC representative, Chinese government officials in Beijing were becoming nervous that the QBPC—an independent association with foreign roots—was growing so rapidly and made it clear that it was to be co-opted within the relevant Chinese government associations. Interview 02BJ09, August 9, 2002.

123. QBPC Pamphlet. There is some confusion regarding the acronym. It is generally written as "CAEFI," but in QBPC publications, it is written as "CAFEI." Both refer to the China Association of Enterprises with Foreign Investment.

124. Margaret M. Pearson, *China's New Business Elite: The Political Consequences of Economic Reform* (Berkeley: University of California Press, 1997), 123.

125. Interview 02SH09, July 2, 2002.

126. There were two versions of this report that arose from information provided by the QBPC—an "open" (*gongkai*) and an internal (*neibu*) version. The *neibu* version gave a much more serious assessment of the counterfeiting problem and made it all the way up to Jiang Zemin for review. Interview 02BJ09, August 9, 2002.

127. In fact, these QBPC representatives had some fence-mending to do after this meeting, as these middle-level officials were so bruised by Zhu's comments that—immediately following the meeting—they were reluctant to work with the QBPC, lest they receive another tongue-lashing. Interview 02BJ09, August 9, 2002.

than happy to supply him with this information). In mid-2001, he told the
QBPC to write another report on counterfeiting, which he then distributed among the top leadership. These two "breaks" put the QBPC squarely
on the radar of the top leadership.[128]

Since then, the QBPC has also been actively involved in preparing suggestions to the Chinese government on changes to other relevant laws,
such as the Product Quality Law, with varied amounts of success.[129] The
QBPC has also worked closely with central and local officials, including
Vice Premier (now chairman of the National People's Congress, NPC) Wu
Bangguo, former NPC standing committee vice chairman Wang Guangy-
ing, and MOFCOM Vice Minister Ma Xiuhong, to educate them on the
negative impact of counterfeiting on the Chinese economy, to provide
advice and expertise to the Chinese government in its development of laws
and regulations, and to press for more prosecutions of counterfeiters. The
vice director of the NPC legislative affairs department even came to Shanghai to consult with two QBPC representatives on how to strengthen anticounterfeiting legislation.[130] At the same time, the QBPC has expanded
its membership roster to include eighty companies united in their goal of
making criminal prosecutions the default dispute settlement mechanism
for counterfeiting in China.

While the QBPC has become the "good cop" in the shift toward increased
criminal prosecutions, many other individual companies operating in the
trenches have taken up the goal of aggressively pursuing criminal prosecutions on the ground.[131] Even though the actual number of cases currently
appears infinitesimal, when seen against a baseline of even three years earlier, it appears significant.

The main reason these numbers remain low is that resistance to increasing invocation of the Criminal Law for anticounterfeiting offenses comes
from several directions, the first of which is illustrated in the following:

> A recent example of this problem involved a company in Guangdong
> province that produced large amounts of oil lubricants and similar
> products under the names of Mobil, Esso, Shell and STP, as well as
> various local brands. The local AIC fined the company yuan 4 [mil-
> lion], one of the largest fines ever imposed in a Chinese trademark
> case. China's chief prosecuting agency, the Supreme People's Procu-
> racy, ordered Guangdong prosecutors to pursue a criminal case but
> the AIC refused to release its files to prosecutors. The AIC said its
> policy was not to release such files until at least two-thirds of assessed

128. Ibid.
129. For example, the QBPC was unable to secure an opportunity to advise the Chinese government in the Prosecutorial Guidelines (promulgated April 18, 2002) and the Case Transfer
Regulations (promulgated July 9, 2001). Interview 02SH09, July 2, 2002.
130. Ibid.
131. Interview 02GZ01, July 25, 2002.

fines had been paid. In this case, the AIC had received only 10% of the assessed fine. The prosecutors, meanwhile, said they would not pursue the case until they received the AIC's files.[132]

This underscores the tremendous disincentive for the administrative enforcement agencies to hand over their cases for criminal prosecution. QTSBs and the AICs, in particular, realized that the big money was not in exacting case fees and bribes from foreign clients but in using the fines levied against the counterfeiters to enhance their own official and unofficial operating budgets.[133]

After working for years to establish relations with foreign companies and their private investigation agencies, and amassing significant financial and other benefits in doing so, the AIC and the QTSB are loath to give them up. First, a criminal conviction means that the counterfeiter will not only go to jail, he will be put out of business as well. Thus, the AIC, in particular, loses both a source of revenue through enterprise registration and regular management fees it collects, while also losing the opportunity to skim money off of the fines that it levies on the counterfeiter.[134] Second, handing cases over to the Public Security Bureau leaves the AIC and the QTSB with no records or samples to indicate that they have done the initial enforcement of the case, and thus their activity does not make it onto their own enforcement quotas. And if the cases get "bounced" back to the AIC or QTSB there is a good chance that they have already gone cold and that it will be close to impossible to pursue them with any expectation of success.[135] Third, it potentially diminishes the relevance and utility of the AIC and the QTSB as important enforcement agencies in the eyes of government superiors, a reputation that these two bureaucracies have painstakingly nurtured over several years. One investigator said that in his two years in Shanghai, he has never seen one instance of the AIC or the QTSB voluntarily passing off a case to the PSB.[136] Often, the AIC or QTSB will increase the fine (with the acquiescence of the investigator or company) in exchange for being able to hold onto the case.[137]

But this does not mean that the PSB has been aggressively taking cases away from the AIC and the QTSB. In fact, it has taken a tremendous amount of coaxing to get the PSB to become interested in taking on IPR cases in the first place. Taking on anticounterfeiting work was regarded by the PSB as an increase in responsibilities without a corresponding increase

132. Economist Intelligence Unit, *China Hand: The Complete Guide to Doing Business in China* (Hong Kong: Economist Intelligence Unit, 1997), 39.

133. Interview 02SH02, June 21, 2002.

134. Interview 02SH01, June 20, 2002 and Interview 02GZ01, July 25, 2002.

135. Interview 02SH05, June 27, 2002.

136. Ibid. The foregoing trend is also the case regarding the General Administration of Customs, and for the same reasons. My source indicated that he is not aware of a single case in which Customs voluntarily transferred a case to the PSB. Interview 02SH10, July 2, 2002.

137. Interview 02SH01, June 20, 2002.

in budgetary revenues. Moreover, there was a perception that IPR cases were "civil" in nature and that they did not have the gravitas of "standard" criminal offenses. There was a gap of about three to four years between the promulgation of the revised Criminal Law and an active interest in IPR cases on the part of the PSB. PSB interest in the issue is gradually increasing, and there is even a shadowy figure within the Shanghai PSB known as the "IPR Czar," as well as a special PSB intellectual property enforcement unit known simply—and ominously—as "803," after its street address.[138] Even though the PSB is more willing to participate in bringing counterfeiters to justice, it will not send the cases to the prosecutor unless the chances for success, in the opinion of one investigator, are 95 percent or higher.[139] Sending a case back to the AIC or to the QTSB gives the PSB the equivalent of a "black eye" and negatively affects its case file.

Moreover, the prosecutors, like the PSB, will only take a case if they are almost certain that they will gain a conviction. Once the PSB hands a case over to the prosecutors, they have an internal discussion about whether to go ahead with prosecution. In the past, the conviction rate was very high, and prosecutors are resistant to the possibility of diluting their overall success rate with cases that might not end in a conviction. If they decide not to take on a case, they hand it back to the PSB, which then has to take the case back to the AIC or QTSB, something that PSB does not like to do, for the reasons mentioned above.[140] This overly cautious approach to prosecutions is changing, but very slowly.

It also appears that counterfeiters from other locales (*waidi ren*) make up the majority of convictions. It is still very difficult to prosecute "local boys." As there is no national database, it is also extremely hard to establish patterns of recidivism, and establishing a pattern of counterfeiting often requires vertical coordination among several different bureaucracies at different levels of the administrative hierarchy across several provinces, an almost impossibly complex undertaking.[141]

Finally, in several instances the laws themselves remain vague on crucial points. What constitutes a "huge" (*judade*) or "serious" (*yanzhongde*) incident is still unclear. Moreover, even the seemingly clear and objective criminal threshold of 50,000 yuan is also open to interpretation.[142] Valuation is tricky when the merchandise itself is fake. If the methodology for calculating the value of the goods only takes into account real production and ignores the costs of utilizing the intellectual property in the production of

138. Ibid.
139. Interview 02GZ01, July 25, 2002.
140. Interview 02SH05, June 27, 2002.
141. One private investigator was afraid that current attempts toward increased criminalization of counterfeiting would create a situation where the punishment would go far beyond establishing the deterrent effect necessary and actually become a tool for repression. Moreover, he implied that some foreign trademark owners were indifferent to this potential outcome. Interview 02SH02, June 21, 2002.
142. Interview 02SH10, July 2, 2002.

the good—the preferred method of the enforcement authorities because calculating intellectual property losses is difficult and open to dispute—this depresses the price and makes the 50,000-yuan threshold more difficult to attain.[143] And until the recent promulgation of the Judicial Interpretation on the Handling of the Crime of Manufacturing and Selling Inferior and Shoddy Goods on April 10, 2001, a significant loophole existed that manufacturers could use to assert that they were involved in the manufacture and not the sale of goods and that the 50,000-yuan threshold for *sales* did not apply to them. In some cases, local authorities have been slow to adopt the new interpretation, if they are even aware of it.[144]

At this point, groups like the QBPC and the growing number of foreign companies in China pushing for criminal penalties for counterfeiting are facing opposition from two groups: the AIC and QTSB bureaucracies, which want to hold on to their enforcement portfolios, and the PSB and the People's Procuracy, which do not want the added caseload and related responsibilities. To the extent that these foreign actors are successful, therefore, in reaching their goal of the default criminalization of counterfeiting, it will provide further evidence to support the contention of this chapter that foreign actors are an important part of the local enforcement process in China. However, questions regarding their prospects for future success notwithstanding, the past successes of foreign actors in mobilizing the AIC and the QTSB demonstrate that foreign actors can play a significant role in shaping the direction and depth of policy implementation and enforcement in China if the bureaucratic environment is conducive to such tinkering and if the form of the pressure itself is cooperative rather than confrontational. It may thus be possible to begin thinking about foreign actors as a part of Chinese "society" along a state-society continuum. Although it is important to note that foreign actors, like other nonstate actors in China, face considerable constraints in their ability to work within the Chinese political system, in cases such as anticounterfeiting enforcement, such interactions have demonstrated quite successfully what foreign pressure can do, and has done, in China.

---

143. Interview 02SH05, June 27, 2002.
144. Interview 02SH09, July 2, 2002.

CHAPTER 6

Evaluating the Argument and Analysis

What are some of the claims that would infirm or falsify this argument? It is always somewhat hazardous to discuss falsification in the context of a qualitative research design, because one must often resort to counterfactual reasoning, and all the epistemological baggage it entails, to explore such falsifiability claims.[1] Nevertheless, as I argue in this section, when comparing the claims I make in this book with their counterfactuals, the latter are untenable or, at the very least, far less persuasive than the argument I have put forward in this book.

To summarize, much of the exogenous pressure directed at China was top-down in direction and resulted from direct demands by the United States Trade Representative on the Chinese negotiation team. However, some of this pressure emanated from other areas. In the case of trademark enforcement after the mid-1990s, there was a shift in the direction and tone of exogenous pressure (although top-down pressure was minimal compared to copyright, as we saw in chapter 2). Increasingly, this pressure was lateral, coming mostly from foreign companies operating in China working with local Chinese anticounterfeiting enforcement agencies to improve the latter's anticounterfeiting effectiveness. This shift to lateral pressure has also begun to take root in copyright enforcement, but it has been a much slower process with fewer tangible results (from the bottom left cell to the bottom right cell in Table 6.1).

1. See James D. Fearon, "Counterfactuals and Hypothesis Testing in Political Science," *World Politics* 43 (January 1991): 169–95. On falsification, see Karl Popper, *The Logic of Scientific Discovery* (New York: Basic Books, 1959); and A. F. Chalmers, *What is this Thing Called Science?* 3d ed. (Buckingham: Open University Press, 1999), esp. chs. 4 through 6.

TABLE 6.1.
Conceptual framework/summary of conclusions

	Top-down exogenous pressure	Lateral exogenous pressure
Dynamic institutional structure	Copyright legislation patent administration	Trademark enforcement
Inert institutional structure	Patent enforcement copyright enforcement (up to 1997)	Copyright enforcement (after 1997)

The Dependent Variable: Changes in the Legislation and Enforcement of IPR

It is possible to analyze this variation in dynamism and inertia regarding the legislation and enforcement of IPR by focusing on China's administrative enforcement bureaucracies and not on the courts. This is because, as noted in the introductory chapter and highlighted in chapters 3 through 5, three entirely different bureaucratic clusters govern the management and enforcement of patents, copyright, and trademarks, respectively.

In the case of copyright legislation and national-level patent administration, considerable top-down exogenous pressure resulted in substantive changes on the Chinese side at the national level (the top left cell in Figure 6.1) in the form of legislation and policy making, as discussed in chapters 3 and 4. External U.S. pressure had a much more direct and substantive impact on national-level copyright legislation than it did on legislation on patents and on trademarks. However, as argued in the preceding chapters, translating national legislation into local administrative enforcement resulted in a situation in which such change was absorbed by the institutional inertia surrounding copyright enforcement. Finally, exogenous pressure had an important impact on the national and local bureaucratic structure of China's patent regime (rate and direction), as described in chapter 3 (also the top left cell), but with little corresponding impact on local enforcement (the bottom left cell).

But the foregoing did not translate into corresponding changes in effectiveness. Why not? Enforcement in China, as elsewhere, is predominantly a local phenomenon, and at least for the moment, it is mostly enforcement by administrative agencies, not by the courts (which I discuss below). Therefore, when we look at *local administrative* patent and copyright enforcement (the bottom left cell), we see that an inert institutional structure has the effect of absorbing exogenous pressure to change and reform, rendering such pressure largely ineffective as far as enforcement is concerned. Specifically, I use "inert institutional structure" here to mean that the bureaucracy of interest is highly dependent for financial and personnel resources on a separate "host" bureaucracy that may have very different organizational goals, often resulting in suboptimal enforcement outcomes in the policy area of interest (a theme discussed in detail in chapters 3 and 4).[2] Exogenous pressure can alter the formal institutions that govern a given issue area and move them along a trajectory (the shape and direction of change) that follows an alternate course to that path that would likely otherwise have been pursued. But the effect on the quality and robustness of enforcement (change in effectiveness) may well be—and has been found to be—negligible.

In chapter 5, I documented change in the trademark case by looking at the mid-1990s as a key moment of transition. Only since the mid-1990s has a combination of interbureaucratic competition and an increased role for foreign actors taken root in China such that trademark enforcement began to improve dramatically. However, what is important here is not simply that trademark enforcement has become more effective, but also that the direction of the exogenous pressure is lateral and not vertical. Again, there has been a similar shift in the case of copyright as well, but the impact on copyright enforcement thus far has been modest at best. To examine this point further, it is necessary to look at the primary explanatory variable, exogenous pressure.

The Independent Variable: External Pressure

With regard to foreign pressure, the principal independent or explanatory variable in this analysis, I have made three broad claims: foreign pressure resulted in the growth of the importance of the Intellectual Property Rights Working Conference Office; foreign pressure initiated an acceleration in the creation of China's copyright legislation and led to, among other things, provisions in China's Copyright Law that expressly favored foreigners; and foreign pressure, much of it lateral, was an important component in the improvement of anticounterfeiting enforcement rates. I will examine each of these claims in turn.

The first of these claims is probably the most debatable. The IPR Working Conference predated the 1995 agreement and Action Plan, having been formed in the summer of 1994. Moreover, such a mechanism is a typical Chinese response to tackling a problem that is not easily contained by an existing bureaucracy. As demonstrated in this book, other such offices, such as the *saohuang dafei* ("sweep away pornography and strike down illegals") leadership small group, the *dajia* ("strike down counterfeits") leadership small group, and the *guifan shichang jingji* ("standardize the market economy") leadership small group (and their attached offices) were conventional institutions formed in response to various policy goals.

2. The exception that proves the rule is the "one-shot" campaign, the 1996–97 "Winter Action" in copyright enforcement, discussed in chapter 4.

However, the IPR Working Conference (IPRWC) differed from these other groups in two ways. First, it was often depicted (or widely interpreted) as being more than simply a coordinating mechanism—the IPRWC was regarded, certainly by the U.S. side, as an institution that could effectively manage and lead the various bureaucracies within its purview. Indeed, its main responsibility in the post-negotiation stage was to manage and coordinate the implementation of the agreements. At the national level, as argued in chapter 3, this was an accurate and credible description. At the subnational level, it was not. Second, and related to the first, the IPRWC became the principal gatekeeper for handling IPR issues and representing these other bureaucracies to the foreign actors with an interest in IPR in China. Although the Ministry of Foreign Trade and Economic Cooperation was the principal contact in the context of the actual trade negotiations, the IPRWC's attached office (the IPRWO) was the main link between these foreign actors and the IPR bureaucracies described in this book. One would be hard pressed to imagine such interaction between foreign actors and the *saohuang dafei* leadership small group.

What accounts for this difference? I have argued that the IPRWC/IPRWO became an integral part of the negotiations and became enshrined in the subsequent agreements, specifically in 1995 and 1996. In effect, similar to the changes to the legislative and regulatory regime that resulted from the 1991–92 negotiations, the institutional framework of the IPRWC/IPRWO and its emerging political power were due in no small part to the position of the IPRWC/IPRWO within the actual substantive framework of the 1994–95 negotiations and the resulting agreements. As Merit Janow has written, the 1995 agreement "was the most detailed enforcement agreement of its kind ever entered into between the United States and a foreign country."[3] At the time, it was the farthest the United States had gone in not simply trying to get Beijing to change China's IPR legislative and regulatory regime, but in actually shaping China's institutional mechanism charged with *enforcing* these laws and regulations through relentless pressure and the threat of trade sanctions. One provincial-level patent official went so far as to say that the IPRWC/IPRWO were created in the wake of, and as a result of, the Sino-U.S. negotiations that were going at the time.[4] This is an extremely significant development because it provides a precedent for moving beyond the norm of "enforcement left to the sovereign government"; it made the enforcement of the policy, and not simply the policy itself, part of what was to be negotiated by the representatives of the two states.

3. Merit E. Janow, "U.S. Trade Policy Toward Japan and China: Integrating Bilateral, Multilateral, and Regional Approaches, in *Trade Strategies for a New Era: Ensuring U.S. Leadership in a Global Economy*, ed. Geza Feketekuty with Bruce Stokes (New York: Council on Foreign Relations, 1998), 188–89.
    4. Interview 98KM01, September 1, 1998.

Unlike other agreements, the 1995 Action Plan focused primarily on implementation and enforcement, which helped move the IPRWC/IPRWO from obscurity to national and international prominence. Indeed, the scope of the Action Plan was so great that it would arguably have been impossible to administer it without a coordinating agency like the IPRWC. It therefore gained outward legitimacy not simply from its creation in the context of domestic Chinese politics, but also from its reception of an international imprimatur. Although the IPRWC/IPRWO were unable to replicate their successes at the local level, as discussed in detail in chapter 3, this should not be taken to mean that they were not powerful bodies at the national level; rather, it underscores yet again, the cleavage between national and local politics in China. Would the IPRWC/IPRWO be equally powerful, salient, and recognizable, at least at the national level, in the absence of U.S. pressure? This would falsify my claim. However, given the fact that U.S. pressure moved the IPR issue area (and, by extension, the institutions charged with managing it) to national prominence in China—to the extent that even taxi drivers, a generally good barometer of the "man on the street," were surprisingly knowledgeable about IPR (and far more so than the U.S. public at large)—such a counterfactual, while certainly possible, nevertheless seems unlikely.

Indeed, although this is largely anecdotal, ordinary Chinese with whom I spoke often conflated "intellectual property" with "software copyright," attesting to the ability of the USTR to frame the issue area of IPR in China: the Special 301–led negotiations overwhelmingly focused on software copyright. The counterfactual in this case would be: in the absence of these negotiations, would software copyright occupy such a prominent position in Chinese conceptualizations of intellectual property? This also seems highly unlikely.

The second broad claim in this book regarding outside pressure is that, while it may have had little effect on the actual administration and enforcement of copyright protection in China, exogenous pressure had a substantial impact on the formal legislation of copyright in China. It is difficult to identify a Chinese expert willing to go on the record that foreign pressure was instrumental in shaping China's IPR regime and, more specifically, its Copyright Law and related provisions. Yet, as argued in chapter 4, it became clear from the debate that followed the establishment of the first Copyright Law that, because of the combination of the Copyright Law, the Regulations on Protecting Computer Software, and the Provisions on Implementing International Copyright Treaties, foreigners' copyright was better protected than that of Chinese authors and artists by China's own copyright legislation. Given the protracted debate over copyright legislation in China throughout the 1980s, during which all the minutiae of copyright were pored over and contested, it is inconceivable that China, on its own, would have established a copyright regime in which its own citizens were offered less protection than that available to foreigners. Indeed, one key national-level copyright agency official told me that the NCA's goals were precisely *the opposite,* that is, to offer Chinese more copyright protection than that extended to foreigners.[5]

There is also the issue of timing. Given the contentious legislative history of copyright during the 1980s, it would appear that the least likely time for China to establish its own Copyright Law would have been within one year of the Tiananmen Square massacre. After all, the Copyright Law was meant to protect precisely that group which was eyed with the most suspicion in 1989–90: the intellectual class. It would have raised no eyebrows if China had put its draft Copyright Law on ice and not returned to it until after Deng Xiaoping's Southern Tour (*nanxun*) in early 1992, after the Fourteenth Party Congress in October of that same year. Instead, China promulgated the Copyright Law at precisely the time when the conservatives were consolidating their power in the aftermath of the Tiananmen Square crackdown and the "ferreting out" campaign that followed. The Copyright Law could easily have been delayed indefinitely, raising the question of why senior members of the Chinese government (including, among others, such conservatives as Li Peng) were so eager to establish China's Copyright Law by 1990. The answer is because the United States had made it clear to China that Washington would not renew the 1979 U.S.-China Bilateral Trade Agreement, which came up for renewal in 1989, unless China made significant steps toward establishing an intellectual property regime. The centerpiece of these demands was the promulgation of a copyright law.

The third broad claim I make in this book is that anticounterfeiting enforcement improved dramatically in China as a result of lateral foreign pressure. There are two counterfactual arguments that are relevant here: how anticounterfeiting enforcement might have been different if, first, foreign pressure had been top-down, as was the case with copyright and patents, and, second, if foreign pressure had not existed at all.

Greater top-down pressure may have led to some marginal changes in enforcement, at most. As was the case with copyright and patents, top-down pressure did little to alter the incentives of local enforcement agencies or the local governments that had personnel and budgetary jurisdiction over them. Even if some top-down pressure somehow trickled down to local Administration of Industry and Commerce units, it would have created pressure to focus on a less-than-popular enforcement mandate, trademark protection, without a commensurate increase in the resources necessary to get the job done. Moreover, as noted, the AIC trademark offices were not immune to the same type of embeddedness issues (i.e., in the context of the overall AIC apparatus) that have so undermined provincial copyright departments from enforcing copyright effectively. As a result, other tasks would have been neglected, or the AIC units would have paid lip service to trademark enforcement while the status quo would have remained largely

5. Interview 99BJ33, July 30, 1999.

intact. Indeed, the resistance that these same agencies have to a shift of anticounterfeiting enforcement activity to the criminal courts suggests the degree of resistance these agencies would have offered if initial exogenous pressure toward better enforcement of trademarks had only been in the form of top-down pressure, as with copyright and patents.

Moreover, as argued in chapter 5, there was a fear among many trademark owners in China that such top-down pressure would actually lead to local Chinese retaliation or discrimination against their continued operations, a "worst of all possible cases" scenario. Although it is this fear that arguably contributed to the trademark lobby's (particularly the International Trademark Association) low profile in the Special 301 process, in retrospect it seems to have been a sound strategy.

What about the counterfactual claim that better trademark enforcement would have occurred anyway—in other words, with or without *lateral* foreign pressure? At the core of this counter claim is the notion that foreign pressure pushed local enforcement agencies onto a trajectory of greater anticounterfeiting enforcement. In order to do this, these foreign actors had to alter the local incentives of these enforcement agencies. As I have argued in chapter 5, the trademark holders on the ground in China, and their agents (i.e., the anticounterfeiting investigation agencies) have spent much time and effort over the past decade nurturing relationships with local enforcement agencies. Some of this has been indistinguishable from corruption, bribery, and kickbacks. However, as one private investigator put it to me, "This is a short-term fixative that makes the job harder for all of us in the long run."[6] So there is a subtle but important distinction between paying outright bribes and helping defray enforcement costs. Other side payments, such as lavish banquets, karaoke, and more intimate services, fall somewhere in that gray area between the two. Moreover, there are other, more symbolic side payments that help reinforce these pecuniary ones. These can include high-profile acknowledgements of service (meant for the attention of superiors), training programs, and institutional and professional development seminars. Other positive incentives even include the personal and professional bonds that have grown between individuals representing their respective offices (the private investigation firm on the one hand and the Chinese local enforcement agency on the other).

As in the counterfactual case of top-down pressure focusing on trademarks, the effect of the absence of lateral foreign pressure would most likely have been maintenance of the status quo of non-enforcement. Not only would the AIC have had no incentive to change, but the QTSB would also have had no reason to enter into the anticounterfeiting enforcement arena with the aggressiveness that it did.

Finally, some may argue that the institutional restructuring in 1993 may have caused these changes, but it is unclear how. There is no mention

6. Interview 02GZ01, July 25, 2002.

about trademark or anticounterfeiting responsibilities in the QTSB. In my initial interviews, I was often rebuffed by QTSB officials until I deleted the specific references to "intellectual property" from my interview protocols and letters of introduction; once I did so, QTSB officials were far more willing to meet with me. As I have argued in chapter 5, AIC-QTSB competition has been fierce but low-profile. If increased aggressiveness on the part of the QTSB was due to official institutional changes, there would have been no need for the QTSB to have acted in this rather furtive way.

The Intervening Variable: Bureaucratic Structure and Process

The final set of falsifiable propositions has to do with the structural argument of this analysis. A claim focusing on institutional structure and process that would falsify my argument is that bureaucratic structure is irrelevant to explaining resistance to IPR enforcement. I have argued that foreign pressure is the independent variable and that the institutional structure of the specific bureaucracies charged with managing and enforcing intellectual property is the crucial intervening variable. This explanation posits that the institutional nexus in which IPR (and other) policy issues are handled is critical to understanding the degree of and the limits to the effectiveness of foreign pressure in bringing about policy change. However, there are several potential alternative explanations, particularly regarding the variation in enforcement among these bureaucracies that form the core of the analysis of this book, that could nullify the importance I have placed on bureaucratic structure. It is worth identifying and discussing them here.[7]

One can argue that such variation in enforcement is an accurate reflection of piracy rates and that the performance of these bureaucracies matches the actual IPR piracy and counterfeit rates on the ground. In other words, all the discussion on the bureaucratic structure may be accurate, but it is also irrelevant. This explanation posits that there is comparatively more trademark enforcement precisely because there are fewer violations of patents and copyright relative to trademarks. While this may or may not be true in absolute terms, when they are compared in terms of piracy levels *as rates of market share,* copyright piracy easily dwarfs trademark counterfeiting. The China Quality Brands Inspection Committee estimates that sales of counterfeit products on average account for 15 to 20 percent of total sales.[8] Meanwhile, the International Intellectual Property Alliance (IIPA) estimates piracy levels in 2000 at 90 percent for motion pictures, 85 percent for sound recordings and musical compositions, 93 percent for

---

7. For a more detailed discussion of these alternative explanations, see Andrew C. Mertha, "Policy Enforcement Markets: How Bureaucratic Redundancy Contributes to Effective IPR Policy Implementation in China," forthcoming in *Comparative Politics.*

8. CAFEI Quality Brands Protection Committee [QBPC] Pamphlet.

TABLE 6.2.
Cases of administrative enforcement of copyright and trademark, 1994–2001

Year	Requests for patent invalidation[1]	Copyright cases	Trademark cases
1994	N.A.	N.A.	5,174
1995	452	N.A.	14,776
1996	546	673	16,209
1997	486	1,361	32,027
1998	N.A.	1,208	28,952
1999	N.A.	1,586	32,298
2000	N.A.	2,457	38,240
2001	977	4,416	41,163

Source: China Administration of Industry and Commerce Yearbook (1995–2001), *China Intellectual Property Yearbook* 2000 and 2001/2002, and 1996 and 1997 *Annual Report of the Patent Office of the People's Republic of China*

1. The administrative management of patents, unlike that of copyright and trademarks, involves people bringing their claims to the patent bureaus. For copyright and trademarks, claims are brought to the relevant administrative agencies, but cases also emerge from market sweeps and other crackdowns. Therefore, the lower figures for patents may actually reflect the lower number of patent disputes.

business application computer software, and 99 percent for entertainment computer software.[9]

Similarly, one might conclude that these asymmetrical enforcement levels correlate with the ratio of actual economic losses related to patents, copyright, and trademarks, respectively, and therefore represent similar *enforcement rates,* again rendering the bureaucratic structure and politics argument irrelevant. This valuation-based argument suggests a causal relationship between the economic loss ratios between trademark counterfeiting and copyright piracy (particularly those pertaining to *foreign* rightholders in China) on the one hand and the rates of enforcement by Chinese enforcement agencies on the other. But this conflates Chinese and U.S. economic interests, which is, at best, a highly questionable assumption. And even if Washington and Beijing have shared interests, such an argument ignores different, and frequently opposing, preferences on the part of national-level Chinese officials and their local counterparts.[10]

9. International Intellectual Property Alliance, "2001 Special 301 Recommendation to the United States Trade Representative," February 16, 2001, 26. Even if we control for bias in these figures (i.e., that these are not actual "lost sales" because much of the software in question would not be purchased if sold at the retail price), the correct figure would most likely be at least as high as that of the figures (losses as a percentage of market share) for trademarked goods.
10. A major theme in this and other analyses of China is that the central government in Beijing may have—and often does have—very different priorities than those of local Chinese governments at the provincial level and below. However, even if we retain the assumption that Beijing and the localities have unified preferences, it does not explain, for example, why the Sino-U.S. IPR trade talks from 1991 to 1996 were dominated by copyright issues, while trademark concerns

Others may claim that the disconnect between national policy and local enforcement and specifically the differences in the rates of copyright and trademark enforcement are explained by differences in the inherent difficulty of enforcing copyright and trademarks, that it is harder to go after copyright-violating goods than it is to enforce trademarks. Manufacturing, distributing, and selling music and video compact disks and computer software are cheap, fast, and profitable undertakings that satisfy an ever-growing consumer demand. Production start-up costs in the late 1990s were estimated at around one million U.S. dollars, which could be recovered after only one month of full-time operation.[11] However, the same holds true for trademark counterfeiting. Production of counterfeit clothing, cosmetics, and thousands of other goods is decentralized along sophisticated manufacturing and distribution networks. A 1999 raid that has become part of "IPR in China" folklore resulted in the netting of hundreds of thousands, if not millions, of dollars' worth of counterfeit batteries in two rural communities in Guangdong (appropriately nicknamed *dianchi cun*, or "battery village"), where scores of illegal migrant workers from interior provinces shrink-wrapped labels onto the batteries using portable hair dryers in the comfort of their own living quarters, which are far more difficult to raid than are factories or warehouses.[12] In cases of both copyrighted and trademarked goods, legitimate factories are often used to make illegitimate products (i.e., outside of their contracted production runs), while profit rates from counterfeiting and piracy are similar in range. In sum, there is little substantive difference in the inherent ease or difficulty of copyright and trademark enforcement.

Finally, having laid out this predominantly structural argument, I should discuss another potential alternative explanation, that an "organizational culture" or "organizational ideology," as distinct from structure and process, is what explains such variation. The argument in this approach is that the more coherent an organizational ideology is, the greater the probability of effective enforcement will be (and, conversely, the less coherent an overarching organizational culture is, the poorer enforcement is likely to be). Yet trademark enforcement appears to be rising without the presence of any discernible coherent organizational culture. This is suggested, in part, by the variation in professional orientation to anticounterfeiting enforcement.

One experienced private investigator found government anticounterfeiting bureaus in the city of Beijing, the provinces of Shandong and southern Yunnan, and the municipalities of Zhengzhou and Wenzhou to be effective and generally proactive with regard to anticounterfeiting enforcement, while finding those in the northern provinces and in Fujian (and, surprisingly, in Shanghai) to be extremely unprofessional.[13] This variation

---

played a negligible role. Indeed, based on the comparison of losses due to counterfeiting and piracy, we would expect trademark issues to have been the principal focus of those talks.

11. Interview 98HK03, June 22, 1998.
12. Interview 99HK02, June 2, 1999.
13. Interview 02GZ01, July 25, 2002.

is true even within specific regions. Indeed, there are so many shades of gray that it is difficult to avoid being overwhelmed by intraregional variation. In the single southern province of Guangdong, for example, in the provincial capital city of Guangzhou, another private investigator found the official Chinese anticounterfeiting enforcement agency to be generally well-skilled, and in Shenzhen, he found it to be powerful, if not quite as reliable as other enforcement bureaucracies in the area. In Shantou and Nanhai, on the other hand, he found this agency to be particularly poorly managed and somewhat corrupt, and the Dongguan Trademark Office was ineffective while the Economic Crimes Unit (both within the same bureaucracy—the Administration for Industry and Commerce) was somewhat better.[14] The behavior of these local enforcement units indicates a great deal of variation in how these units approach their responsibilities, suggesting the absence of an effective, overarching organizational culture. Given the institutional ambivalence of the Administration for Industry and Commerce with regard to its administrative responsibilities, the absence of a coherent organizational ideology is not surprising.[15]

Moreover, within the copyright bureaucracy, there is no dearth of commitment to copyright protection, nor is there a discernible organizational culture that is anathema to copyright enforcement, within either the copyright bureaucracy or the culture market management bureaucracy. The latter, especially in recent years, has been taking on increased copyright enforcement functions, but the priority on *saohuang dafei* as opposed to copyright enforcement reflects universal scarcity of budgetary, personnel, and other resources that is more easily resolved when the institutional structure favors one set of enforcement actions over another. It would appear that insofar as organizational or institutional culture is important, it is reflected in the actual institutional structure of the bureaucracy in question. Finally, there is no shortage of commitment to patent protection among any of the Chinese patent bureaucracy officials I interviewed; indeed, there appears to have been a great degree of genuine enthusiasm and commitment reinforced by the advanced technical educational background of many of these officials. Support for a possible alternative explanation for higher overall rates of anticounterfeiting enforcement or lower rates of copyright or patent enforcement (and higher degrees of contestation against these subfields of intellectual property) based on organizational culture or organizational ideology does not appear to be borne out.

14. Interview 99HK01, June 1, 1999.
15. This is not to deny the existence of *organizational* learning among discrete local units within a given bureaucracy that can, in turn, be aggregated to the larger organizational level—or that a critical mass of county- and municipal-level enforcement agencies undergoing similar learning patterns can form a core from which tentative generalizations about larger organizational behavior can be made. But this is different than a distinct agency-specific organizational ideology. It is based on a local economic calculus—not a normative "ideological" one.

Legal-Judicial vs. Administrative Management and Enforcement of IPR in China

Finally, am I selecting on the dependent variable, and, in doing so, documenting a spurious relationship and thus omitting a potentially more important explanatory variable, the legal-judicial process?[16] It is important to engage the notion that by focusing on China's administrative apparatus and not its judicial-legal one, the foregoing is not looking simply at the margins of the structure and process of IPR management and enforcement in China, but rather at the very nexus of intellectual property policy in China.

At the very beginning of my research in 1998, a provincial-level trademark department official, growing increasingly exasperated with my questions about personnel allocations and budgetary flows, reached into his pocket and threw a copy of China's Trademark Law on the table. "Everything you need to know [about trademarks]," he said gruffly, "is in there." Thus endeth the interview. Several months later, I found myself at a luncheon in Hong Kong attended by some of the foremost legal experts on intellectual property in China. I was one of very few nonlawyers in the room. The conversation quickly centered on the ways in which parts of China's IPR laws were poorly worded and how this was a significant impediment to IPR enforcement in China. At many points in the discussion, somebody would say, "If only Article Y could be rewritten to say X . . . ," with the implication that everything would then be different. When I raised the issue of power, administrative structure, and the extrajudicial aspects of IPR enforcement in China, I was met with silence; they seemed to be saying, "Who invited this guy?"

These anecdotes are revealing because they underscore the discomfort that many people, both inside and outside China, have in trying to disaggregate politics and administration from law and legal development in China, whether it involves intellectual property or any number of other policy issue areas. Often, the default dimension along which scholarly inquiry falls is a formalistic legal one. However, throughout more than six years of research, I found that an overwhelming amount of the activity surrounding the enforcement of IPR takes place *outside* the courtroom and in the halls of China's complex cluster of IPR enforcement bureaucracies analyzed in chapters 3 through 5 or in the marketplaces and factories in the form of raids and other types of enforcement activity. The previous three chapters have provided a detailed map of the Chinese institutional landscape for

---

16. See Christopher H. Achen and Duncan Snidal, "Rational Deterrence Theory and Comparative Case Studies," *World Politics* 41, no. 2 (January 1989): 143–67; Barbara Geddes, "How the Cases You Choose Affect the Answers You Get: Selection Bias in Comparative Politics, *Political Analysis* 2 (1990): 131–50; and Gary King, Robert O. Keohane and Sidney Verba, *Designing Social Inquiry: Scientific Inference in Qualitative Research* (Princeton: Princeton University Press, 1994), 128–49.

the administrative management and enforcement apparatus for intellectual property. But why is this focus on administrative enforcement bureaucracies appropriate in analyzing China's intellectual property enforcement regime? There has been a vigorous scholarly debate about the extent to which formal adjudication took place in traditional China.[17] Although this debate continues to evolve, all sides accept that in the reform era, China has established a formal IPR regime in a fraction of the time that such a regime developed in the West. China's IPR laws are generally considered to be, on balance, quite good by the many legal experts with whom I discussed the issue, although, they add, there still remains plenty of room for improvement. Moreover, recent developments in greater China, and especially in Taiwan, underscore that although intellectual property may have been an alien concept in the traditional Chinese cultural sphere, it has quickly been appropriated by Chinese legal scholars, officials, businesspeople, and ordinary citizens.[18] Indeed, during the 1995–96 Sino-U.S. IPR negotiations, the United States Trade Representative had to replace one of its lead lawyers because his Chinese counterpart was reportedly better versed in the TRIPS (Trade-Related Aspects of Intellectual Property) framework, the World Trade Organization's IPR regime.[19]

Although any legal infrastructure or evolving legal norms that developed during the late Qing and Republican China were, after 1949, effectively eradicated or driven deep underground by Mao Zedong and his insistence of "politics in command," this trend has been reversed during the reform era, and the top leadership has emphasized the importance of establishing a viable legal apparatus in order to regulate society, resolve conflict, and promote stability. But these goals often outpace reality. Although there have been dramatic developments in the evolution of the Chinese legal regime in the past quarter-century—foreigners and Chinese are going to the courts in increasing numbers to adjudicate civil conflict, and the proliferation of learned Chinese lawyers and legal scholars is unprecedented in Chinese history—the legal-judicial system is institutionally weak and remains firmly under the control of the Chinese Communist Party. Hence it suffers from a lack of social prestige and professional experience and is largely unable to enforce its own decisions.[20] Given the uneasy history

17. Stanley B. Lubman, *Bird in a Cage: Legal Reform in China after Mao* (Stanford: Stanford University Press, 1999), 23; Kathryn Bernhardt and Philip C. C. Huang, eds., *Civil Law in Qing and Republican China* (Stanford: Stanford University Press, 1994); and Matthew H. Sommer, *Sex, Law, and Society in Late Imperial China* (Stanford: Stanford University Press, 2000); Melissa Macauley, "Civil and Uncivil Disputes in Southeast Coastal China, 1723–1820," in *Civil Law in Qing and Republican China*, ed. Bernhardt and Huang; Mark A. Allee, "Code, Culture, and Custom: Foundations of Civil Case Verdicts in a Nineteenth-Century County Court," in *Civil Law in Qing and Republican China*, Bernhardt and Huang.

18. William P. Alford, *To Steal a Book is an Elegant Offense: Intellectual Property Law in Chinese Civilization* (Stanford: Stanford University Press, 1995).

19. Interview 98US15, December 8, 1998; Interview 98US20, December 12, 1998; Interview 99BJ16, March 24, 1999; Interview 02US01, April 5, 2002.

20. Lubman, *Bird in a Cage*; Interview 98SH17, May 28, 1998; and Interview 98SH21, May 31, 1998.

of legal development in China, "law" in the Chinese context can best be understood as a complex amalgam of formal laws, informal norms, institutional incentives, and economic and political calculations.

It should be clear that I am *not* arguing that laws are not important, but rather that how they are used depends on far more than simply the substance of the laws themselves. It is necessary to look at the institutions charged with upholding the law. Usually, such an approach focuses on the legal-judicial process. Indeed, this was where I had begun my own research. But it quickly became apparent—even obvious—to me that the lion's share of activity was not taking place in judicial courts. The vast majority of mediation and enforcement was being undertaken by the administrative enforcement bureaucracies that have been analyzed in this book. Exclusively concentrating on the formal legal process—or, for that matter, on the administrative enforcement bureaucracies—provides an incomplete picture of how the law is utilized and enforced in China. Because the focus to date has neglected the administrative enforcement dimension of the equation, my goal has been to correct this deficiency in the literature.[21]

However, I am also making a more controversial claim. Although the formal legal-judicial apparatus may become dominant in the future, it is far from the default conflict resolution and law enforcement mechanism in China today. Therefore, in order to understand the relationship between law and society currently unfolding in China, we must look not only at the laws but also at the government bureaucracies—as distinct from the courts—as the principal arena for conflict resolution and policy enforcement, at least at present. This is true with regard to intellectual property as well as to a host of other policy areas.

This is further underscored in the following passage, which describes an increasingly central component to administrative enforcement, the "enforcement action," or raid:

> Ordering a raid on a suspected IPR infringer by an administrative enforcement agency is so simple, and so immediately gratifying, it is little wonder such actions are by far the most popular method of dealing with IPR problems in China. . . . The procedure is straightforward. Once an infringement has been discovered, the rights holder presents evidence of piracy to the local office of the appropriate administrative authority. The authority will then decide whether the evidence is sufficient to merit a raid. As it is empowered by law to take these decisions without applying a judicial standard of proof, a positive decision from the administrative authority is almost assured.

21. See, for example, Peter Feng, *Intellectual Property in China* (Hong Kong: Sweet and Maxwell, 1997); and Daniel C. K. Chow, *A Primer on Foreign Investment Enterprises and Protection of Intellectual Property in China* (New York: Kluwer Law International, 2002). A notable exception is Michel Oksenberg, Pitman B. Potter, and William B. Abnett, "Advancing Intellectual Property Rights: Information Technologies and the Course of Economic Development in China," *NBR Analysis* 7, no. 4 (November 1996).

TABLE 6.3.
Legal vs. administrative cases of anticounterfeiting and enforcement

Year	Cases of adjudication		Cases of administrative enforcement	
	Copyright	Trademark	Copyright	Trademark
1996	436	42	673	14,000
1997	411	45	1,361	32,027
1998	571	92	1,208	28,952
1999	750	65	1,586	32,298
2000	963	49	2,457	38,240

Source: China Administration of Industry and Commerce Yearbook (1997–2001) and *China Intellectual Property Yearbook* 2000.

A team of officials from the local office will conduct the raid on their own, though in certain cases, if advisable, it may call a police escort. No warrant is required.[22]

In traditional as well as contemporary China, administrative mediation has three principal benefits. It does not necessarily entail the type of formal and overt sparring between litigants, as is the case in the courtroom. Second, the administrative process is both much faster and often less expensive than the legal process. Third, administrative agencies are better able than the courts to enforce their decisions.

On balance, therefore, administrative enforcement is just as important—and arguably even more so—than the legal-judicial process, at least for the short-to-medium term. Conceptually, an overarching legal and judicial infrastructure that is the default mechanism through which IPR disputes are adjudicated cannot explain why some IPR issues (trademarks) are enforced better than others (copyright). In order to explain this variation, it is necessary to find some variation in the independent or intervening variable(s) of interest. The legal-judicial process does not explain such systematic variation. A focus on China's administrative institutional structure—and the discrete bureaucratic clusters that manage and enforce patents, copyright, and trademarks, respectively—does explain it. Just as many Chinese and foreign commercial actors have discovered the benefits of the administrative route, as scholars we should also maintain an analytical focus on these enforcement agencies when studying China's legal development.

22. Economist Intelligence Unit, *China Hand: The Complete Guide to Doing Business in China* (Hong Kong: Economist Intelligence Unit, 1998), 10.

CHAPTER 7

Casting a Wider Net

This book has focused on a simple but important question: what has been the impact of external pressure on China's policymaking and implementation processes? The argument framing the analysis of the previous several chapters is that the *direction* of external pressure is crucial to understanding the effects of foreign pressure on policy enforcement outcomes, especially when combined with the characteristics of the institutions it is designed to change. I have argued that exogenous pressure can take more than one form and that the direction of pressure—in this case, top-down versus lateral—is also critically important in accounting for specific implementation patterns and policy enforcement outcomes. Top-down pressure can result in dramatic, substantive changes in China's legislative, regulatory, and policymaking processes, but this same form of pressure has little, if any, sustained effect on the implementation and enforcement stages. Indeed, a strategy of leveling pressure against China cannot be successful in these latter stages if it does not take into account the bureaucratic structure through which this pressure, and the laws and regulations that result from it, must pass before they are translated into concrete policy outcomes. Although my cases have focused on the issue area of intellectual property, there is nothing inherent in the IPR issue area that makes the conclusions of this analysis unique to intellectual property.

There is a tendency to build unrealistic expectations regarding China's ability to enforce policy. In particular, there is a propensity to oversimplify the issue and place the blame for failure squarely at the feet of the China's national leadership. This strand of the conventional wisdom points to resistance or neglect by China's leaders as a principal reason that external pressure does not always succeed; it is often followed by the prescription that further escalation of this pressure is necessary to force Beijing into action. Two high-profile policy successes reinforce this tendency to focus on the national leadership to explain policy outcomes. The first has to do with

China's population control; the second with the recent outbreak of Severe Acute Respiratory Syndrome, or SARS, in 2003.

Beginning in the late 1970s, China began to enforce its draconian "one child" birth control campaign. This policy is widely unpopular, given the traditional Chinese desires for large families and male heirs. It is also extremely intrusive, in effect regulating the most intimate behavior of over a billion people. Finally, it is a policy that has been in place, more or less, for a generation. More recently, the SARS crisis in China, and particularly Beijing's response to it beginning in late April 2003, demonstrated to the world that China's authoritarian political regime and extensive Chinese Communist Party structure could reverse a viral outbreak through a combination of policy, coercion, and propaganda in just over two months. Many have concluded that if China can successfully implement the "one child" policy or effectively isolate SARS, enforcing something as comparatively benign as intellectual property should be easy, even effortless.

But this conclusion is flawed. The error lies in conflating leadership intent with state capacity. By the 1970s, overpopulation had become such a problem that it threatened social, economic, and political stability, and the Chinese government was forced to act. Similarly, SARS provided a clear and present threat to the very foundation of China's economic reform strategy of opening up to the outside world. In order to restore investor confidence, to demonstrate to the outside world that China was a mature member of the global community, and, not least, to forestall an epidemic that jeopardized public heath, social stability, and even the regime's political future, a tremendous amount of political capital and other resources had to be transferred to the fight against SARS. Limits to state capacity, however, allow the Chinese state to husband resources to only two, maybe three, such crisis issues in a sustained fashion at any given time.

Therefore, although IPR infringement may be a crisis for Hollywood and Microsoft, and while it is recognized by leaders in Beijing as an impediment to further economic development, it, like so many other policy areas in China, is eclipsed by more immediate and pressing priorities. Although intellectual property policy may have received national-level attention during the policymaking process, this elite attention did not extend to enforcement, which was the responsibility of China's complex, indeed overwrought, bureaucratic matrix. Thus, with intellectual property, as in the case of most policy areas in China, enforcement falls under the domain of China's institutional network of functional bureaucracies. The importance of this institutional nexus as an intervening variable underscores the problem with the assumption of "outside pressure on Beijing = enforcement results."

Indeed, I have argued that certain types of exogenous pressure are more likely to succeed when applied locally. Although this notion of "locally based international exogenous pressure" might seem a contradiction in terms, in today's world, in which the penetrative effects of globalization set the course for increasingly obtrusive relations between states, some may see the erosion of the traditional Westphalian system, in which states are bound by sovereign noninterference. While this is not the place for that debate, what is clear from the preceding analysis is that the notion of sovereignty has become much more flexible, both in terms of the legislation of domestic laws and regulations, which increasingly converges with international laws and norms, as well as the actual enforcement of that legislation. In this international context, international pressure is likely to grow rather than to recede. It is, therefore, all the more important to understand the channels through which such pressure travels, from the talking points that are negotiated between national elites to the trenches in which they are enforced by local actors. Although I have focused on a narrow, albeit important, issue area in the context of China, the conclusions of this study are by no means limited to China or to intellectual property.

The implications for China's ability to abide by its obligations to the World Trade Organization and other international bodies and treaties are clear. This analysis has not only laid bare the problem of neglecting the process of enforcement and the structure of the enforcement apparatus; it reorients our focus squarely onto this dimension, beyond the formal commitments made by Beijing, in order to anticipate policy outcomes and to explain patterns of compliance. The challenge in doing so is that this is actually more—not less—difficult than it sounds. There are several facets of this dimension that are germane to such an analysis: the clustering of the bureaucracy, the rank of the relevant unit(s), the jurisdiction of the unit(s), the jurisdiction of competing agencies, and the overall autonomy and resource pool available to the unit(s) in question. All of these dimensions help us evaluate the impact of the intervening variable—bureaucratic structure—to explain patterns of compliance.

The clustering of function- or policy-related bureaucracies (*xitong*) is the first of these facets. Traditionally, these *xitong* were largely independent, and it was difficult to cross over from one to another.[1] It should be noted that

---

1. The following example is illustrative. In 1998, when I was a graduate student undertaking research for my Ph.D. thesis, I was invited to a dinner banquet given by an individual who seemed completely secure in his own power. I went with two senior China specialists from the United States. One of them asked a question to our host: "What did you do during the Cultural Revolution?" Although most Chinese would have noticeable stiffened at such a question, our host was gracious. He responded that he worked on building railway lines in Heilongjiang province. Many people who had been branded "rightists" were sent to do this type of backbreaking work, and many of them died. We all felt no small degree of sympathy. He went on to say that he later joined the public security apparatus in Anhui province. At this point, we almost dropped our chopsticks. The three of us knew that because of the difficulty of laterally transferring across *xitong*, he could have moved from being an exiled rightist on the railway to becoming a policeman in Heilongjiang province; or he could have been a policeman in Heilongjiang and later in Anhui province; but it would have been extremely unlikely to move from being a worker on the railway line in Heilongjiang to a police officer in Anhui at that time. In other words, he was not one of the unfortunate rightist workers hammering railway spikes into the permafrost in Heilongjiang; he must have been one of the guards overseeing this work. We were only able to know this because of what we knew about *xitong*. Needless to say, when he proposed that we get up and sing a few songs on the karaoke machine, we quickly obliged.

xitong have become more porous over the years; in fact, the term is used far more casually to refer to "bureaucracies," as opposed to "bureaucratic clusters." And today it is somewhat easier to move among them. Moreover, different *xitong* intersect with one another as policy in China becomes more diverse and wide-ranging. Nevertheless, many of these boundaries still stand, and the fact that they have eroded somewhat in recent years should not be taken to mean that *xitong* are no longer relevant to conceptualizing (and compartmentalizing) the Chinese political system—they are. In order to understand the enforcement of policy in China, it is necessary to know which bureaucratic actors are involved in a given *xitong* because each of these bureaucracies has different goals and means of achieving them. Insofar as any single bureaucracy may exercise de facto veto power over others, or at least act as "spoilers" (i.e., by defecting when it comes to policy implementation), it is important to be able to identify the members of a particular *xitong* and the types of incentives they face vis-à-vis the policy at hand. In this book, I have discussed this in terms of the *saohuang dafei xitong,* as well as the IPR *xitong* headed at the top by the IPRWC.

How these various units interact with one another also depends on their formal rank and their informal power. There have been many cases of this throughout this analysis. For example, not only was the national IPRWO housed in the Science and Technology Commission, but it reported directly to a vice premier, Song Jian. Even though it had a formal rank of an "office," which was outranked by the various ministries and bureaus it was charged with handling, its placement within a commission, which formally outranks ministries and bureaus, gave it some extra formal leverage. This was enhanced by the informal power of its leader, Duan Ruichun, who everybody knew spoke for Song Jian. The ranking of various Provincial Patent Bureaus described in chapter 3 underscores the variation in the subordination of these units with their "host" units, the provincial science and technology commissions. The nominal ranking of the provincial copyright departments is an administrative fiction described in chapter 4 as a way to give these units some leverage among their competitor bureaucratic agencies, with which they sometimes have to coordinate policy. These formal and informal power relations are absolutely critical in evaluating an agency's ability to shape and enforce policy processes and outcomes.

Rank also becomes important when delineating the jurisdictional parameters among various bureaucratic agencies. For example, the Provincial Copyright Bureaus are unable to compel the Press and Publications Bureaus to undertake copyright enforcement if the latter have different priorities. These constraints are further exacerbated by resource scarcity (described below). Indeed, below the provincial level, as I have argued, the jurisdiction of the culture bureaucracy often trumps that of its embedded copyright sub-bureaucracy so that copyright enforcement often piggybacks on *saohuang dafei* campaigns, which do not target "apolitical" products such as computer software. When jurisdiction becomes an issue that is jointly claimed by two or more bureaucracies with the same administrative rank, the outcome is often intense bureaucratic competition, as with the AIC and the QTSB. However, this can actually lead to positive outcomes, at least for short- to medium-term policy enforcement, as chapter 5 has demonstrated. Nevertheless, such competition is understated, to the point that official sources deny its existence (particularly the QTSB, which does not have a formal trademark/IPR enforcement mandate), so identifying such dynamics is as difficult as it is crucial to understanding enforcement patterns in China.

Finally, early on in my research it became clear that it was absolutely critical to "follow the money" in order to understand the constraints faced by bureaucracies and the incentives they face. When the Guizhou Copyright Department has an annual operating budget of about $3,600, it is not surprising that copyright enforcement suffers. One of the reasons that trademark enforcement has improved is that many of these expenses are now underwritten by foreign actors, who work together with the AIC or the QTSB, either directly or through investigation agencies. However, it is also important to understand where budgetary outlays originate. Very often, they are provided by the government at the same administrative level—the essence of decentralization. Provincial governments give the press and publications agencies their personnel and budgetary allocations and the press and publications agencies then make the personnel and budgetary outlays they earmark for copyright management and enforcement to the provincial copyright agencies, and so on. If local governments have priorities that deviate from IPR protection (or any given policy), they can manipulate enforcement by withholding resources or making them contingent on some sort of behavior by the agency in question. Since 1998, the AIC and the QTSB have been centralized up to the provincial level in order to take them out of local government control. The impact of this shift on anticounterfeit enforcement remains to be seen.[2]

How much does this analysis tell us about China since securing its membership in the World Trade Organization (WTO) in 2001? As I have argued, the IPR issue area is representative of other commercial and trade policy areas that have rocked the Sino-U.S. bilateral relationship. Moreover, this is not simply limited to China's pre-WTO trade regime. As noted in chapter 2, many of the unilateral strategies that the United States uses to identify and emphasize unfair trade practices abroad are the same whether the target country is a member of the WTO or not; only the *forum* for mediating the dispute is different. But since this book has dealt with enforcement, one question remains: how do China's pre- and post-WTO enforcement regimes differ from one another? The answer is: not much, if at all. The 1992 MOU on intellectual property between the United States and China

2. See Andrew C. Mertha, "China's 'Soft' Centralization: Shifting *Tiao/Kuai* Authority Relations Since 1998," forthcoming in *China Quarterly*.

incorporated many of the TRIPS provisions even before TRIPS came into law. And these, in turn, found their way into China's revised IPR laws and regulations. In effect, what this means is that China adopted TRIPS long before other WTO members did. Thus, during most of the time frame analyzed in this book, China was de facto operating under WTO IPR laws. Put differently, the dynamics (or lack thereof) of enforcement documented in this study are fully "compatible"—in behavior if not in the spirit and letter of TRIPS—with China *as a member of the WTO*. As we analyze China's ability to enforce its domestic and international legal commitments, including those regarding the WTO, therefore, this book has raised the claim that we must pay closer attention to the institutional matrix through which these laws and legal commitments are channeled between the policymaking and the policy enforcement processes.

Finally, although this analysis has focused on China, and certain dimensions of this institutional analysis are unique to China, many of the dynamics and outcomes discussed herein can be found in other countries with similar institutions and state organizations as well as in other issue areas in China and elsewhere. Insofar as administrative institutions play a role in policy compliance with a given country's international commitments and obligations, the general conclusions of this analysis should not be understood as being unique to China. Insofar as a country's legal system is in the developing stage or infancy and/or insofar as it is overwhelmed by the government's own administrative apparatus, it is important for scholars to take these bureaucracies seriously, as way stations through which policy becomes squeezed, pulled, or otherwise altered in unanticipated directions and enforced in unexpected ways. It is only at such a point that we can state with the requisite degree of confidence that we have begun to understand the structure and process of enforcing such countries' international and domestic commitments.

This book has demonstrated that exogenous pressure can indeed have an effect on the formulation, implementation, and enforcement of policy. This analysis has also shown that the nature and the "location" of that pressure also matters. Top-down pressure in the form of confrontational negotiations with the USTR may have an immediate impact on the formal legislation that frames China's formal IPR regime—but such pressure has been less effective in promoting and facilitating effective and sustained enforcement. Likewise, lateral pressure between foreign actors and local Chinese enforcement agencies may have little, if any, impact on the national legislation of IPR laws and regulations, but it has proven to be absolutely crucial in establishing effective enforcement.

China is no longer a country in isolation. The days of the Celestial Empire or, more recently, the "hermit (Middle) Kingdom" of the 1960s and early 1970s are as unimaginable today as the current economic state of China would have been back then. Nevertheless, the last century and a half have made China's leaders and people somewhat suspicious of foreign involvement and highly sensitive to exogenous attempts to alter China's political and social nexus. Some of this resistance is simply rhetoric; some of it is substantive. But perhaps the most conceptually interesting and policy-relevant flashpoint at the current time and into the near future is where foreign pressure and China's gargantuan institutional apparatus—the arena in which such foreign pressure is altered, refracted, and distorted—come together to shape policy implementation and enforcement in China. This is especially true as China becomes increasingly interconnected with the international community of nations and as the world watches to see how China meets its international commitments and obligations. With regard to intellectual property, as with other policy areas, to understand the workings of the Chinese state, we must focus our attention most on this level of analysis in the years to come.

Index